Women in the Metropolis

WEIMAR AND NOW: GERMAN CULTURAL CRITICISM
MARTIN JAY AND ANTON KAES, GENERAL EDITORS

Women in the Metropolis

Gender and Modernity in Weimar Culture

EDITED BY

Katharina von Ankum

UNIVERSITY OF CALIFORNIA PRESS

Berkeley   Los Angeles   London

The publisher gratefully acknowledges permission to reprint the following:

"Ich liebe Berlin mit einer Angst in den Knien: Frau und Stadt in Irmgard Keuns *Das kunstseidene Mädchen*," by Katharina von Ankum, reprinted in somewhat revised form from *The German Quarterly* 67: 3 (Summer 1994);

"In Search of the Female Flaneur: Women on the Streets and Screens of Weimar," by Anke Gleber, to appear in *The Image in Dispute: Visual Cultures in Modernity*, ed. J. Dudley Andrew, University of Texas Press (Spring 1997), by permission of the publisher;

"*Lustmord*: Inside the Windows of the Metropolis," by Beth Irwin Lewis, from *Berlin: Culture and Metropolis*, ed. Charles W. Haxthausen and Heidrun Suhr, University of Minnesota Press, ©1990 by the Regents of the University of Minnesota;

"Perceptions of Difference," by Patrice Petro, reprinted in slightly shortened form from Petro's *Joyless Streets: Women and Melodramatic Representation in Weimar Germany*, ©1989 by Princeton University Press. Reprinted by permission of Princeton University Press.

University of California Press
Berkeley and Los Angeles, California

University of California Press
London, England

Library of Congress Cataloging-in-Publication Data

Women in the metropolis: gender and modernity in Weimar culture /
edited by Katharina von Ankum.
    p.   cm. — (Weimar and now : 11)
    Includes bibliographical references and index.
    ISBN 0-520-20464-6 (cloth). — ISBN 0-520-20465-4 (pbk.)
    1. Urban women—Germany—History. 2. Germany—Social
conditions—1918-1933. 3. Women—Germany—History—20th century.
4. Feminism—Germany—History—20th century. I. Ankum, Katharina
von. II. Series.
    HQ1623.W66 1997
    305.4'0943—dc20   96-3118
                                                             CIP

Printed in the United States of America
1 2 3 4 5 6 7 8 9

The paper used in this publication meets the minimum requirements of American National Standard for Information Sciences—Permanence of Paper for Printed Library Materials, ANSI Z39.48-1984 ♾

CONTENTS

v

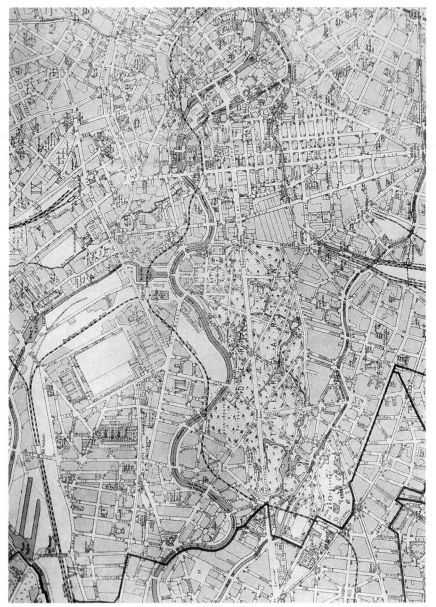

Berlin, 1921. Reprinted courtesy of Landesarchiv, Berlin, Kartenabteilung.

Introduction

I'm sitting in the express train from Berlin to Stuttgart. With tremendous speed, the train is racing through the flat countryside. . . . The rapid change of scenery reinforces the overall image that the big city we have just left has once again impressed on me. The hustle and bustle of the metropolis is simply breathtaking. Just like on the express train, you don't have the leisure to follow a thought through to the end or to finish looking at something, since your attention is immediately caught up by something else. . . . To me, this phenomenon seems to lie at the bottom of all that is metropolitan: the constant hurry and running around, everything imposing its attraction onto people, tearing on them and pulling them in different directions, preventing them from finding themselves. No wonder that both physical and moral resistance are on the wane; the entire environment is directed at destroying it. . . . [T]he city most certainly does not harbor Germany's soul, despite the restless thought and incessant activity that takes place there. The soul of Germany rests in the countryside, in the grace of its rolling hills where man is still part of the land which instills him with the strength to defend himself against the developments of our time that are infringing on our lives.[1]

This personal account of a young woman's urban experience reverses the classic "arrival in the city" scene frequently employed in fictional and filmic texts of the 1920s that establish urban space as a place of great expectation for women, a place where changes in traditional gender roles had become most visible and most accepted.[2] Rather than coming to Berlin to begin a new life, the narrator is relieved to be leaving the city and returning to her hometown in southern Germany. Such a critical contemplation of the hectic urban environment would not come as a surprise, were the narrator a protected daughter from a good provincial family or a housewife and mother returning from a family visit. However, its publication in *Junge Kräfte*, a professional journal for sales and office employees, suggests that this is the perspective of a working woman whose own life very much embodies the societal changes she observes and critiques. Evidently traveling alone, she appears to be one of the emancipated young women of the 1920s who have begun to expect a hitherto unimaginable mobility and independence, but have also had to adjust to the idea of having to support themselves and stand on their own feet in the hectic and aggressive urban environment.

"Grosstadtgetriebe" (Urban Bustle), the text from which I drew this quotation in fact dates from 1926, a time when the precarious balance between women's hopes and claims to equality in modern society and their healthy skepticism toward modernization increasingly began to tip in the direction of the resurrection of traditional notions of (German) womanhood. While the narrator's reflections do not in themselves establish a connection between an antimodernist definition of Germanness and the desire for a return to traditional gender roles, they do show a characteristic emphasis on the stressful rather than liberating aspects of women's experience of the modern city. Such emphasis on exhaustion rather than exhilaration with the new ways of life embodied by the flapper, the Girl, the Garçonne, is a prominent aspect of the rejection of these "imported" models of femininity. The deconstruction of the "New Woman" paralleled the disillusionment with modernization ensuing from the unsuccessful implementation of modern American economic principles in postwar Germany and the retreat from a French-influenced overt sexualization of the female body.

In 1925, the New York correspondent of the trendy cultural magazine *Uhu*, Maria Leitner, described the hard working day of a young woman from Saxony employed as a waitress in New York City. In 1928, *Uhu* attached a pedometer to the leg of a revue girl to demonstrate the hard labor that went into a seemingly effortless performance. And a 1930 article in the same publication used the description of the life of an American showgirl to demonstrate the downside of the "Girl" lifestyle to its German audience. The dismantling of the Hollywood myth of American women's glamorous modernity was reinforced by accounts of German women's pragmatism. In 1930, *Uhu* published a photo-essay entitled "Ich werde Mannequin, um mein Studium zu verdienen" (I am becoming a model to finance my education) while a 1931 report on twenty-five young women's career plans emphasized the fact that, contrary to what might be expected, all were planning to train for careers other than film.[3] Two years later, however, *Uhu* published a much less optimistic "cross section" of contemporary female existence, "Ich schreibe auf jedes Inserat! . . . Querschnitt durch vier Monate Daseinskampf eines jungen Mädchens von heute" (I respond to every job ad—Four months in the struggle of existence of a young woman today).[4] As much as these reports acknowledged and responded to the conflicting desires and harsh realities of women's lives, they also helped to construct a cultural and increasingly political discourse that pitted women's new societal roles against the survival of the German nation.

Sympathetic accounts of the burdens born by the New Woman were paralleled by "scientific" reports that issued warnings to women that the physical strains of their new professional and leisure activities would permanently damage their reproductive abilities. Representations of pioneering women driving sports cars, flying planes, or working in laboratories increasingly made way for idyllic scenes of mothering that took on increasingly national and racial connotations. The reconstruction of traditional femininity was paralleled by a political reorientation toward the provinces and away from the city. A characteristically German regionalism was to present a modern alternative to provincialism. In the same way that the countryside was expected to regenerate the cities, women were expected to become the redeemers of modernization.[5]

Fantasies of returning to the countryside to escape the pressures and frustrations of urban reality also mark fictional texts by women writers in the early 1930s: sitting in the waiting room of Bahnhof Zoo, faced with the ultimate failure of her aspirations to a life of glamour, Irmgard Keun's Doris in *Das kunstseidene Mädchen* (The Artificial Silk Girl, 1932) dreams about a garden colony outside the city limits of Berlin where she envisions herself enjoying respite and a protected domesticity as the companion of her old friend Hans. Christa Anita Brück's highly autobiographical novel *Schicksale hinter Schreibmaschinen* (Destinies Behind Typewriters, 1930) ends with the protagonist's return to her native East Prussia where she hopes to regain the physical and emotional strength she has spent in her unsuccessful struggle to advance professionally in the city. As the sociologist Alice Rühle-Gerstel critically observes in a book review in *Die literarische Welt* in 1933, such texts by contemporary women writers constitute a delayed fictional representation of women's disillusionment with the promise of modern independence and urban anonymity.

> Literature can only show developments after the fact. While they take place, they are too subconscious to be observed. Thus, war novels started to come out ten years after the war, and those books that convey a well-meaning message to their women readers to return to their traditional roles, are published several years after women have already begun to withdraw; because they knew or because they were tired of being at the forefront where no one wanted to join them or because they were afraid to go further.[6]

The representational discourses of journalism and literature did indeed lag behind political and economic reality when it came to recording the shift in women's identification with Weimar modernity and their subsequent withdrawal from the public sphere. Providing them with the right to vote and the assurance of sexual equality—albeit within the boundaries of contemporary gender essentialism—the Weimar Republic initially promised to be an era of professional and political emancipation that women were eager to support. Between 1918 and 1920, female membership in the Social Democratic party (SPD) had risen from only 66,000 to 207,000. The number of women among the Independent Social Democrats (USPD) showed a similar increase within that same two-year period. However, the economic and social reality of Weimar society quickly brought this period of optimism and active participation to a halt. While 9.6 percent of the members of the

Weimar National Assembly of 1918 had been women, by 1930 only 7 percent of all parliamentarians were women. Membership trends within labor organizations even more drastically reflect women's early withdrawal from the public sphere. While female membership in the Central Union of Clerical Staff had quadrupled between 1918 and 1919 to reach 175,204 members, the number dwindled to about 60 percent over the course of the next decade. The Union of Female Retail and Office Staff experienced a similar drop in membership over the course of the decade. However, this development did not mean that women were no longer active in these professions or that working conditions had improved to a degree that rendered activism superfluous. The number of female white-collar workers continued to grow by over 200 percent between 1907 and 1925, and 12.6 percent of all working women were employed in that sector by 1925. As a result of such gender-specific "supportive" work assignments, women averaged approximately 30 pfennig to each mark made by their male colleagues.

Although white-collar employment made working women more visible than ever before—moving them out of the relative privacy of the agricultural sector into the public clerical sector and thus from countryside into the city—it did not substantially increase female employment. By 1925, only 35.6 percent of all women were working, only 0.7 percent more than in 1907. Female employment continued to be regarded as the exception rather than the rule. In 1925, two-thirds of all white-collar workers were single women under the age of twenty-five.[7] Impeded by bourgeois morality and lack of education, their professional lives were in most cases limited to a few years. Weimar's true emancipatory potential for women lay in the fact that this "intermediary stage of personal independence" [Gertrud Bäumer] between adolescence and marriage/motherhood, albeit economically required, became socially acceptable. As women's need to work outside the home—increased by the demographic and economic realities of the interwar years—began to threaten the traditional gender balance, women had to retreat from the public sphere. The 1932 Law on the Legal Position of Female Public Servants that disallowed the employment of married women in that sector emphasizes the precarious position of working women in a tight labor market. It also stresses the essentialist approach of Weimar gender politics in the interest of nationalist politics that assigned priority to women's "natural" roles as mothers over the female individual's autonomy. Women's temporary participation in a culture of leisure, consumption, and body consciousness created the powerful image of the New Woman that populated the Berlin of the 1920s, yet this modernist female persona was as short-lived and ambiguous as it was generational.

Despite its limited reality, the icon of the New Woman that emerged from the war years as the embodiment of the sexually liberated, economically independent, self-reliant female was perceived as a threat to social stability and an impediment to Germany's political and economic reconstruction. The discursive obsession with female identity was prompted by the sexualization of the public sphere resulting from the entry of large numbers of women into the modern workplace, the perception of a "birth strike" among middle-class women, and the decisively mas-culine appearance of the New Woman that repressed the physical markers of fem-ininity. In *Die Frau von morgen-wie wir sie wünschen* (Tomorrow's Woman According to Our Wishes, 1929), prominent intellectuals of all political hues expressed their hopes that women, after having conquered traditionally male domains, would not become imitators of male ways but rather develop viable alternative lifestyles. Rather than indulge in promiscuity and careerism, women were asked to maintain their internal balance and use their maternal instinct in the interest of the future of humankind.

While the political atmosphere of the influential Sex Reform movement posi-tively acknowledged female sexuality, it was also clearly oriented toward its regu-lation. Providing women with the means of controlling the size of their families through birth control or legal abortion was motivated by the desire to allow women to combine their reproductive responsibilities with their new role in the working world. The concept of the companionate marriage, proposed by Judge Lindsay, which introduced a personal five-year plan of a childless marriage that could be revoked, and Theodor Van der Velde's manual *Die vollkommene Ehe* (The Perfect Marriage, 1928) demonstrate similar attempts to liberate women sexually within acceptable bourgeois forms. Feminist organizations like the Mutterschutz-bund introduced legal initiatives to legitimize and offer government support for single mothers. Positing women's *Kinderwunsch* (the wish for a child) as the basis of female sexual desire, feminist activists interpreted women's reproductive rights primarily in the context of procreation. To be sure, the reconstruction of female sexuality in exclusively reproductive terms not only reinforced bourgeois morality but also affirmed female sexuality as healthy and normal for women of all social classes. Yet at the same time, it lent emphasis to women's crucial role in the cre-ation of a "eugenic utopia." The celebration of "primitive" beauty, sexuality, and consequently "natural" motherhood also conveyed the message that women should strive to successfully combine their function as workers with their repro-ductive responsibilities to build a strong German nation.

The essay collection *When Biology Became Destiny* (1984), edited by Renate Bridenthal, Atina Grossmann, and Marion Kaplan, was the first attempt by fem-inist scholars to document the natalist backlash against women that took place be-tween 1918 and 1933 in the interest of reconstituting a strong sense of nationalism in Germany. More recently, Cornelie Usborne's study *The Politics of the Body* (1992) has added another layer of historical detail and critical analysis to the documen-tation of women's experience of modernity as dominated by reproductive control. Both studies, significant and influential as they continue to be, have limited them-selves to reconstructing the historical and political context of women's lives rather than analyzing the cultural and representational discourses on gender that shaped women's identities of the time.

Despite their participatory role in societal reconstruction after World War I, women's historiography of the period differed significantly from men's. While the war experience confronted men with societal displacement and cultural "castration," it had reinforced women's growing trust in their own abilities and opportunities. While men experienced the postwar years as a time of chaos and loss of individual boundaries, women had to sustain the conflict between defending their new models of self against the onset of a societal reconstruction. Women's willing return to traditional gender roles was ultimately determined by their increased awareness of the limitations placed on their emancipation after the onset of the economic decline in the mid-1920s that brought Weimar's intrinsically patriarchal structures to the fore. The dominant cultural discourses of the time sought to negotiate the acknowledgment of women's newly won independence with their desire to reconstruct traditional gender roles.

Curiously, studies that explicitly explore the connections between the historical impact of World War I and the cultural (re)constructions of gender in Weimar Germany have focused on the documentation and representation of male experience.[8] Klaus Theweleit's much-debated *Male Fantasies* (1977, 1987) is extracted from autobiographical texts by Freikorps officers. Theweleit's analysis of these personal accounts of the interwar years documents an intricate connection between men's struggle to reconstruct their familiar gender identities in the face of dramatic societal change and their perception of Weimar Germany as a non-nation. The soldiers' relationships to real women are replaced by their relationship to their "fatherland," carrying the metaphysical representation of woman to an extreme in the images of the white and the red nurse.[9] Helmut Lethen's more recent analysis of the interwar culture of New Objectivity, *Verhaltenslehren der Kälte: Lebensversuche zwischen den Kriegen* (1994), draws on Hartmut Plessner's philosophy from the 1930s, which centers around the "cold persona"—the individual who cultivates traditionally negative qualities like anonymity, uprootedness, artificiality, and distraction as a shield against the shock effect of modernity and the trauma of the war. Conscious of the fact that women are not theorized as embodying these personality traits but appear solely as creatures (Kreaturen), that is, as antipodes to the male "cold persona," Lethen apologetically notes that his study has by default turned into a "male book" (p. 14). Because of woman's inherent quality as "other," *Women in the Metropolis*, by contrast, could not be called a "female book." It is a book about women, about women's representations and experiences of the interwar years, but it is also a book about men, since the cultural construction of woman embodies the projections of male hopes and anxieties. *Women in the Metropolis* has a dual focus: one is to excavate women's experience of modernity and urbanization from the life stories of women artists and writers and to discover reflections of these life stories in their work; the other is to document and analyze the cultural discourses that developed to make sense of and regulate the emerging images of femininity. The contributions in the collection seek to reveal the origins and effects of the gendered discourses of modernity in fictional, visual, and scientific texts of the time. Yet they are careful not to employ the category of gender as an exclusively representational concept that diffuses or erases women's concrete historical experiences. Instead, they insist on a historical reality for women that both reflects and contradicts these discourses. Consequently, women are not portrayed as mere objects of male-made policies and discourses but as active participants in the construction of their own modernity.

Women in the Metropolis combines the perspectives of art and cultural historians with those of literary and film scholars to outline the emancipatory potential of modernity for women and explore women's problematic relationship with the process of modernization in Germany during the 1920s and 1930s. The individual contributions analyze women writers' and artists' critical engagement with the discourses of rationalization and technology, theorize female spectatorship, investigate the trope of masquerade in the mass media and the fashion industry, and explore the correlation between race, gender, and the nation-state. All texts undertake an archaeology of Berlin as the "city of women" in the 1920s and 1930s, a city that had become the emblem of characteristically German trepidations about the effects of modernization and social change after World War I. *Women in the Metropolis* thus adds an important German perspective to already-existing studies on gender and national identity in the interwar years in Britain and France.

Lynne Frame's digest of popular medical research from the 1920s shows how the categorization of physical features, originally devised by nineteenth-century criminologists, was adapted by Weimar scientists to create a typology that would ascertain women's reproductive potential, deemed crucial for the reconstruction of the German nation. Placing Vicki Baum's popular novel *stud. chem. Helene Willfüer* (1927) in the context of this regulatory scientific discourse, Frame demonstrates how popular culture participated in the construction of a female ideal that sought to preserve the moral notion of "true womanhood" while acknowledging the economic need for female professionalism and independence. The cultural and political imperative to halt the masculinization of women and preserve femininity as a utopian category of difference reinforced rather than negotiated the contradictions Weimar women experienced in their daily lives.

Patrice Petro captures the tensions between the male projection of the New Woman, as described by Frame, and the conflict women experienced between their old and new roles by setting "men's modernism" against "women's modernity." Petro's theory of a female cinematic spectator argues that the cultural construction of woman as metaphor of modernity actually conceals or distorts women's (and men's) actual experience of modernization. Focusing on the category of gender in theoretical texts on spectatorship by Martin Heidegger, Walter Benjamin, and Siegfried Kracauer, she posits that women's different reality affects their perception of the real world as well as their perception of the realm of illusion. The disqualification of the institution of the cinema as the epitome of a modern culture of distraction, she suggests, reflects the male discomfort with the visual invasion of his individuality through this medium that mirrors the provocative gaze of the increasingly visible women in the modern city. Against the presumed inability of the female spectator to focus on the screen image or disassociate herself from it, Petro posits the independent, provocative, and emancipated female gaze.

Anke Gleber's reading of Walter Ruttmann's *Berlin, Symphony of a City* provides a striking example for the problematic correlation between the representation of femininity and women's actual presence in the urban environment. Gleber discovers the precursor of the female flaneur who, as she purports, ultimately comes into her own as the female spectator of the cinema. This discussion prefaces her reinterpretation of a much-quoted scene from Ruttmann's film: a fashionably dressed young woman stops in front of the shop window of a corner store. Her direct gaze meets that of a gentleman on the other side of the shop window, who eventually joins her and walks off with her. The common reading of this scene immediately attached the label of sexual availability and prostitution to the woman's active gaze. Gleber, by contrast, identifies several different women participating in this scene, one of whom boldly meets her male counterpart's gaze and another who walks down the street with yet a different man. Her careful dissection of the filmic collage reveals the interpretive power of the dominant discourse on women in the public sphere that effectively erases the presence of actual women in the city.

Annelie Lütgens introduces Jeanne Mammen as an artist whose life epitomizes the strains of the pioneering female flaneur of the 1920s. The images of working women's reality she collects while wandering through the streets of Berlin in her characteristically androgynous garb reflect a solidarity with the members of her generation and her sex who feel alienated and overwhelmed by the demands of postwar society. Her protagonists are strangers in the urban context, finding support only among each other. The utopian quality of the girlfriend motif that dominates Mammen's work of the period culminates in her representation of a lesbian subculture as a harmonious counterworld to an otherwise cold and unbearable city. Mammen's emphasis on female solidarity introduces an element of resistance to the images, which, commissioned as illustrations for popular magazines and journals, could otherwise easily have been co-opted by the consumer culture they were trying to critique.

While Mammen's artistic development is tied to her status as outsider—reinforced by her sexual preference—Hannah Höch's work is marked by her struggle to find acceptance in an all-male artist group. Unlike Mammen whose work betrays a discomfort with postwar Berlin from the onset, Höch's early work still projects a confident and optimistic attitude toward the emancipatory promise of Weimar democracy that is reflected in her representation of women and technology. Maria Makela's analysis of Höch's political stance toward the impact of technology on modern society relates the artist's disillusionment with Weimar and the subsequent societal critique in her work to her relationship with Raoul Hausmann. The emotional abuse and physical violence Höch suffered in her liaison with the intellectual spokesperson of Berlin dada and the repression and ridicule she was subjected to as a woman artist led her to doubt the presupposition that the process of modernization would by default accomplish women's emancipation and equality. Her experience of the clash between modernist theory and personal practice led her to an early and fundamentally gendered critique of technology's impact on human relationships that differentiates her work from that of her male colleagues.

For Janet Lungstrum, the creation of the woman robot in Fritz Lang's *Metropolis* epitomizes male fantasies of control over female sexuality and technological change. Her analysis of several central scenes from the film focuses on the male loss of control over the machinic other that is of his own creation. Women's identification with technology, Lungstrum argues, is thus not by default repressive, but offers new ways of self-empowerment for women. Rather than reject gendered images of technology as dystopian and by necessity protofascist, Lungstrum insists that women reappropriate their Medusan heritage and begin to explore the emancipatory potential of the loss of distinction between organism and machine inherent in their cultural construction as technological bodies of modernity.

If Fritz Lang's *Metropolis* conflates male fear of and fascination with modernity and female sexuality in the image of the female robot, the all-black revue of the mid-1920s represents an attempt to regulate and contain the desire for and fear of primitivity and progress that dominated popular imagination in the 1920s. Nancy Nenno's reading of Josephine Baker's success story in Berlin hinges on the performer's symbolic potential as an African-American woman. Although her race and gender linked her to the notion of the primitive and the natural, her citizenship made her a representative of the most modern of nations, allowing the spectator to imagine an unproblematic, safe fusion of the "natural" and the "civilized." Nenno, however, does not limit herself to an analysis of the commodification of difference through the medium of the female black body, but shows how Baker participated in her own cultural construction, successfully exploiting the marketability of her image as "erotic savage."

The fictional fate of Irmgard Keun's artificial silk girl Doris challenges this concept of such an emancipatory potential inherent in women's active participation in the media construction of femininity. Doris's intimate relationship with her stolen fur coat, which marks her entrance into a self-perceived semicinematic existence of glamour and eroticism, undoubtedly represents an act of self-empowerment in the face of traditional models of femininity. However, as my reading of Keun's novel in the context of contemporary discourses on prostitution illustrates, this vital accessory of Doris's urban existence also functions as a signal of sexual availability within the dominant patriarchal discourse. The clothed body as sign thus takes on different meanings, whether it is performed by the male spectator or the female wearer. Doris's experience of commodification in the streets of Berlin exposes the hierarchical relationship between both discourses and reveals the limitations of masquerade as a strategy to attain the societal and economic status promised by the mass media.

Sabine Hake's discussion of fashion as metaphor of modernity focuses on its dual function as visual expression of women's new societal roles and as regulatory discourse of femininity. The *Bubikopf* (pageboy) for example, initially the expression of the adaptation of femininity to the necessities of the modern workplace, quickly turned into the external marker of a culturally prescribed modern female identity. Despite the danger inherent in such a commodification of emancipatory symbols, Hake insists on fashion's crucial role for the deconstruction of gender identities. In allowing women to act out different visual patterns of femininity through a different staging of their body, she argues, fashion encouraged women's critical stance toward identity construction and allowed them to maintain a playful attitude toward modernity.

The images of advertising, the mass media, and the shop windows confronted women with their own visually fragmented bodies, while the windows of the metropolis became the keyholes to the visual performance of gruesome male fantasies. Beth Irwin Lewis draws attention to the prominent role of representations of sex murders in the early works of male expressionists like Otto Dix and George Grosz. She identifies the frequent representation of violence against women as a strategy of the male artist to express the damage suffered to his gendered ego through the experience of war and its ensuing social changes in the mutilation of the female body. These images, Lewis insists, do not merely represent the artistic documentation of a violent urban reality, but reveal the misogynist subtext of modernity that had its bearing on the daily lives of women in the metropolis in Weimar Germany.

All the contributions in *Women in the Metropolis*, in one way or another, focus on women in public spaces, be they spectators in the cinema, artists recording street life, shoppers in the streets, or working women in the office or on the stage. Women's visibility and their visual re/presentation in the public sphere emerge as the central issue of the gender-focused discussions that make up this volume. Lütgens and Makela focus on women's own visual representations of this new "public" and publicized femininity. The contributions of Petro, Lewis, and Frame elucidate the processes of male control inherent in the fragmentation and categorization of women's bodies, and Lungstrum posits a liberating potential of the mechanized female body. Hake, Gleber, and Nenno, in turn, attempt to negotiate the regulatory aspects of the display of women's bodies in fashion and on the stage with the liberating and playful dimension of these performances of self. My own analysis of Keun's *Das kunstseidene Mädchen* perhaps most directly reflects a Foucauldian reading of women's experience of controlled public space.

The volume's New Historicist perspective may well elicit skepticism among some readers who may question the adequacy of this methodology when attempting to document women's experience of modernity. Feminist criticism of Foucault as the main theorist behind this approach has hinged on his failure to acknowledge the omnipresence of the male gaze as enforcing processes of self-surveillance for women in the public sphere that resemble those of men in enclosed institutional spaces. If, however, one accepts Foucault's analysis of systems of surveillance as self-sustaining—based on the participatory role of their subjects—such an extension of surveilled space for women would negate their potential to resist the dominant patriarchal discourse in their conquest of the public sphere and stamp them as collaborators in their own repression.

Yet women's multifaceted presence and participation in the public sphere was as central to their emancipatory vision of modernity as their increased visibility was to men's fears of modernization. Their consciousness or internalization of their position as performers or spectacles in modern urban society only partially reflected a problematic domination of their identities by outside forces. As Helmut Lethen has theorized in his critical analysis of post–World War I culture—*Verhaltenslehren der Kälte*—the adaptation of self to changing outside conditions does not necessarily predetermine a repressible and antidemocratic personality structure. The contributions in this volume suggest that the positive ability of what Lethen terms the "radar type"—namely, the ability to adapt to external circumstance while preserving internal autonomy and resistance—may in fact be what informs specifically female reactions to and ways of coping with modernity.

NOTES

1. S.V. "Grosstadtgetriebe," *Junge Kräfte* (April 1926), 44–45.

2. Texts that include such "arrival" scenes are Clara Viebig's *Es lebe die Kunst* (1910), Rudolf Braune's *Das Mädchen an der Orga Privat* (1929), Irmgard Keun's *Das kunstseidene Mädchen* (1932), and to some extent *Gilgi–Eine von uns* (1931). Naturally, the city is also portrayed as a place where women risk to endanger their good name. M. I. Breme's *Vom Leben getötet* (1927) focuses exclusively on that aspect of women's city experience.

3. "Von der höheren Töchterschule zum Film: Ein Querschnitt durch fünfundzwanzig junge Mädchen von heute," *Uhu* 12 (September 1931): 34–42.

4. *Uhu* (9 June 1933): 64–71.

5. Hans Schiebelhuth, "Die Kräfte der Provinz: Das Land als Mutterboden deutscher Persönlichkeit," *Uhu* 8 (1931): 9–14. Hannes Küpper, "Provinz und Berlin," *Querschnitt* 5 (1931): 307–309.

6. Alice Rühle-Gerstel, "Zurück zur guten alten Zeit?" *Die literarische Welt* 4 (27 January 1933), 5.

7. All statistical data in these paragraphs are taken from Ute Frevert, *Women in German History: From Bourgeois Emancipation to Sexual Liberation* (New York, Oxford, and Munich: Berg, 1989), 156–175.

8. Mary Louise Roberts's cultural history of postwar France, *Civilization Without Sexes* (1994), provides such an integrated analysis of history, culture, and gender. Contrasting the representational discourse on femininity with the statistical documentation of women's realities, she reads the three patterns of femininity she identifies in her research—*la femme moderne*, *la mère*, and *la femme seule*—as cultural responses to men's postwar trauma. Mary Louise Roberts, *A Nation Without Sexes: Reconstructing Gender in Post-War France 1917–1927* (Chicago: University of Chicago Press, 1994).

9. For a recent critical response to Theweleit and another analysis of modernity's impact on male identity, see Bernd Widdig, *Männerbünde und Massen: Zur Krise männlicher Identität in der Moderne* (Opladen: Westdeutscher Verlag, 1992).

ONE

Gretchen, Girl, Garçonne?
Weimar Science and Popular Culture
in Search of the Ideal New Woman

Lynne Frame

*The days of the "misunderstood woman" are numbered. . . . [S]he [like the others] will hold
no more secrets for the scientists.*
—DR. MED. J. LÖBEL, IN *DIE DAME* (1927)

In 1927 the Berlin bourgeois newspaper, the *8-Uhr-Abendblatt*, claimed,

> Today three women stand before us. The three types: Gretchen, Girl, Garçonne.
> The *Gretchen* type is not only the young naive German girl with braids and a knitting-
> needle horizon, it is also the heroic and militaristic ranting fascist woman. . . . Sexu-
> ally powerless, personally passive, this type as a group is a historical hindrance, is the
> stumbling block of every historically urgent development. Allied with the church
> and reaction, she has an optimistic attitude toward life, that is not, however, produc-
> tive. . . . The *Girl*, originating in America as the child of pioneers and immigrants, is
> aware from the beginning that you can rely only on yourself, and that getting ahead
> is the sole guarantee that you won't rot. . . . A daring athlete, sexy but without siz-
> zle—rather coolly calculating—she succeeds whenever she encounters the sexually
> bourgeois man of the old school. . . . The *Garçonne* type cannot be grasped by lan-
> guage. . . . [Her] combination of fifty to fifty [percent] sexual and intellectual po-
> tency often gives rise to conflict. . . . [T]he most significant one in this group: the
> business- and life-artist. Uniting a sporting, comradely male entrepreneurial sense
> with heroic, feminine devotion, this synthesis—if successful—often makes her so su-
> perior to the man she loves that she becomes troublesome.[1]

The article focuses on the relationship of these types of women to social and cultural progress: the Gretchen type is "an impediment to history"; the Girl is based
on a "medieval" ideology.[2] In keeping with an odd image of American culture
that appeared in a wide variety of Weimar texts, the author interprets American
women's (perceived) high status in society as a holdover from the "feudal" conditions of colonial and frontier cultures (when women were in short supply). The
cultural origins of the Girl are thus "primitive."[3] Only the Garçonne, still a rare
type, represents a truly progressive form of feminine development.[4] The *8-Uhr-
Abendblatt's* sweeping categorization of all European women into three groups and

12

its glib conclusions about their historical significance were far from rare. Weimar culture was obsessed with taxonomies. Without hesitation, journalists, social critics of all hues, and scientists alike constructed human typologies and made pronouncements on their relative social "worth." Like the above article, such typologies often shared the anthropological project of appraising the German population, especially in terms of its relationship to metropolitan modernity. Women often stood at the center of these analyses, as many writers treated the seemingly drastic changes they were undergoing—in lifestyle and appearance—as a barometer of modern society, its progress and its discontents.

In turn, women were clearly looking for role models and ways of evaluating their own position—and potential—in society. As the author and editor Ilse Reicke observed in 1928, the informational content of newspapers had become increasingly interesting to working women, who were especially eager to read about other women and their pioneering accomplishments.[5] An article like the one quoted above certainly invited women readers to "measure" themselves against a given typology, or rather, to place themselves in it. It encouraged them to construct an image of themselves and their identity, and to consider their own contributions to the promotion or impairment of modernity and progress.

In providing women with new models for identification, typologies could also place restrictions on their behavior. Helmut Lethen has recently characterized the classification mania ("Furor des Rasterns") that gripped Weimar culture as a response of the symbolic order to the economic and social chaos of the postwar period.[6] While J. C. Lavater's popular Enlightenment era *Physiognomik* teaches classification of the human visage as an exercise in appreciation of God's creations,[7] classification schemes of the Weimar period order every aspect of humanity, from physique to handwriting, to give contours to a society in disarray. They provide the individual with means for differentiating and discriminating, for drawing new boundaries and putting up barriers for security. Such schemes "help to *differentiate* the elementary things: self and other, inside and outside, male and female. They are supposed to prevent the mixing of spheres, to regulate forms of expression and spontaneity, and guarantee the 'balance' of the individual."[8] The function of typologies is thus twofold: they operate as both hermeneutic tools and behavioral guides (*Verhaltenslehren*). Their interpretive and normative applications are directed both inward and outward, regulating both self and other, thereby providing a new structural security in the destabilized social landscape. This double function of the classification schemes of the twenties points to the normative aspect of the typologies of women: women can use them to "interpret"—but also to regulate—themselves. And they become, in turn, the objects of interpretation and regulation by others.

While Lethen's discussion of this phenomenon emphasizes its connection to the social conditions following World War I, my investigation here finds that a number of Weimar typologies are indebted to an older discourse. Its roots lie in the efforts of nineteenth-century scientists social critics who responded with

"scientific principles" and structures to the pressures of social, economic, demographic, and political change similar to the upheavals later experienced in even
greater magnitude in postwar Germany. In the context of industrialization and
urbanization, a broad spectrum of commentators turned to the biological sciences
for answers to social problems, focusing their analyses increasingly on an "economy of the body and the social effects of its reproduction."[9] In the wake of the
First World War, these discourses of urban decay, "degeneration," and its proposed antidote, "racial hygiene" (eugenics), shifted from the realm of philosophical speculation and medical investigation to that of political practice. Biomedical
schemes for boosting the "quality and quantity" of the population came to inform
state legislation and administration, creating policies that focused largely on
women and their role in reproduction. In their concern that modern women were
losing sight of their "obligation" to propagate the race, research biologists and
medical practitioners increasingly called for the programmatic education of individuals to acquire a "biological conscience" (*biologisches Gewissen*) or personal sense
of biological responsibility to society and the race, which would govern their sexual behavior and choice of marriage partner.[10] I will argue here that this clearly
normative biological thinking, which viewed the modern woman as an adversary,
manifested itself in some popular cultural typologies of women. Where it governed how social value was attached to various female identities, biomedical ideology restricted the potential of newly constructed "types" to encourage women
to cross the boundaries of their traditional roles.

I

Various articles in the popular press offered typologies as tools for negotiating the
challenges of interpersonal contact in the complex urban environment. Consider
the 1929 *Berliner Illustrirte Zeitung* rendition of leg posture, the way women (in most
of the examples) position their legs in the everyday posture of office work and rest:
sitting in a chair. How one holds one's legs, the text proclaims, represents the last
bastion of the modern, urban person's natural, unconscious physical expression of
character (fig. 1.1).

> The person . . . who grows up in the milieu of high metropolitan culture keeps a tight
> rein on her or his bodily gestures and controls the expression of her or his movements
> as well as her or his facial gestures; she or he "wears a theatrical mask." . . . Only the
> legs have thus far escaped this already unconscious restraining compulsion.[11]

Scientists, the report continues, are busy prying away at this remaining "hole in
the security system" of the "highly civilized" person's psyche, unlocking the secrets
of leg position to provide the trained observer with a view behind the increasingly
opaque "mask" of behavioral self-control acquired by the modern urbanite.[12] The
captions underneath the photos educate the reader in this newly developed technique of character assessment.

Figure 1.1. "New Approaches to Character Research: What Leg Position Can Tell You." From *Berliner Illustrirte Zeitung* 38:13 (1929), 517. Reprinted courtesy of Bildarchiv Preussischer Kulturbesitz.

The practice of crossing the legs below the knee indicates quarrelsomeness, but ready appeaseability, hot temperament and volatility. Must be led by a strong hand. . . . Legs held in a rigorously parallel position speak for particular suitability for marriage, adaptability, inner restraint.[13]

These and other captions suggest that, beyond the obvious strategic advantages a good leg-reader might have in his everyday dealings, one of the significant applications of this new character theory could lie in its usefulness as a tool for evaluating the marriageability quotient of a potential partner.

In his 1930 typology of human physique and character, *Sieh dir die Menschen an!* (Take a Look at Your Fellow Human Beings!), the physician and popular writer Gerhard Venzmer also addresses the classification of women in terms of their viability as marriage partners. With its goal of educating a lay reading public in the psychological typology established through clinical studies of the insane by the Marburg psychiatrist Ernst Kretschmer in the early twenties,[14] it served a function similar to the hermeneutic tool of metropolitan living offered by the "science of leg position." The central conclusion of Kretschmer's widely respected research had been that character or temperament had a biological basis that could be correlated to a physical body type, as both were expressions of the individual's genetic heritage. The trained eye could thus identify an individual with a slender, angular physique as a *Gedankenmensch*, a person with a tendency toward intellectual preoccupations, just like a muscular build would indicate a man of action, the *Tatmensch*, and a person with a rounded physique would reveal an uncomplicated and good-natured individual, a *Gemütsmensch*.

These categories were applied to both sexes, but not without differing implications. As the rounded physique, emotionality, and passivity of a *Gemütsmensch* practically defined the age-old concept of ideal femininity, a woman who displayed the physical and psychological attributes of the "naturally masculine" *Gedankenmensch* or *Tatmensch* was bound to be dangerously out of balance. Although more likely to display brilliant, exciting personalities, such women, according to Venzmer, were risky marriage partners for any man in search of peace and solidity in his relationship. Only very adventurous and hearty souls were advised to undertake such a marriage—those who enjoyed the challenge of dealing with conflict, tension, and radical mood swings.[15] (See fig. 1.2.)

Indeed, as Venzmer's text warns, many women who represent "pure" expressions of the slender or muscular body types make an impression that is downright "unfeminine." For many of the Weimar era classification systems used to describe women, femininity—or apparent lack thereof—was the crux of the matter. In their grasping for visual predictors of a woman's marriageability, these classification systems reveal one of the common subtexts that informed typologies as they were applied to women in the twenties: the fear that along with the disappearance of long hair and restrictions to home and hearth, femininity itself was on the wane, or had at least gone underground, becoming harder to discern under the boyish looks and freewheeling behavior of the so-called New Woman. To the extent that this general concern about the "masculinized" modern women took a specific shape, its contours were largely defined by the "biopolitics of population,"[16] which since the late nineteenth century had warned that women's forays beyond husband and family would ultimately threaten reproduction, society, and the human race.

"Sexuality" or "sexual character" (*Geschlechtscharakter, Geschlechtstyp, Geschlechtlichkeit*) were the terms most often used in Weimar medical literature to categorize women according to their inherited body and character type, or "constitution."

Figure 1.2. "Female Types Considered Unsuitable for Marriage." In the public domain.

Although it was only just gaining broader acknowledgment from other medical practitioners in the twenties, gynecologists exhibited a great interest in the practical implications of "constitutional biology" (*Konstitutionsbiologie, Konstitutionslehre*), which conceived of the human body and psyche as intimately connected and biologically predetermined.[17] In this context, the notions of "sex," "sexuality," "sexual character," and "sexual identity" described very nearly the same thing, and the notion of a "true" psychobiological sexual "nature" within each person went largely undisputed.[18] This theoretical framework held at least two attractions for gynecologists. First, it provided a practical basis for the ideas of social and racial hygiene, to which many gynecologists adhered. Their widespread involvement in the politics of reproduction and a consistent emphasis on genetics and selection in the major gynecological manuals indicate that they often saw themselves as the professionals most directly responsible for reproduction, as the caretakers of the *Volkskraft* (biological strength of the race or population).[19] Second, constitutional biology justified the construction of the all-encompassing category of sex, which could function as "a unique signifier and a universal signified,"[20] thus serving as a basis for the normative "guidance" and "care" of women. By defining the individual in both body and mind as a manifestation of biological sex, the field of gynecology could expand into a new all-encompassing *Frauenkunde,* or science of woman, which allowed the gynecologist's range of professional expertise and responsibility to include all aspects of women's physical and mental lives.[21] Thus experts in obstetrics and gynecological surgery came to publish and lecture widely on such topics as female psychology and the implications of modern female types for cultural evolution.[22]

Probably the most influential work on female constitutional types was a lengthy study by the Innsbruck gynecologist P. Mathes, published in 1924 as a contribution to the major gynecological reference work, *Biologie und Pathologie des Weibes*.[23] Drawing on contemporary research and his own clinical experience, Mathes classified women's bodies and psyches according to their mix of male and female characteristics. Echoing Otto Weininger's infamous turn-of-the-century study, *Geschlecht und Charakter* (Sex and Character), Mathes explained that all men and women possess the characteristics of both sexes to some degree, since variable development of the "energy carriers" for the sex-determining factors causes differing levels of the expression of "M" (male factor) or "F" (female factor) throughout the body.[24] Thus the occurrence of a fully sexually "differentiated" man or woman proved rare, even impossible (p. 75). In agreement with Kretschmer, however, his analysis concluded that a "real" or "complete" woman (*Vollweib*) generally has the predicted rounded physique.[25] In contrast to these "true" women, Mathes and others characterized a large proportion of all other women as more or less "inadequate" or "deficient" (*mangelhaft*) in their sexual differentiation—in other words, in their degree of difference from men—and therefore "intersexual."[26] Another prominent gynecologist found that 40 percent of all women of slender or athletic build were "deficiently differentiated."[27] Despite his assertion that some degree of intersexuality characterizes *most* women,[28] Mathes finds it necessary to base his definition of female "normality" on an admittedly fictitious "ideal"—that of the greatest possible sexual differentiation from the masculine ideal.[29] "Normal" femininity thus becomes a consciously *normed* femininity, allowing the specification of a single characteristic (e.g., hairless legs) as an attribute of the "normal woman" and categorization of its opposite (hairy legs) as an attribute of "deficient sexual differentiation"—despite its occurrence among the vast majority of women.[30] In this diagnostic approach the sum of the discrete characteristics determines the overall degree of intersexuality. Intersexual women were represented as being prone to irregularities in their sex drive, frigidity, physical complications or psychoses associated with giving birth, or even infertility, and—consistent with Venzmer's popular representation in *Sieh dir die Menschen an!*—generally unstable psyches.[31] All of these factors reportedly led to crisis-ridden and, more important, relatively infertile marriages. At stake in the normed identification and, ultimately, the regulation of intersexuality was thus the mental and physical health of both the individual and society. Beyond that, gynecologists, in their concern for the stability and fertility of individual marriages, portrayed their surveillance of female intersexuality as a defense of European culture and civilization as a whole.

In keeping with their broadly defined social responsibilities, gynecologists worried about the impact that more "serious" cases of individual intersexuality would have on the population at large. Mathes was particularly concerned by the results of an experiment in which crossing different strains of butterflies had increased the occurrences of intersexual offspring. One of the concrete symptoms of intersexuality in the butterflies—infertility—increased dramatically with the intermixing of different "races" of the same species.[32] Asserting that unusually high levels of human intersexuality were "evident" in the modern metropolitan centers of the world—the great racial melting pots—Mathes found that these butterfly experiments had alarming implications for the human race. Urban intersexuality might account for the declining birthrates, he declared, pointing toward the potential demise of contemporary European civilization. "It is well known that the greatest civilized races, with their greatly multiplied connections—one can say, to the entire world—perished as a result of infertility."[33] Other gynecologists and cultural critics went even further in their concerns than the isolated question of fertility, insisting that sexual differentiation was both the ends and the means of biological and cultural evolution. The prominent gynecologist Hugo Sellheim argued that the "new Germany" could only progress by cultivating a "natural" division of sex roles, and declared, "Where there is true culture the sexes move away from one another and develop their differences to the extreme."[34] Sex differences thus constituted the very basis of all advanced civilizations, which were now threatened by the gender-blurring trends of Western modernity.[35]

Given the scarcity of clear-cut physical cases of intersexuality, the gynecologist Otto Herschan warned his colleagues in a 1927 article to be wary of its characterological symptoms.

The intersexual woman, if [still] intellectually intact, is identifiable by her uniquely reflective nature. The judgment of the intersexual woman is less subject to emotional influence than that of the real ("complete") woman, more self-reliant, and the development of independent opinions is more marked.[36]

In fact, a woman's lifestyle and ambitions were significant clues to her intersexuality.

We often encounter the intersexual female type in the lecture halls of the university, and teachers represent a high percentage. Emancipated women, suffragettes, female academics, woman politicians, leaders of the women's movement, woman artists, woman drivers . . . are not infrequently intersexual. A great enthusiasm for completely unfeminine professions must always in and of itself alert one to intersexuality.[37]

As extreme as these ideas may seem, they were related in the respected *Zeitschrift für Sexualwissenschaft* (Journal for Sexual Science) and were common currency in the Weimar medical establishment.[38]

If the modern "masculine" occupations of some women provided the gynecologist with an important clue to their sexuality, then modern mass-produced and gender-ambiguous women's fashions were the adversary against which the doctor or marriage-minded layman—in search of a "real" woman—must pit his constitutional assessment skills, whether acquired through clinical practice, medical literature, or popular guides. Venzmer's self-help book reassured men that a little practice with the Kretschmerian system would enable them to see through the deceptive tricks of clothing or even posture and gait that fashion-conscious women were using to create the impression they were naturally the slender type of women considered "modern" by current fashions.[39] Dr. Herschan warned that the younger generation of men was particularly vulnerable to the dangers of a tragic marriage, as they seemed to favor the new unfeminine lines in a woman. Indeed, one of the only "problems" with intersexual men mentioned by Mathes was their mutual attraction to intersexual women.[40] Perhaps more than the clothing or the haircut, the slimming influence of women's burgeoning enthusiasm for exercise made the identification of the "truly" intersexual woman doubly difficult.[41] Weimar women's fashion, in lessening the distinctions and sowing confusion with the ubiquitous *Bubikopf* (pageboy) and simple, sporty, or tailored dresses worn by women of all types, constituted a radically subversive power in the realm of sociobiological management.[42]

In pursuit of their multiple missions of biological and psychological therapy on the individual and social level, Weimar gynecologists thus had to conduct what the medical literature represented as bewilderingly complex and subtle analyses of female "sexuality." Only the skilled reading of the overall impression made by the woman "in question," combining her myriad discrete physical and mental characteristics, could produce a decisive determination of her "degree of differentiation," or intersexuality.[43] Sex was in the eyes of the beholder—most reliably in the eyes of the talented and experienced examining doctor.

The literature on constitutional medicine emphasized the importance of clinical experience and natural talent for what was, after all, the "art" of medicine.[44] The schematic typologies proposed by the various constitution theorists provided a doctor with a means of systematizing his clinical experience and honing the sensitivity of his diagnostic gaze.[45] Constitutional medicine was deemed particularly useful for doctors because it awakened and refined the *Stilgefühl*, the sense of style.

> The sense of style, that is the capacity by which the doctor, in the absence of objective signs, grasps the clinical picture through instinct and intuition more than discernment and deliberation, and establishes the possibilities for treatment. One used to call it the "doctor's eye." It is trained and continuously nurtured by the impressions and experiences gained in the professional life, and held as images in memory—*memory-images* that are largely tied to the constitution and character of the patient.[46]

Constitutional medicine thus provided doctors with the means of ordering, deciphering, and ultimately assigning values—with a semblance of objectivity—to the images that were otherwise so complex that they were only accessible to intuition.

Constitutional medicine was a sort of cataloging system for the medical doctor's archival memory of cases. Venzmer's book, *Sieh dir die Menschen an!* suggests that he—and, we might suspect, other doctors—used this sort of archival analytic tool not only in his clinical practice but also in his interaction with all the people he encountered in everyday life. In the introduction to the book, Venzmer tells about his own observations of his fellow humans at a beach resort, and his reflections on their fascinating variety through the schema of Kretschmer's typology.[47] The book advises his readers in the lay public to learn to apply the same (Kretschmer's) order to their personal archives of body and character images as well.

The reading public was thus encouraged and "educated" to incorporate the same archival system used by the medical community into their observations of those around them. In his 1986 essay, "The Body and the Archive," Allan Sekula discusses a notion of the "universal archive" that provides a useful paradigm for understanding the function of such typological images as they might operate in the popular imagination. Working from Michel Foucault's insights into the insidiousness of social surveillance systems, Sekula describes the processes of looking at and evaluating photographic portraits in the nineteenth century. The new "democratic" technology of photography "welded the honorific and repressive functions" of the formerly class-bound practice of portraiture together, "introduc[ing] the panoptic principle into daily life."[48] In a procedure analogous to the nineteenth-century criminologist's evaluation of a mug shot, any person looking at a photographic portrait simultaneously placed that image among others in a "lineup" in her or his imagination. Thus every portrait implicitly took its place within a social and moral hierarchy. "The *private* moment of sentimental individuation, the look at the frozen gaze-of-the-loved-one, was shadowed by two other more *public* looks: a look up, at one's 'betters,' and a look down, at one's 'inferiors.' "[49] The ordinary viewer's looks up and down the social hierarchy scanned a "shadow archive" of the images for comparison. This imaginary archive was generalized, "universal," encompassing "an entire social terrain while positioning individuals within that terrain."[50] It contained images of figures of all social types and was organized by the then widely accepted hermeneutic paradigm for judging inner character by physical appearances: phrenology (skull analysis) and physiognomy (analysis of facial features). Photography emerges as a medium that involved the viewer in a surveillance operation of global proportions.

I suggest that the various typologies of women—both popular and scientific—that circulated in Weimar culture can be understood as just such a "universal archive." The *8-Uhr-Abendblatt*'s analysis of modernity and the Gretchen, Girl, and Garçonne could have easily proceeded without the help of illustrations, as these physical—and even characterological—profiles had achieved such common cultural currency through the mass media that they already influenced the categories applied to women in the popular imagination. Understanding how this universal archive of Weimar women was related to the hierarchical scale of constitutional intersexuality should offer some insight into the degree of success that met the therapeutic and educational efforts of the gynecologists and other doctors, like Venzmer, who sought to improve or at least maintain the public well-being through such typologies of women. To what extent did this medical discourse succeed in co-opting the general public's gaze for its surveillance of the modern "plague" of female intersexuality?

II

In 1931 the psychologist Alice Rühle-Gerstel reported in *Die literarische Welt* on her experience teaching an evening class on the reading of love stories. She found that the thirty-five young working women and housewives in her class were not interested in the aesthetic pleasures that motivated her own reading.

> But the need to find help for a woman's everyday life, advice in personal matters, is very strong. The women want to find in a novel that which is at the moment only available in the popular scientific or so-called self-help books; answers to questions like: to marry or not to marry, bringing children into the world or preventing pregnancy; faithfulness in love, demanding faithfulness, whether one can hope for faithfulness; being fair to husband and children and still increasing one's income through work.[51]

Novels were for these women, as Rühle-Gerstel understood it, a direct alternative to the self-help books that men were more likely to read. And indeed, a study of the lending habits of Leipzig library patrons in the early twenties found that *belehrende Literatur,* or educational, "nonfiction" texts such as Venzmer's *Sieh dir die Menschen an!* were far more popular reading for men than for women.[52] Novels provided a scenario into which a woman could project a bit of herself and reflect on the alternatives to and within her real-life situation. As in Janice Radway's more recent systematic study of the late twentieth-century romance reader, Rühle-Gerstel determined from her anecdotal evidence that this kind of reading was always a matter of identification: "the unliterary reader looks into the book from his own position, from his individual fate—even more so the woman reader."[53] Realistic or not, women in the twenties often looked to novels as a source of education and personal advice, much the way that the women in Radway's contemporary study see the romance novel as a source of knowledge and self-improvement.[54]

If women used novels to help make sense of their lives—to organize their "archives" in a sense—then an analysis of how women's information and pleasure sources participated in the "ideological work" of biomedical discourses will offer important insights into how these cultural forces helped shape women's self-images and experiences.[55] The degree of agreement—or conflict—between biomedical and popular images of women will register how popular culture disseminated or subverted the promotion of social and racial "hygienic" ideas that were applied to women in the professional discourse.

I will use the following investigation of Vicki Baum's novel, *stud. chem. Helene Willfüer,* to illustrate the complex ways in which the influence of biological discourse on popular representations of women could undermine attempts to construct positive images of modern women. Serialized with great success in the weekly *Berliner Illustrirte Zeitung* beginning in October 1928 and later released in book form,[56] the novel offers itself as a catalog of human types, practically inviting comparison with the typologies that newspapers, popular science books, and the medical community were advancing. As in the medical discourse of constitution in the twenties, the ubiquitous power of biology over personal fate exists in tension with the text's representation of an "ideal" New Woman, whose apparent command of her life might otherwise imply that an individual should actively pursue strategies of self-improvement and self-determination, in spite of the biological "givens."

Baum's novel tells the story of a university student, Helene Willfüer, who struggles against destitution and a series of setbacks in her personal life to achieve academic and professional success. After a youthful love affair leads to pregnancy, an unsuccessful search for an abortion, and a brush with suicide, she manages to finish her doctorate in chemistry and land an unlikely position in a private laboratory. There she conducts research on a youth-preserving hormone, while simultaneously raising her little boy. After ten years of hard work the product becomes commercially viable and brings her a top position in the chemical industry. The novel ends with Helene accepting a proposal of marriage from her mentor and former chemistry professor.

Quite early the narrative draws the reader's attention to its interest in character types and their comparison. The entire second chapter uses a montage technique reminiscent of filmic narrative to convey the idea of events simultaneously unfolding. With the present-tense narrator we peek into the windows of the university town of Heidelberg, already well established in the German popular imagination as the quintessential locus of student life. The city itself is a classic "type," whose true nature "we" will investigate. And "we"—the reader and her or his narrative guide—will approach it with the penetrating gaze, at once both analytic and awestruck, of the novice anatomy student.

> Didn't this city at times seem to lie there, like an exposed brain? A twitching, feverish, restless workshop of the intellect—an organism whose every hour gives painful birth to something new—learning, research, understanding, knowledge . . . ?[57]

This image of the university town as restless organism echoes the trope of the "nervous" modern city as a pathological body, allying the gaze of the narrator/ professor and the reader/anatomy student with the nineteenth-century sociologists who viewed the problems of urban society in biological terms and sought "cures" for the "social ills" of the metropolis.[58] As the narrative eye zooms in on the morning activities of the eight individuals whose lives it will follow throughout the rest of the novel, the voice of the guide points out what typifies them.

> There are people who find getting up astonishingly easy—like Fräulein Willfüer, for example, who, at the first trilling notes of her alarm clock, sits up in bed, clear headed and alert; who always rises in the best of humors, promptly sets the water on the spirit stove for her morning cup of tea and dashes a few handfuls of cold water over her tall body, chuckling softly and uttering little grunts of delight. While Gudula Rapp, . . . who shares her room, wakes up with a headache. . . . She moans with weariness. . . . And only when Helene Willfüer is already marching along her way . . .—only then does the struggle within Gudula Rapp's character come to an end— her better nature triumphs, and she leaves her meager student bed. . . . Then there are others . . . who are vanquished in the daily conflict: weak, nervous people.[59]

The guided tour continues in this vein, scanning the city and giving us an initial picture of each of the major players, intimating strong connections between character and body, and hinting that these have great significance for the future unfolding of events. Thus the pattern has been set: the text invites the reader to share in this experience of guided investigation and learning about character in a manner that evokes an interactive museum tour, or perhaps one of the popular educational films of the time—both favorite tools of the Weimar social and medical hygienists, whose programs aimed to strengthen the "resistance" of the population to the stresses of the metropolitan environment.[60] This narrative strategy also suggests an invitation to the reader to compare herself or himself to the characters, echoing popular self-help books that encouraged women to measure themselves against normative standards of beauty or health.[61] The novel's stylistic alliances to popular and scientific educational texts that promoted biomedical values are thus established from the beginning.

With an academic and successful working woman at its center, the novel was publicized and read as the story of an emancipated New Woman—a topic that had wide appeal in the Weimar era.[62] Its systematic characterological survey of the bourgeois women types circulating in the Weimar imagination manages to provide very few details of their physical appearance. Because a handful of stereotyped visual and characterological profiles of New Women were so solidified in the collective mind's eye by the illustrated press and other mass media, only the slightest intimation of a woman's character or appearance sufficed to activate the reader's "universal archive" and fill in the complete picture.

"Friedel," for example, is a young Heidelberg woman from a "good family" who is engaged to one of Helene's student friends. The slightest of hints—that she is eighteen, delicate, and has a little face like a flower that resembles an anachronistic lithograph[63]—are enough to suggest the complete image: it is Gretchen. With or without braids, she embodies the traditional woman who can only be the stumbling block under the wheel of history and progress (to paraphrase the *8-Uhr-Abendblatt*). Her traditional upbringing, strict moral standards, and naïveté cause her fiancé, the young chemistry student, Marx, to stray and become infected with venereal disease. At least, that is the meaning of the event suggested by the eminently more modern Helene Willfüer in a letter to Friedel informing her of her fiancé's illness. The only somewhat older Helene appeals to Friedel to grow up and muster her womanly capacity for tolerance, forgiveness, and support in hopes of saving Marx from his suicidal depression.[64] Here are echoes of a wide-ranging Weimar discourse that obliquely blamed the prudery of Wilhelmine bourgeois morality, especially in the education of girls, for indirectly causing men to turn to prostitutes and other promiscuous women, thus contributing to the spread of syphilis.[65] The Friedels of the world—along with the prostitutes—represented a public health hazard.

Yvonne Pastouri, the young, glamorous violinist married to Helene's chemistry professor, suffers from constitutional flaws that would place her toward the less feminine side of the gynecologists' continuum of intersexuality. Again, the text barely sketches her physical image, but the details provided point the reader toward a complete picture consistent with her character. Myriad typologists from both the popular and professional spheres could assist the reader in constructing the full image. The *8-Uhr-Abendblatt* would classify her as a "Girl," relating both her coquetry and her unwillingness to sleep with her husband to a calculating, manipulative egotism. Dr. Venzmer's popular typology would assess her delicate, slender build and "precious beauty" as good predictors of both her "dazzling" and "bewitching" presence and her lack of womanly warmth.[66] The gynecologists' typologies would of course agree, and find her strong-mindedness and success as a performing artist very consistent with her sexual "disorder"—her lack of sexual attraction to her spouse. Yvonne's rejection of the advances of her husband, Ambrosius, leads to a moment of dramatic tension, when only her threats to leave him forever succeed in warding off marital rape.[67] Recognizing Yvonne as an "intersexual type," the reader familiar with Dr. Mathes's typology via its 1927 treatment in the high society magazine, *Die Dame*, could explain this brush with marital rape in psychogynecological terms. "She *wants* to submit to the man she loves, but she *cannot;* the other sex [in her] always rebels. . . . It even comes to the point where the husband hits his wife; naturally the man [male part] in the woman loses, is conquered, the woman [female part] comes to the fore and—is even thankful for her liberation. That is the scientific explanation for the common wisdom that love and beatings are compatible," comments the gynecologist and author of the *Dame* article dryly, as he continues to express his pleasure that an expert, state-sanctioned gynecologist (Mathes) has finally provided unbiased scientific insight into the biology and pathology of woman: "The days of the 'misunderstood woman' are numbered. . . . [S]he [like the others] will hold no more secrets for the scientists" (p. 34).[68]

Helene Willfüer's roommate, Gudula Rapp, or *"das* Gulrapp," as she is called by her friends, evokes a Garçonne image, although she is not the unusually idealized, sexually and intellectually balanced *Lebenskünstlerin* described in the *8-Uhr-Abendblatt*. As a stereotype of the "masculinized" woman academic whose intellect and determination reflect an inner conflict with her femininity, she represents the Garçonne whose androgynous image was at once fashionable and controversial in the popular media.[69] Gudula appears early in the text as "a small girl, overtaxed by the demands of a great mind."[70] Nestled deep in the text, almost hidden, however, are clues to her struggle that go beyond this suggestion of feminine delicacy. The black-haired, cigarette-puffing Gudula clearly has a mutual affection for her roommate but tenses up and reminds her friend that she cannot bear it when Helene touches her in a gentle, friendly gesture. Helene understands, and feels sympathy for her poor friend, reflecting on "poor Gulrapp,"

> struggling so bravely with herself, day after day, night after night, driving her deviant, morbid affection down in to the depths of her heart. Her small figure grows more and more insubstantial, the gaze behind her glasses more and more hysterical, the thin hands of old ivory more and more tremulous; while the triumphant fulfillment, the inner serenity, the essential peace, recede farther and farther from her restless spirit.[71]

This passage evokes Venzmer's and Herschan's warnings that women of the slender, thinking type often suffer from severe inner conflicts, including conflicts of sexual identity. This is as close as the text ever comes to naming it: her deviant, "sick" inclination or tendency. As with its treatment of most other stereotypes charged with a negative valence in the popular imagination, the text tends to sympathize rather than denounce, lament rather than attack Gulrapp's homosexuality. She is the victim of a tragic biological fate. In the Weimar context, the sexologist Magnus Hirschfeld's influential theory that homosexuals represented a biologically determined, naturally occurring "third sex" was closely allied with this sympathetic representation of the lesbian.[72] A mainstream gynecologist following Mathes's typology would not be so forgiving. For such a doctor, Gudula would represent an extreme case of "constitutional intersexuality," whose "masculine desire," although biologically determined, must be condemned in its practice as far from "natural" in the sense of "normal" or acceptable.[73]

If we recall Mathes's warnings that urban centers tended to breed intersexuality, it is not surprising that the highly intersexual Gudula also clearly exhibits the pathological signs of the stereotypical *Stadtmensch,* or urbanite. In popular texts this label applied to particularly high-strung people, whose malaise was seen as a product of life in the fast-paced modern city. In fact, the medical profession had a technical diagnosis for Gudula's severe stress symptoms (trembling hands, difficulty making decisions) and tendency toward overexertion, both of which seem to arise directly from her driving ambition.[74] The image strongly suggests that Gudula suffers from the so-called modern disease of neurasthenia, which greatly concerned the medical community around the turn of the century. Neurasthenia was attributed to a generally weak psychological constitution, and counted among the symptoms of biological degeneration. Like the larger category of degeneration, the neurasthenic "weakness" was often explained as a product of the demands of high-pressure, chaotic metropolitan life. From the late nineteenth century on, neurasthenia was for many doctors the disease of the "moderns." Besides Americans, European Jews were seen as particularly plagued by neurasthenia due to their concentration in the urban centers and their positions of prominence in the stressful "competitive battlefield" of developing capitalism.[75] We can hardly be surprised, then, that this determined and nervous young woman, with her black-lacquer hair, bloodshot owlish eyes peering out through horn-rim glasses, and her scholarly passion for "oriental" cultures (the subject of her dissertation),[76] evokes the image of a Jewish intellectual.

As Atina Grossmann has pointed out, such a conflation of the Jewess and the lesbian is characteristic of one of the more malicious stereotypes of the sexually deviant New Woman.[77] It layers notions of female sexual independence with the image of the "perverse" or "degenerate" sexuality of the Jew that circulated widely in medical and anthropological discourse.[78] A 1920 lecture by a professor of anthropology at the University of Vienna, Robert Stigler, located a biological source for Jewish sexual deviance *and* liberal gender politics in their "intersexual" physiognomies.

> The physical signs of the sexual characteristics are noticeably vague. Among them, the women are often found to have relatively narrow pelvis and relatively broad shoulders and the men to have broad hips and narrow shoulders. . . . It is important to note the attempt on the part of the Jews to eliminate the role that secondary sexual characteristics instinctively play among normal people through their advocacy of the social and professional equality of man and woman.[79]

Although this passage reveals the nexus of racist and sexist potential inherent in the discourse of intersexuality, Sander Gilman has shown that it is not far from views on the biological "degeneration" of the Jews voiced around the turn of the century by a number of assimilated Jewish intellectuals themselves.[80] In their dependence on nineteenth-century medical knowledge and their professional need to distance themselves from such "aberrations" among their own race, even Jewish doctors subscribed to notions of a racial predisposition toward sexual deviance and mental illness.[81] Whether they considered the source of such biological "weaknesses" to be hereditary in origin or the biological result of environmental pressures on a group (such as the stresses of cosmopolitanism mentioned above), race was accepted as a central category in the discussion on "degenerate" body and character.[82] Adoption of this anti-Semitic discourse by Jewish doctors could serve the double function of distancing the author from these pathologized subgroups while still allowing the expression of political sympathy for the group as a whole, such as in an appeal for improvement of the social and living conditions of the Jews (as in the case of the Zionists).[83] In *Helene Willfüer* Gudula's apparent Jewishness has a parallel double-edged effect, perhaps serving a similar function for the novel's (assimilated) Jewish author.[84] Race works to reinforce Gudula's image as aberration, as Other, but simultaneously provides a "scientific apology" for her sexual deviance and a basis for her sympathetic portrayal. By combining the discourses of intersexuality, neurasthenia, and race, the Gudula figure represents the novel's fears for women who—for whichever reason—were not constitutionally strong enough to bear the stresses of academia and modern city life in general.

In the case of Helene Willfüer herself, the suggestions of her form are just as sparingly offered as for the other women, but through much of the novel the reader is less successful in constructing a complete visual image of her because the cues conflict with one another. Helene seems to be a new type. She is driven, yet peaceful and patient; she is proud, yet humble; large and plain-looking, but considered beautiful by many.[85] A woman who can hold her own in the competitive male world of the laboratory, Helene has a talent for making it feel like "home" by gathering a couple of colleagues around her Bunsen burner for a cup of tea.[86] The text repeatedly reminds the reader of these nurturing, traditionally feminine characteristics, which the medical discourse of intersexuality would deem unlikely to coexist in an extremely independent, hardworking young woman, who in stressful times finds solace in diving into her chemistry books. Helene has modern values, treating sex as something quite serious but not confining it to marriage, and accepting abortion as a necessary evil, although at heart she is an old-fashioned, nurturing, "natural" mother. Already on the second page of the book, the picture of Helene's motherly delight at holding a baby in her arms promptly impresses this most decisive signifier of Helene's femininity on the mind's eye. The rest of the book works at reinforcing this image of Helene's nurturing instincts alongside her *Sachlichkeit* (practicality), iron will, and boundless reserves of energy and self-discipline.

Described previously only in terms of her simple but attractive appearance and dress, her strong, working hands, straight brown hair, and large, distinctly German stature, the image of Helene Willfüer is finally given a very specific form at the end of the novel. Several years after the end of his disastrous marriage to Yvonne, the Heidelberg chemistry professor Ambrosius, on vacation in Italy, sits on a bench overlooking the sea. Struck by the image of a woman sitting quietly on the cliffs below, he sits in the twilight, spellbound by the combined peace and longing that he sees in her reflective pose.[87] The picture haunts him until he identifies its strange familiarity: "It is Feuerbach's Nanna. The same carriage, the stature, the strength, the reserve. And the same line of the averted face."[88] The reference is quite specific, invoking a set of images that were quite familiar to an educated readership of the Weimar period, when a number of popular books presenting the nineteenth-century artist's work were in publication. And the reference is more than fleeting: Ambrosius later orders a set of Feuerbach reproductions to be sent down from Munich, which he studies carefully, confirming for himself—and, of course, the reader—that the likeness is quite striking.

> Yes, here was the same forehead, the same vigorous sweep of the brows, the same line of marked but controlled sensuousness about the nostrils. Only Helene's mouth was less surely drawn, less feminine—a mouth shaped more by will than by emotion.[89]

In the act of acquiring the reproductions and comparing them to Helene, feature by feature, Ambrosius concertizes the process of evaluating his potential marriage partner with the help of a memory-archive (fig. 1.3).

Anselm Feuerbach's many famous paintings of Nanna Risi often used distinctly neoclassical motifs, such as that of Iphigenia on Tauris. One of this woman's great attractions for the artist was the classical Greek quality of her face and body. Here Helene Willfüer's large frame takes on the distinct features of a Greek ideal that was familiar throughout Weimar culture and had long enjoyed a special status within the discourses of social and racial hygiene.[90] In 1925 the Ufa film studio's highly popular educational film, *Wege zu Kraft und Schönheit* (Ways to Strength and Beauty), directly promoted the emulation of Greek physical culture as an antidote to the ills of the modern metropolitan "struggle for life."[91] The widespread pursuit of sports, dance, and, above all, body-conditioning programs according to the various methods of the neoclassically styled *Körperkultur* schools of expressive gymnastics and dance would pave the way to achieving "a harmonious proportion of the body [that] was the ideal of the ancient Greeks" (*Wege*). Using a trope made familiar by popular self-help books and medical texts,[92] the film dramatized the degenerative impact of "unnatural" civilization on the female body with the image of a female torso permanently disfigured by a corset, and warned further that "even today vanity injures many a woman's health." This film, like many popular texts concerned with lifestyle reform, positioned the image of the "healthy," unfettered Grecian-style female form—nude or draped in a neoclassical tunic—in direct contrast to the contemporary female body, disfigured by the demands of work and fashion in early twentieth-century European civilization.

Of the many books dealing with women's athletics and exercise, those promoting the "schools" or methods of neoclassical Körperkultur were especially concerned with designing exercise programs and styles of movement that sought to develop the "specifically female" body and feminine "nature."[93] Advocates explicitly touted the gender-specific exercises of Körperkultur as compensation for the

Figure 1.3. Ludwig Feuerbach, *Iphigenie* (1862). Reprinted courtesy of Hessisches
Landesmuseum, Darmstadt.

damaging influence of civilization's neglect of the female body and mind. In their promotion of such gymnastic programs they sought literally the *recultivation* of women's capacities for the gender-specific roles of reproduction and the "transmission of culture" to the next generation.[94] While most discussion of Körperkultur focused on the development of women's physical reproductive capacities, one popular self-help guide to female beauty made an explicitly pathologizing connection between the psyche and shape of the "modern woman": "Most 'moderns' have a great preference for the consumptive figure; they find it especially beautiful and interesting. In so doing, however, they themselves become interesting—for the psychiatrist."[95] The biomedical ideology of the many doctors who helped shape the objectives of the fitness movement is evident in the normative language of pathology used here and throughout the books, films, and articles on Körperkultur[96]

For many of its advocates, Körperkultur was about producing racial, cultural, and social health through the cultivation of a presumably lost or degenerated femininity. Informed by the medical discourse of the female constitution, it proposed an ideal of the "highly differentiated," "complete" woman, the *Vollweib*, to stand in direct contrast to the negative example of the modern "intersexual" woman, who was at once a symptom and a cause of biological and cultural degeneration. The discursive construction and disciplining of the pathological intersexual woman could only take place in conjunction with this positing of the healthy, complete woman. The Vollweib figured as both the basis for comparison (the doctor's analysis or a woman's self-analysis) and the model for emulation (the doctor's hygienic directives or a woman's self-regimentation) in the "universal" typology of women's "sexuality."

In Baum's novel the professor's identification of Helene with the neoclassical image of Feuerbach's Nanna constitutes his recognition of her as a "real woman," a Vollweib. While Ambrosius, and presumably the reader, contemplates these images of Helene as classical woman, however, the text relayers them with elements of the Weimar New Woman iconography: the cigarette-smoking, energetic single mother clambers on rocks, races her eight-year-old boy on the beach, and reads chemistry books on her vacation. And now, at the age of thirty-two, she is a renowned scientist and successful business leader. "True," "whole," "classical" womanliness is therefore not necessarily incompatible with these modern traits and ways, as the typologies discussed earlier and the other images of women in the novel would have us believe. The reader has little opportunity to allow Helene's masculine-encoded practicality, intellect, and strength of will to disturb that picture of her. Ambrosius, in contrast, standing in for that part of the male population that has not yet grasped that these characteristics can exist compatibly in one woman, undergoes a reeducation in the recognition of femininity that almost *requires* being severely burned by the "wrong" type before he is ready to see his former student, Helene Willfüer, in a new light.

In its reeducation of the professor to recognize a "real woman" underneath the modern guise of a professional, independent, and ambitious colleague, Baum's novel thus attempts to subvert the campaign against the "masculinized" modern woman with a *new* construction of the New Woman, and a fantasy of its acceptance. The critics took note of the new ground that the figure of Helene was breaking by taking the threatening edge off of the many stereotypes of intersexuality, coldness, and lack of motherliness that accompanied the images of the modern women in Weimar. And yet both the figure of Helene and the style of the novel were praised for their lack of sentimentality, their Sachlichkeit—"objectivity" or sobriety.[97]

I would argue that it is this very association with Sachlichkeit that compromises the potentially enlightening impact of the novel's construction of the strong, independent woman on a reader's consciousness in at least two ways. First, the stylistic association with *Neue Sachlichkeit* or the artistic direction of the New Objectivity carries with it an implicit claim to objective reporting of reality that prompts its reading as reportage. This was consciously promoted through the publisher Ullstein's extensive marketing of Vicki Baum as a serious writer and journalist, who conducted extensive research to become an "expert" on student life and the current state of scientific rejuvenation research.[98] Ullstein was clearly aware of the hunger of its readers for seemingly authentic and informative texts, which would combine learning with the pleasurable reading of fiction. The text itself takes this idea even further by subtly suggesting that it be read as an adventurous equivalent to the "informational" articles that surrounded its weekly installments in the *Berliner Illustrirte* or as a popular nonfiction, self-help guide to physique and character. Such a claim to objectivity reinforces the novel's self-representation as a source of truth and knowledge. It also reinforces the "reality" of those scanty characterizations that rely on and validate the heavily stereotyped and ideology-ridden mythologies of the New Woman that haunted the movie screens, the pages of the illustrated press, and, of course, the medical manuals.

Second, the style of Sachlichkeit evokes a strong association with the rationalizing forces of scientific and technological modernity—forces with which this biologically based typological representation of women is complicit. Despite the "new" New Woman who emerges in the figure of Helene Willfüer, her image cannot counteract the message of biological determination carried with the discourse of constitutional typologies in the text. She may represent a new "complete" femininity, but her strength of character is both consistent with and represented through her morphology, both of which indicate her likelihood to succeed from the beginning. The text indicates that this is her nature, not a result of her experiences, of learning. She was born with it. From the beginning, Helene is an "upright" person whose strong hands have "a look of race and character . . .—full of spirit and strength and resistance."[99] She survives extreme destitution and duress on the "patient, unyielding, proud, humble strength of her breed," qualities that seem to coexist naturally with her domestic, nurturing characteristics. Even her suggestive name reinforces the idea that Helene was a woman of "classical" stature and character from the very day she was born. Helene's fate, as much as any other character in the book, is tied to her form. Through Helene, therefore, the text attempts to challenge gender as a limitation to women's abilities but replaces it with biological types and biological fates.

The novel's characterizations, style, and story all are closely allied to "authentic" and official science, which reinforced the idea that biology is the centrally determining factor in an individual's fate. This places it in a web of ideologies and their institutional manifestations that identified the biological profile of a population as the main determinant of social progress and ills, and doctors or biologists as the most viable leaders in efforts toward social improvement. As Gilman has noted, the "peculiar power" of medical representation systems like those employed in *Helene Willfüer* lies not only in its status as science but also in the overt helplessness of the individual in the face of illness (or in the face of being labeled ill).[100] This power manifested itself in the everyday lives of average people as programs sprung up to place doctors in schools, in the workplace, and in a network of private and government "marriage counseling centers," all of which had missions to watch over individuals and steer them away from behaviors and activities deemed "constitutionally" or biologically less appropriate for them—including reproduction.[101] Given women's role in reproduction and the biological arguments often made to control their access to all sorts of work, women were deeply affected by such policies, which defined their social worth—regardless of profession—as contingent on their qualification as mothers.

Vicki Baum's *stud. chem. Helene Willfüer* tries to imagine new opportunities for women but does its best to "qualify" its New Woman in these traditional terms, as a mother and wife. By emphasizing Helene's essential "nature" and turning to the neoclassical image of "ideal" femininity for her shape, the text pulls her into the confines of a biomedically influenced type and explicitly places her in opposition to the ambiguous images of modern women as intersexual. In aligning female intersexuality with neuroses, racial "weakness," and failure, and "true" femininity with success,[102] the novel not only undercuts its attempt to construct a modern woman who succeeds through determination and will but also makes its own typology of women into another insidious disseminator of the normative principles of racial hygiene. As a widely read work of fiction that was presented and packaged as a view of reality to a wide reading audience, hungry for "real life" and new models in its literature, this novel's potential to influence women's worldviews and self-images made it a powerful element in the compendium of cultural images that shaped the "universal archive" of women. Such images contributed a biological dimension to the assessment of women by educating readers of both sexes to "read" women's health and social "worth" according to the dictates of—mostly male—scientific "experts." Operating inside the intimate sphere of pleasure reading, *Helene Willfüer* emerges as an important source of "local power" in the diffuse "deployment" of sexuality as an all-encompassing ideology that Foucault has described.[103] This popular novel thus supports the matrix of Weimar ideologies that looked to biology, and science in general, as a unifying, seemingly objective, and politically neutral source of solutions to the problems of modern, urbanized society. It belongs to the ideological framework of popular and medical constitutional guides and an endless number of other efforts to create new technologies imagined necessary for survival—survival of the sentimentally imagined bourgeois family, of patriarchy, of the German race, even of the human race.

NOTES

All translations are the author's unless otherwise indicated.

I would like to acknowledge my colleagues Deborah Cohen and Nancy Nenno, whose many thoughtful comments contributed greatly to this chapter. A shorter version was presented at the annual conference of the German Studies Association held in Dallas in October 1994.

1. M. G., "Drei Frauen stehen heute vor uns. Die drei Typen: Gretchen, Girl, Garçonne," *8-Uhr-Abendblatt* (4 June 1927). I am grateful to Julia Sneeringer for coming upon this source in my presence—and for sharing it with me.

2. Specifically, the "Girl type" is an "Anglosaxon lifestyle experiment on an ideologically medieval basis" (M. G., "Drei Frauen").

3. "Numerically rare in all of the colonies, and often in danger among the socially very mixed masses of the colonists, [this type] once enjoyed an elevated level of protection and respect and has cleverly figured out how to preserve this male attitude [ever since]" (M. G., "Drei Frauen"). Fritz Giese's *Girlkultur* provides the most detailed example of this notion; he explains that the frontier experience of macho male competition for land and (rare) women lives on in the status of women as the "queens" of the American household, honored by their subjugated husbands with "knightly service." Fritz Giese, *Girlkultur: Vergleiche zwischen amerikanischem und europäischem Rhythmus und Lebensgefühl* (Munich: Delphin, 1925), 105–108.

4. "Gretchen or Girl, antiquated or primitive, neither is a progressive form of feminine development. The Garçonne is . . . an individual attempt, whose generalization is still impossible" (M. G., "Drei Frauen").

5. Ilse Reicke, "Fraueninteressen in der Tagespresse," *Frauengenerationen in Bildern*, ed. E. Wolff (Berlin: Herbig, 1928), 116–117.

6. Helmut Lethen, *Verhaltenslehren der Kälte: Lebensversuche zwischen den Kriegen* (Frankfurt am Main: Suhrkamp, 1994).

7. J[ohann] C[aspar] Lavater, *Physiognomische Fragmente* (Leipzig and Winterthur: Weidmann, Reich, Steiner, 1775–1778). For an extensive discussion of Lavater's work and its European reception in both the eighteenth and nineteenth centuries, see Graeme Tytler, *Physiognomy in the European Novel: Faces and Fortunes* (Princeton: Princeton University Press, 1982).

8. Lavater, *Physiognomische Fragmente*, 36.

9. Daniel Pick, *Faces of Degeneration: A European Disorder, c. 1848–c. 1918* (Cambridge: Cambridge University Press, 1989), 6. See Cornelie Usborne, *The Politics of the Body in Weimar Germany* (London: Macmillan, 1992).

10. See Hugo Sellheim, "Hygiene und Diätetik der Frau," *Handbuch der Gynäkologie*, 3d ed., ed. J. Veit and W. Stoeckel, 9 vols. (Munich: Bergmann, 1926), 2:58.

11. "Neue Wege der Charakterforschung: Was die Beinhaltung enthüllt," *Berliner Illustrirte Zeitung* 38, no. 13 (1929), 517.

12. Ibid.

13. Ibid.

14. Gerhard Venzmer, *Sieh dir die Menschen an! Was die biologische Verwandschaft zwischen Körperform und Wesenskern des Menschen verrät* (Stuttgart: Franckh'sche Verlagshandlung, 1930); Ernst Kretschmer, *Körperbau und Charakter: Untersuchungen zum Konstitutionsproblem und zur Lehre von den Temperamenten* (Berlin: Springer, 1921). The latter went through at least twenty-six printings up to as late as 1977 and remains to this day a canonical work covered in the *Physikum*, the first set of comprehensive examinations for medical students in Germany. It was already in the eighth (revised) printing by 1930.

15. Venzmer, *Sieh dir die Menschen an!* 70.

16. Michel Foucault, *The History of Sexuality.* Vol. 1: *An Introduction* (New York: Vintage, 1980), 139.

17. The field of constitutional biology, which developed in the early twentieth century, encompassed the efforts of psychiatrists, philosophers, biologists, anthropologists, and medical doctors to understand the "whole person." Despite the widely acknowledged impact of Freud's ideas on the field of psychotherapy, much of the medical community remained unwilling to reject the close connection between biological and psychological processes that psychoanalytic theory required.

18. Voices that opposed this view from within the medical profession seem to be almost nonexistent. One prominent example of a modifying—if not fully conflicting—representation of sexuality is the psychologist Alice Rühle-Gerstel in her major work, *Das Frauenproblem der Gegenwart: Eine psychologische Bilanz* (Leipzig: Hirzel, 1932). Her account of sex and character is based on the theories of Alfred Adler's individual psychology, which does credit biology with a "limiting" but not determining role in psychological development (p. VI). While astutely pointing to the (male) social and political interests influencing the dominant contemporary theories of sexual difference (p. 4), she theorizes that the *social* effect of male dominance has attached artificially hierarchical values to male and female bodily functions (pp. 6–13), in addition to actually encouraging—through selection—much of the physical sexual differentiation (p. 6). Thomas Laqueur's recent *Making Sex* (Cambridge, Mass.: Harvard University Press, 1990) has convincingly demonstrated that the political interests Rühle-Gerstel points to not only affected the view of psychological differences, but indeed shaped the scientific understanding of anatomical sex differences as well.

19. Albert Niedermeyer, *Die Aufgabe des Frauenarztes bei der Eheberatung, Veröffentlichungen aus dem Gebiete der Medizinalverwaltung,* ed. T. Lentz (Berlin: Schoetz, 1929), 28:24. See also Johannes Meisenheimer, "Grundlagen der Vererbungslehre," in *Handbuch der Gynäkologie,* ed. J. Veit and W. Stoeckel, 9 vols. (Munich: Bergmann, 1926), 2:355–475; C. H. Stratz, "Rassenlehre," in *Biologie und Pathologie des Weibes: Ein Handbuch der Frauenheilkunde und Geburtshilfe,* ed. J. Halban and L. Seitz, 5 vols. (Berlin: Urban & Schwarzenberg, 1924), 1:491–516; and Fritz Lenz, "Erblichkeitslehre und Rassenhygiene (Eugenik)," in *Biologie und Pathologie des Weibes,* 803–868.

20. Foucault, *The History of Sexuality,* 1:154.

21. The "natural" affinities between the fields of gynecology, eugenics, sexology, constitutional medicine, and the new discipline of Frauenkunde were promoted especially by the prominent Berlin gynecologist Max Hirsch, who established and edited the journal *Archiv für Frauenkunde und Eugenik* in 1914 and eventually changed its name to *Archiv für Frauenkunde und Eugenetik, Sexualbiologie und Konstitutionsforschung* (Archive for the Science of Woman and Eugenics, Sexual Biology and Constitution Research) in 1923, on the occasion of taking over the leadership of the Ärztliche Gesellschaft für Sexualwissenschaft und Konstitutionsforschung (Medical Society for Sexology and Constitution Research). Hirsch was

also one of the leading members of the Prussian Beirat für Rassenhygiene und Bevölkerungsfragen (Advisory Council for Racial Hygiene and Population Issues). See Robert Lenning, "Max Hirsch: Sozialgynäkologie und Frauenkunde," dissertation, Free University, Berlin, 1977; and Cornelie Usborne, *The Politics of the Body in Weimar Germany.* See also Paul Weindling, *Health, Race and German Politics between National Unification and Nazism, 1870–1945* (Cambridge: Cambridge University Press, 1989), regarding the socioeconomic factors behind structural changes in the medical profession.

22. See, for two examples among many, Hugo Sellheim, *Das Geheimnis vom Ewig-Weiblichen: Vorträge über Frauenkunde für weitere Kreise,* 2d ed. (Stuttgart: Enke, 1924), or Wilhelm Liepmann, *Psychologie der Frau,* 2d ed. (Berlin: Urban & Schwarzenberg, 1922). Both published extensively on obstetrics (*Geburtshilfe*), and Liepmann especially on gynecological surgery, before branching out to include psychology, culture, and politics.

23. P. Mathes, "Die Konstitutionstypen des Weibes, Insbesondere der intersexuelle Typus," in *Biologie und Pathologie des Weibes,* ed. J. Halban and L. Seitz, 5 vols. (Berlin: Urban & Schwarzenberg, 1924), 3:1–112. This article by Mathes was frequently and deferentially quoted in the various articles and medical manuals cited here, including reference to it as the founding, "the classic," work on female constitutional typology in Niedermeyer (1929). (Although his full name cannot be found on any publication, all references to his work confirm that Mathes was a man.)

24. Mathes, "Konstitutionstypen des Weibes," 72–73. Mathes and others who quoted him noted Otto Weininger's anticipation of this notion in his 1903 book, *Geschlecht und Charakter* (repr. Munich: Matthes & Seitz, 1980), but clearly considered Mathes's own contribution the most significant, as it provided the essential scientific basis for Weininger's "intuitive" speculations (Mathes, "Konstitutionstypen des Weibes," 75). Weininger even anticipated the notion of ideal marriage combinations based on matching partners with complementary "M":"F" ratios (pp. 34–35).

25. Mathes, "Konstitutionstypen des Weibes," 23–28. Mathes also defined this ideal form of femininity as constituting a necessarily less advanced stage of evolutionary development than that of the man (female *Jugendform* vs. male *Zukunftsform*), rendering the ("pathological") intersexual woman an *evolutionarily* "more advanced" form (pp. 17–22)—a paradox with broad implications and many parallels in other Weimar discursive domains.

26. Ibid., 55–75.

27. Quoting Max Hirsch in Otto Herschan, "Die weibliche Intersexualität," *Zeitschrift für Sexualwissenschaft* 14 (1927/1928):408.

28. Mathes, "Konstitutionstypen des Weibes," 63.

29. Ibid., 9–10.

30. Ibid.

31. See Venzmer, *Sie dir die Menschen an!* 95–107; Herschan, "Die weibliche Intersexualität," 409.

32. Mathes, "Konstitutionstypen des Weibes," 56–59. Mathes is referring to the research of Richard Goldschmidt, which actually involved gypsy moths, not "butterflies." His references included the following: "Untersuchungen über Intersexualität," *Zeitschrift für induktive Abstammungs- und Vererbungslehre* 23 (1920):1–19; *Die quantitative Grundlage von Vererbung und Artbildung* (Berlin: Springer, 1920); "Die biologischen Grundlagen der konträren Sexualität und des Hermaphroditismus beim Menschen," *Archiv für Rassen- und Gesellschaftsbiologie* 12 (1916):1–14.

33. Mathes, "Konstitutionstypen des Weibes," 76.

34. Sellheim, "Hygiene und Diätetik der Frau," 285–286, 57.

35. See also, for example, Ernst Klimowsky, "Sexualtyp und Kultur: Elemente einer Darstellung der europäischen Kulturgeschichte auf der Grundlage der vergleichenden Psychologie der Geschlechter," *Abhandlungen auf dem Gebiete der Sexualforschung* 5, no. 3 (1928); J. Crux and F. Haeger, "Körperbau und Gattenwahl," *Zeitschrift für Sexualwissenschaft* 17, no. 6 (1930/1931):337–349. For an opposing voice: M. Vaerting, *Die weibliche Eigenart im Männerstaat*, 2 vols. (Karlsruhe: Braun, 1921, 1923). This was also a wide-ranging discourse, ridden with paradoxes.

36. Herschan, "Die weibliche Intersexualität," 410.

37. Ibid.

38. Women physicians most certainly felt less threatened by the phenomenon of modern women professionals, but there is no evidence that they raised their voices against this concept of intersexuality. Women physicians generally did subscribe to the basic tenets of social and racial hygiene. See Atina Grossmann, "Berliner Ärztinnen und Volksgesundheit in der Weimarer Republik: Zwischen Sexualreform und Eugenik" in *Unter allen Umständen: Frauengeschichte in Berlin*, ed. C. Eifert and S. Rouette (Berlin: Rotation, 1986), 183–217. Cf. Anton Schücker, *Zur Psychopathologie der Frauenbewegung* (Leipzig: Kabitzsch, 1931).

39. Venzmer, *Sie dir die Menschen an!* 69.

40. Mathes, "Konstitutionstypen des Weibes," 79.

41. Otto Herschan, "Typologie der psychisch eheuntauglichen Frau," *Zeitschrift für Sexualwissenschaft* 16, no. 5 (1929/1930):326.

42. For an interesting analysis of the ideological power of fashion during the same period in France, see Mary Louise Roberts, "Samson and Delilah Revisited: The Politics of Women's Fashion in 1920's France," *American Historical Review* 98, no. 3 (1993):657–684.

43. Mathes, "Konstitutionstypen des Weibes," 71–72.

44. Ibid., 9, 14; Max Hirsch, "Ärztliche Heilkunde und Charakterforschung," in *Konstitution und Charakter*, Monographien zur Frauenkunde und Konstitutionsforschung (Berlin: Kabitzsch, 1928), 10.

45. Hirsch, "Ärztliche Heilkunde," 10. I use the masculine here since that was almost always the case, and it was always the assumption held by these writers about their audience.

46. Ibid., 10; my emphasis.

47. Kretschmer, *Körperbau und Charakter*, 1–2.

48. Allan Sekula, "The Body and the Archive," *October* 39 (1986):10.

49. Ibid.

50. Ibid.

51. Alice Rühle-Gerstel, "Frauen und Liebesgeschichten: Ein kleiner Bericht," *Die literarische Welt* 7, no. 12 (1931):9.

52. Walter Hofmann, *Die Lektüre der Frau* (Leipzig: Quelle & Meyer, 1931).

53. Rühle-Gerstel, *Frauenproblem der Gegenwart*, 9.

54. Janice Radway, "Interpretive Communities and Variable Literacies: The Functions of Romance Reading," in *Rethinking Popular Culture*, ed. C. Mukerji and M. Schudson (Berkeley, Los Angeles, and Oxford: University of California Press, 1991), 474–475.

55. The term "ideological work" is borrowed from Mary Poovey, *Uneven Developments: The Ideological Work of Gender in Mid-Victorian England* (Chicago: University of Chicago Press, 1988). It refers to both the constructing, contesting process of representation itself, which produces the ideology, and the "system of interdependent images" which make an ideology accessible to individuals (p. 2).

56. Lynda J. King, *Best-Sellers by Design: Vicki Baum and the House of Ullstein* (Detroit: Wayne State University Press, 1988), 89; Vicki Baum, *stud. chem. Helene Willfüer* (Stockholm: Forum, [ca. 1925] 1939). All further page references are from this edition (except translations as indicated).

57. Baum, *Helene*, 18; 21–22. Page numbers refer to the German edition (see n. 56, above); Ida Zeitlin's English translation, Vicki Baum, *Helene* (Garden City, N.Y.: Doubleday, 1933), which I have used with some adaptations.

58. See Robert A. Nye, "Sociology and Degeneration: The Irony of Progress," in *Degeneration: The Dark Side of Progress*, ed. J. E. Chamberlin and S. L. Gilman (New York: Columbia University Press, 1985), 49–71.

59. Baum, *Helene*, 18–19/22.

60. A brochure for the 1930 International Hygiene Exhibition in Dresden explained its urgency in terms of the demands of urban living: "We all feel it: a new era is upon us! Surrounded by the cacophony of the metropolis, agitated, driven by the pursuit of daily bread, harnessed to the trials of often monotonous drudgery, the requirements of hygiene are completely new—completely different from those our ancestors knew. Whether we approve of the mechanization and tempo of our era or not, we have to come to terms with it. And further: under these new conditions we must find ways and means to shape our lives as efficiently and hygienically as possible, so that we remain *vigorous, healthy, energetic and ready for action*" (emphasis in original). From a pamphlet cataloged in the Staatsbibliothek Preussischer Kulturbesitz Unter den Linden in Berlin under the title, "Dresden, Internationale Hygiene-Ausstellung 1930."

61. The publisher's foreword to *Der weibliche Körper und seine Beeinflussung durch Mode und Sport* suggested: "Here for the first time every woman will find the key to her beauty, since after reading she can establish—without a competition—whether her body corresponds to the norms of beauty." Rudolf M. Arringer, Else Rasch, and A. M. Karlin, *Der weibliche Körper und seine Beeinflussung durch Mode und Sport*, 7th ed. (Berlin: Verlag für Kultur und Menschenkunde, 1931), 3.

62. For a discussion of the New Woman image in the criticism and publicity surrounding the novel, see King, *Best-Sellers by Design*, 81–107.

63. Baum, *Helene*, 20/32.

64. Ibid., 140–142.

65. This suggestion appeared in a wide variety of literature, ranging from the popular to the scientific and from the socially conservative (Alexander) to the anarchist (Albrecht). See, for example, Paul Albrecht, *Freiheit der Liebe* (Berlin: Der freie Arbeiter, [1926]); Hans Alexander, *Vom Baume der Erkenntnis* (Leipzig: Orla-Verlag, n.d.).

66. Baum, *Helene*, 52, 10/47–50, 131.

67. Ibid., 52–53/65–66.

68. J. Löbel, "Die verstandene Frau," *Die Dame* (January 1927), 34.

69. See Patrice Petro, *Joyless Streets: Women and Melodramatic Representation in Weimar Germany* (Princeton: Princeton University Press, 1989), 103–127, for a discussion of such images and controversy over the "masculinized" woman in the pages of the *Berliner Illustrirte* and *Die Dame*.

70. Baum, *Helene*, 28.

71. Ibid., 142–143, 174–175.

72. See Magnus Hirschfeld, *Die Homosexualität des Mannes und des Weibes: Ein Lehrbuch für Ärzte und Studierende*, 2d ed. (Berlin: Marcus, 1920), vol. 3 of *Handbuch der gesamten Sexualwissenschaft in Einzeldarstellungen*.

73. "Although conceptually the same thing, in practice homosexuality must be considered separately from intersexuality. Whether a woman is homosexually active . . . depends very much on external circumstances—depends in many cases solely on seduction. Just as homosexuality and its activation is usually artificially elicited, it also can be warded off" (Mathes, "Konstitutionstypen des Weibes," 108).

74. "Ambition would drive her like a peppery curse." Baum, *Helene*, 54; 67.

75. For a classic example, see Martin Engländer, *Die auffallend häufigen Krankheitserscheinungen der jüdischen Rasse* (Vienna: J. L. Pollak, 1902), 15–18. Also see Sander L. Gilman, *Jewish Self-Hatred: Anti-Semitism and the Hidden Language of the Jews* (Baltimore: Johns Hopkins University Press, 1986), 286–297; "The Madness of the Jews," in *Difference and Pathology: Stereotypes of Sexuality, Race, and Madness* (Ithaca: Cornell University Press, 1985), 150–162; "Sigmund Freud and the Sexologists: A Second Reading," in *Sexual Knowledge, Sexual Science*, ed. R. Porter and M. Teich (Cambridge: Cambridge University Press, 1994), 336–337.

76. The objects of Gudula's studies and fantasies are tied up with the icons of mystical Eastern religions (26–28; 31–33), an association "inherent in the image of the Eastern Jew" (Gilman, "Madness of the Jews," 155).

77. Atina Grossmann, "The New Woman and the Rationalization of Sexuality in Weimar Germany," in *Powers of Desire: The Politics of Sexuality*, ed. A. Snitow, C. Stansell, and S. Thompson (New York: Monthly Review Press, 1983), 167.

78. Gilman, "Sigmund Freud and the Sexologists," 334–335.

79. "Die rassenphysiologische Bedeutung der sekundären Geschlechtscharaktere," *Sitzungsberichte der anthropologischen Gesellschaft in Wien* (1919/1920), 6–9, 7. Published as a special number of the *Mitteilungen der anthropologischen Gesellschaft in Wien* 50 (1920). Quoted in Gilman, "Sigmund Freud and the Sexologists," 335.

80. Gilman, "Sigmund Freud and the Sexologists," 334–335; cf. Gilman, *Difference and Pathology*, 156–157.

81. Gilman, *Difference and Pathology*, 162.

82. Ibid., 156–158; "Sigmund Freud and the Sexologists," 333–334.

83. Gilman, *Difference and Pathology*, 162.

84. See the first chapter of Vicki Baum's autobiography, *I Know What I'm Worth* (London: Michael Joseph, 1964).

85. Baum, *Helene*, 253.

86. Ibid., 29.

87. Ibid., 242.

88. Ibid., 243; 292.

89. Ibid., 252; 303.

90. Francis Galton, the "father of eugenics" in the nineteenth century, placed the ancient Greeks high atop his hierarchy of human intelligence. Francis Galton, *Hereditary Genius* (London: Friedman, 1978), 342 (quoted in Sekula, "The Body and the Archive," 44).

91. *Wege zu Kraft und Schönheit*, dir. Wilhelm Prager, English intertitles, Stiftung Deutsche Kinemathek, Berlin.

92. See, for example, Arringer, Rasch, and Karlin, *Der weibliche Körper;* Sellheim, "Hygiene und Diätetik der Frau" (1926).

93. The many possible examples include Gertrud Bäumer, "Zur weiblichen Körperkultur," and Bertha Sachs, "Die körperliche Erziehung der Frau vom ärztlichen Standpunkt," both in *Die körperliche Ertüchtigung der Frau*, ed. Bund deutscher Frauenvereine (Berlin: Herbig, 1925); Dora Menzler, *Die Schönheit deines Körpers* (Stuttgart: Dieck, 1924); Fritz Giese

and Hedwig Hagemann, eds., *Weibliche Körperbildung und Bewegungskunst* (Munich: Bruckmann, [1920]); Arringer, Rasch, and Karlin, *Der weibliche Körper;* and Sellheim, "Hygiene und Diätetik der Frau."

94. Bäumer, "Zur weiblichen Körperkultur," 7–14; Hugo Sellheim, *Das Geheimnis vom Ewig-Weiblichen: Vorträge über Frauenkunde für weitere Kreise,* 2d ed. (Stuttgart: Enke, 1924).

95. Arringer, Rasch, and Karlin, *Der weibliche Körper,* 5–6.

96. While on the one hand doctors invented some of the more influential gymnastics techniques (esp. Dr. Beth Mensendieck), served as "scientific advisers" to popular promotional projects (such as Ways to Strength and Beauty—Dr. med. Nicholas Kaufmann), and contributed numerous articles on physical culture to the popular press, on the other, they borrowed promotional Körperkultur photographs of women engaged in "harmonious movement" to illustrate gynecological "hygiene" manuals, making the exchanges among the popular gymnastics schools, the media, and medical literature multidirectional. See Beth M. Mensendieck, *Funktionelles Frauenturnen* (Munich: F. Bruckmann, 1923); Giese and Hagemann, *Weibliche Körperbildung;* and Sellheim, "Hygiene und Diätetik."

97. Alfred Arna, "Modernes Mädchen," *Vorwärts* (1 February 1929); Gabriele Reuter, "Stud. chem. Helene Willfüer," *Vossische Zeitung* (17 March 1929).

98. King, *Best-Sellers by Design,* 87–95.

99. Baum, *Helene,* 16–17; 17.

100. Sander Gilman, "Introduction: What Are Stereotypes and Why Use Texts to Study Them?" in *Difference and Pathology,* 15–35.

101. Kristine von Soden, *Die Sexualberatungsstellen der Weimarer Republik 1919–1933* (Berlin: Hentrich, 1988); Paul Weindling, *Health, Race and German Politics between National Unification and Nazism, 1870–1945* (Cambridge: Cambridge University Press, 1989).

102. Yvonne Pastouri ends up as a varieté artist and prostitute in Paris; Gudula Rapp finishes her doctorate in archaeology and goes off to Berlin, but has little hope of pursuing the glorious career for which she longs. Baum, *Helene,* 26–27, 175, 259/32–33, 213, 310.

103. Foucault, *History of Sexuality,* 94–99.

TWO

Perceptions of Difference:
Woman as Spectator and Spectacle

Patrice Petro

[The] remarkable juxtapositioning of women and cities . . . is probably rooted in the historical fact that the entire ancient world built its great cities on rivers and coastlines, because water transport was superior then. The freer forms of commerce among cities released a certain proportion of women from the most stringent patriarchal relationships and monitoring. As early as the gospel of St. John, we find Babylon described as "the whore sitting beside the waters."
—KLAUS THEWELEIT, *MALE FANTASIES* (1977)[1]

For those who experienced the rapid technological and industrial expansion of Germany, Berlin became the symbol of an almost indescribable dynamic. As one historian explains, if the old Berlin had been impressive, the new Berlin was irresistible, and the mere mention of the city inspired powerful reactions from everyone: "It delighted most, terrified some, but left no one indifferent, and it induced, by its vitality, a certain inclination to exaggerate what one saw."[2] The connection suggested here between vision and an *inflated view* of the city acquires a special significance when we consider some of the most influential theories of perception and subjectivity written during the Weimar period. Indeed, for intellectuals, artists, and journalists in Germany in the 1920s, the evocation of Berlin served not only as a convenient shorthand for a number of technological innovations thought profoundly to alter perception and experience (trains, automobiles, and telephones as well as photography, photojournalism, and film); Berlin also served as the decisive metaphor for modernity. Modernity, in turn, was almost always represented as a woman.

There are, of course, immediate historical reasons for associating Berlin in the 1920s with modernity: as the capital of the Reich and the most populous and industrialized of all German cities, Berlin was the center for mass cultural entertainment; hardly remarkable, given that large-scale urbanization was the precondition for the expansion and differentiation of the mass cultural audience.[3] What is remarkable, however, is that contemporary observers repeatedly imagined the city taking a female form. For example, in a 1929 issue of *Der Querschnitt*, an Ullstein magazine for intellectuals, the journalist Harold Nicolson describes the particular charm of Berlin by invoking the figure of woman as metaphor for the enigmatic and, hence, desirable "otherness" of the city.

What on earth gives this city its charm! Movement in the first place. There is no city in the world so restless as Berlin. Everything moves. The traffic lights change restlessly from red to gold and then to green. The lighted advertisements flash with the pathetic iteration of coastal lighthouses. . . . Second to movement comes frankness. London is an old lady in black lace and diamonds who guards her secrets with dignity and to whom one would not tell those secrets of which one was ashamed. Paris is a woman in the prime of life to whom one would only tell those secrets which one desires to be repeated. But Berlin is a girl in a pullover, not much powder on her face, Hölderlin in her pocket, thighs like those of Atalanta, an undigested education, a heart which is almost too ready to sympathize, and a breadth of view which charms one's repressions. . . . The maximum irritant for the nerves corrected by the maximum sedative. Berlin stimulates like arsenic, and then when one's nerves are all ajingle, she comes with her hot milk of human kindness; and in the end, for an hour and a half, one is able, gratefully, to go to sleep.[4]

Where Nicolson calls on the image of the female adolescent (the "girl in a pullover, not much powder on her face") to describe the curious mixture of old and new in the city, the playwright Carl Zuckmayer invokes a far more sexualized and, indeed, far more demonic female figure to describe what he sees as Berlin's peculiar mixture of seduction and cruelty.

This city devoured talents and human energies with a ravenous appetite, grinding them small, digesting them, or rapidly spitting them out again. It sucked into itself with hurricane force all the ambitions in Germany, the true and the false . . . and, after it had swallowed them, ignored them. People discussed Berlin . . . as if Berlin were a highly desirable woman, whose coldness and capriciousness were widely known: the less chance anyone had to win her, the more they decried her. We called her proud, snobbish, *nouveau riche*, uncultured, crude. But secretly everyone looked upon her as the goal of their desires. Some saw her as hefty, full-breasted, in lace underwear, others as a mere wisp of a thing, with boyish legs in black silk stockings. The daring saw both aspects, and her very capacity for cruelty made them the more aggressive. All wanted to have her, she enticed all. . . . To conquer Berlin was to conquer the world. The only thing was—and this was the everlasting spur—that you had to take all the hurdles again and again, had to break through the goal again and again in order to maintain your position.[5]

Berlin, it is obvious, inspired powerful reactions and induced a tendency to exaggerate what one saw. It is equally obvious, however, that this tendency to exaggerate in representing Berlin as a woman reveals less about women in Weimar than it does about a male desire that simultaneously elevates and represses woman as object of allure and as harbinger of danger. Although it would seem that Zuckmayer's claim that "to conquer Berlin was to conquer the world" defines the particular contours of this male desire, it is, rather, his admission that "you had to take all the hurdles again and again . . . to maintain your position" which reveals its fundamental paradox: the paradox of a male fascination with femininity that threatens to subvert masculine identity, and that therefore requires constant vigilance to keep the fears and anxieties provoked by woman at a safe and measured distance.

The passages I have cited from Nicolson and Zuckmayer are far from anomalous. One need only look at the images of the city made famous in the paintings of George Grosz and Otto Dix, or read the city poems of Bertolt Brecht, Erich Kästner, and Walter Mehring, to realize how numerous artists and writers responded to modernity by imaginatively reconstructing Berlin as demonic, as alienating, and as female. Even an abstract film like Walter Ruttmann's *Berlin, die Symphonie der Grossstadt* (Berlin, Symphony of a City, 1927) builds its investigation of the city's spatial and visual fragmentation around the spectacle of woman—a spectacle barely hidden at the center of the film. Yet if there exists a wealth of evidence to read responses to modernity in Weimar as constructed on male subjectivity and desire—where woman is absent as subject and yet overpresent as object—I raise the following questions: What kind of historical response to modernity is concealed in the textual and artistic inscription of woman in Weimar? And can we discern in this historical response a different discourse on subjectivity, perception, and sexual difference in Germany of the 1920s? In other words, is there a way to reread early discussions of modernity in Weimar so as to situate woman as an inhabitant of the city she so frequently serves to represent?

To begin to answer these questions, we should recall that the Weimar years not only were marked by political, economic, and social crises, but that these crises were often perceived as contributing to the loss of (male) cultural authority. That responses to the loss of this authority should invariably involve woman hardly comes as a surprise, especially when we consider the fact that it was only in the early twentieth century that the women's movement gained a contending voice in German political and cultural life.[6]

In this regard, it is all the more significant that artists and intellectuals typically construed modernity as feminine, and as effecting an almost complete transformation of the cultural and perceptual field. While mass culture in general was frequently associated with modernity (and hence, as several theorists have pointed out, with woman),[7] the cinema in particular seemed to crystallize the relationships among modern life, modes of perception, and male responses to gender difference.

The cultural historian Egon Friedell, for example, expressed the widely held belief that perception and representation had been transformed under the impact of modernity when he remarked in 1912, "[The film] is short, quick, at the same time coded, and it does not stop for anything. There is something concise, precise, military about it. This is quite fitting for our time, which is a time of extracts. In fact, these days there is nothing which we have less of a sense for than that idyllic relaxation and epic repose with objects which earlier stood precisely for the poetic."[8] While the loss of a poetic repose with objects disturbed a thinker like Friedell, other critics, particularly those on the political left, celebrated the loss of this repose since it signaled the demise of outmoded aesthetic values and inaugurated an address to an emerging mass cultural audience. Significantly, however, even critics on the left warned against the tendency of the cinematic image to capture and immobilize the spectator, to induce a passive response characteristic of technological modes of production more generally. As the Spartacist poet Bruno Schönlank describes in his poem "Kino,"

Factory workers, tired
from the drudgery of the day.
Salesgirls, seamstresses, spinning
golden fairy tales of luck and the wages of true love.
Beautiful girls follow the pictures
and swallow in the lies.
They gladly let themselves be led astray
by that which enchants their souls.
Drunk with the glitter they return home
and in the dark room see yet another light,
which breaks through their dreams as bright as the sun
till grey everyday life puts it out again.[9]

This evocation of cinematic spectatorship further indicates how discussions about representation and perception in Weimar were often divided along sexual lines. In Schönlank's view, the appeal of the cinema derives from its illusory plenitude ("golden fairy tales of luck and the wages of true love"), which draws one closer; it is the female spectator—not her male counterpart (as represented, for instance, by the poet himself)—who proves most susceptible to the cinematic illusion, unable to achieve a critical distance from it. Far from being a spectator who assumes an "epic repose" considered poetic in the past, the female viewer is understood as that spectator who is not only willingly duped by the image but also most easily deceived by its lies.

While early assessments of perception and spectatorship in Germany hardly promote a neutral understanding of spectatorship and sexual difference in the cinema, it would be a mistake to assume that our current discussions of these issues have somehow moved beyond the implicit premises of the early debates. Indeed, notions about modernity that circulated in turn-of-the-century Germany—with women equated with the image and, at the same time, situated as that spectator unable to separate from it—continue to inform some of the most sophisticated analyses of perception and spectatorship in current film theory. Most strikingly, contemporary film theorists retain the assumption that film technology so profoundly alters perception and experience that it completely reorganizes the spectator's relationship to space, vision, and structures of desire. In his essays on psychoanalysis and the cinema, for instance, Christian Metz invokes the metaphor of the cinema as an "apparatus"—a technological, institutional, and psychical "machine" for stabilizing subjectivity—to suggest how the film spectator internalizes certain historically constituted and socially regulated modes of psychical functioning.[10] According to Metz, the cinema is more richly perceptual than other arts because it mobilizes a larger number of axes of perception: analogical image, graphic image, sound, speech, dialogue. But, as Metz explains, if the film is thus more perceptually present, that which it depicts is manifestly absent. He concludes that the cinema involves the spectator more profoundly than the other arts in the imaginary, since it is the spectator's identification with his own look—with himself as pure act of perception—that serves as the very condition for perceiving in film.

Metz goes on to argue that while the spectator's look lends coherence and meaning to the cinematic image, the coherence of the viewing subject can only be secured through processes of voyeurism and fetishism; in other words, through those psychic mechanisms that enable the viewer to assume a distance from the image. "It is no accident," Metz remarks, "that the main socially acceptable arts are based on the senses at a distance, and that those which depend on the senses of contact are often regarded as 'minor' arts (e.g., the culinary arts, the art of perfumes, etc.)." Continuing this thought, he writes,

> Nor is it an accident that the visual or auditory imaginaries have played a much more important part in the histories of societies than the tactile or olfactory imaginaries. The voyeur is very careful to maintain a gulf, an empty space, between the object and the eye, the object and his own body; his look fastens the object at the right distance, as with those cinema spectators who take care to avoid being too close to or too far from the screen. . . . [For] to fill in this distance would threaten to overwhelm the subject, to lead him to consume the object (the object which is so close that he cannot see it any more), to . . . [mobilize] the sense of contact and [put] an end to the scopic arrangement.[11]

Although Metz does not concern himself with the historical reasons for the implicit (gender) hierarchizing of the visual and auditory imaginaries, his description of perceptual differences nevertheless raises fundamental questions about the function of gender in perceptual response. Are we to assume that the woman's relationship to the image is the same as the man's, and that she, too, partakes of a voyeuristic or fetishistic pleasure in looking?

In an attempt to respond to this question, Mary Ann Doane has proposed that "both the theory of the image and its apparatus, the cinema, produce a position for the female spectator which is ultimately untenable because it lacks the attributes of distance so necessary for an adequate reading of the image."[12] Doane goes on to explain that the female spectator's inability to distance herself from the image—her tendency to "overidentify" with events on the screen—suggests that the woman is constituted differently than the man in relation to forms of perception and structures of looking. "For the female spectator," Doane writes, "there is a certain overpresence of the image—she is the image. Given the closeness of this relationship, the female spectator's desire can be described only in terms of narcissism—the female look demands a becoming. It thus appears to negate the very distance or gap specified by Metz . . . as the essential precondition of voyeurism."[13]

Although Doane takes pains to modify the Metzian model by theorizing a kind of fetishism available to the female viewer in what she calls the "masquerade," her discussion of female spectatorship significantly rests on notions of perception and sexual difference that tend to corroborate—rather than challenge—certain time-honored assumptions about seeing and knowing in the cinema. In line with Metz, for example, Doane attributes both knowledge and pleasure in the cinema to a necessary distance from the image. As she proposes, the mode of looking developed by the classical narrative cinema depends on an image of woman that is fixed and held for the pleasure and reassurance of the male viewer. While this image automatically produces voyeuristic or fetishistic separation in the male spectator, she explains, it also threatens to overwhelm and consume the female spectator for whom that image is too close, too present, too recognizable. Doane surmises that when the female spectator fails to distance herself from the image of woman, she necessarily merges with that image and, consequently, loses herself. Equating the cinematic apparatus with a theory of the male imaginary, Doane winds up affirming the model of spectatorship she initially sets out to expose: conflating vision with intellection, Doane maintains that the female spectator can only "see" (and thus assume a position of knowledge) in the classical narrative cinema by manufacturing a distance from the image of woman and taking up the position of fetishist. In a formulation of the problem that is in some respects similar to Metz's own, she writes, "A machine for the production of images and sounds, the cinema generates and guarantees pleasure by a corroboration of the spectator's identity. Because that identity is bound up with that of the voyeur and the fetishist . . . it is not accessible to the female spectator, who, in buying her ticket, must deny her sex."[14]

Unlike early German film theorists, Metz and Doane ground their analyses of perception and spectatorship in a systematic application of psychoanalytic concepts. Yet behind these lies a historical argument about modernity and perceptual response that locates gendered spectatorship within the terms of a phallocentric discourse; indeed, Freud himself pointed out that the transition from a matriarchal to a patriarchal society involved the simultaneous promotion of senses at a distance (i.e., sight and hearing) and devaluation of senses of contact (i.e., touch, taste, and smell).[15] The perceptual distance thought to provide a privileged means of access to knowledge and pleasure in psychoanalytic accounts of film spectatorship thus derives its force from a historical argument that gives sense perception a quite specific meaning; to borrow from Doane, it is not sight in general, but the sight of the female body as the sign of castration that provokes the defensive, and thus more mediated, visual response of the film voyeur and fetishist.[16]

I believe there is sufficient cause to challenge psychoanalytic accounts of perception and subjectivity in the cinema and to distinguish the perceptual possibilities of film viewing from the theory of a male imaginary so often employed to describe them. To pose such a challenge adequately, however, we need first to identify the historical argument underpinning discussions of perception and visual response in psychoanalytic film theory, and then to work back through the clichés about gendered spectatorship to recognize how they conceal a fairly complex history rooted in responses to modernity and male perceptions of sexual difference. My concern in the following pages is to offer such a challenge and to trace concepts relating to perception and spectatorship back to philosophical and theoretical debates over mass culture and modernity as they were waged in Germany in the 1920s.

I focus on the writings of Martin Heidegger, Walter Benjamin, and Siegfried Kracauer, since each of these theorists aims to underline the historical nature of subjectivity and identity and thus to situate perceptual changes within a fundamentally historical understanding of modernity. There are, of course, several other important theorists who wrote about spectatorship and perception during the Weimar years, notably, Béla Balázs, Rudolf Arnheim, and Bertolt Brecht. For several reasons, however, I see the work of Heidegger, Benjamin, and Kracauer as most useful for reconsidering the relationships among mass culture, perception, and modern experience, and for discerning the contours of a discourse on sexuality that continues to shape our understanding of cinematic representation and spectatorship.

All three theorists exert considerable influence on the way in which contemporary scholars approach questions of representation and subjectivity as they relate to the problem of modernity.[17] A reexamination of their writings from a feminist perspective, however, should allow us to pursue issues of gendered spectatorship in a manner far more precise than has hitherto been the case. Rather than appeal to the operative dualities familiar to contemporary film theory (active/passive, absence/presence, distance/proximity), Heidegger, Benjamin, and Kracauer define the impact of technology on perception in a more differentiated and subtler manner. The concepts of contemplation and distraction, for instance, enable these theorists to describe the difference between artistic and mass cultural reception, and yet to conceptualize the simultaneous response of passivity and activity, proximity and distance in the spectator's relation to the image. This is not to say that they completely agree on the historical meaning of changes in representation or perceptual response. Indeed, not only do all three theorists take different approaches to questions of modernity, they also exhibit distinct attitudes toward the social and political functions of mass cultural spectatorship—attitudes ranging from contempt to ambivalence to celebration.

Most important, however, their writings disclose a historical dimension in modernity that allows us to take up questions of gender and spectatorship as they exist between the lines of the debate over mass culture. For all three theorists, male spectatorship remains the (unspoken) topic of theoretical exploration. Nevertheless, because they align the cinema with a crisis of perception (in which the subject experiences becoming an object), their writings unwittingly reveal how the crisis of male vision is inseparable from the emergence of a mass cultural audience and from the growing demands of women for an equal share in German cultural life. The writings of Heidegger, Benjamin, and Kracauer thus provide us with a philosophical framework for contesting traditional notions of perceptual response and gendered spectatorship, allowing us, in turn, to recognize in the metaphors of modernity both the city and the cinema in Weimar, which were, undeniably, also inhabited by women.

PERCEPTION, MASS CULTURE, AND DISTRACTION: MARTIN HEIDEGGER

> Everything is going on as if reading Heidegger had nothing to do with sexual differ-
> ence, and nothing to do with man himself, or, said in another way, as if it had noth-
> ing to do with woman, nothing to interrogate or suspect. . . . Perhaps one could even
> speak of [Heidegger's] silence as uppity, precisely, arrogant, provocative, in a century
> where sexuality is common to all the small talk and also a currency of philosophical
> and scientific knowledge, the inevitable *Kampfplatz* [battlefield] of ethics and poli-
> tics. . . . And yet, the matter seems to be understood so little or so badly that Hei-
> degger had immediately to account for it. He had to do it in the margins of Being
> and Time.[18]

There are a number of reasons for the continual appeal to Heideggerian phe-nomenology in contemporary theories of culture and representation. Most obvi-ously, contemporary theorists are drawn to Heidegger's attempt to think more pri-mordially about modern existence—his effort to transcend the division between subject and object by subordinating epistemology to ontology so that critical un-derstanding ceases to be a simple "knowing" in order to become a way of "being." Part of the appeal of this primordial thinking, however, undoubtedly derives from Heidegger's effort to get beyond questions of sexual difference and thus to tran-scend that inevitable Kampfplatz where the sexual is political and vice versa.

And yet, as Jacques Derrida himself insists, Heidegger only appears to be silent on questions of sexuality and sexual difference, for in his early writings on experi-ence and in his later writings on language, Heidegger has quite specific things to say about gender (even if he does relegate these remarks to the margins of his phi-losophy). To understand Heidegger's views on gender, it is necessary to outline his position on modernity; indeed, as we shall see, Heidegger's approach to the ques-tion of sexual duality in experience is fundamentally linked to his exploration of modernity and mass culture.

In his magnum opus on temporality and experience, *Being and Time* (Sein und Zeit, 1927), Heidegger identifies his thoughts in opposition to the technological thinking of the modern age, and thus communicates something of the sense of discontent and disillusionment with modernity that pervaded German culture in the wake of World War I. As one historian explains, "Heidegger's life—his isola-tion, his peasant-like appearance, his deliberate provincialism, his hatred of the city—seemed to confirm his philosophy, which was a disdainful rejection of mod-ern urban rationalist civilization."[19] Or, in the words of Hans Georg Gadamer, who refers less to the man himself than to the reception of his writing, "The contemporary reader of Heidegger's first systematic work was seized by the vehemence of its passionate protest against . . . the levelling effects of all individual forms of life by industrial society, with its ever stronger uniformities and its techniques of communication and public relations that manipulated everything."[20]

Heidegger's critique of modernity and technological forms of communication cannot be separated from his critique of epistemology for holding vision to be a superior means of access to certainty and truth. In *Being and Time,* for example, he refers to a modern obsession with the visual over other sensory faculties and describes this as a privileging of seeing (*sehen*) over understanding (*verstehen*) that contributes to the impoverishment of the senses and a fundamental "distraction" (*Zerstreuung*). In contrast to "concern," or a mode of perception guided by circumspection and contemplation, "distraction" lends itself to what Heidegger calls a "restless" and "curious" gaze.

> When curiosity has become free . . . it concerns itself with seeing, not in order to understand what is seen . . . but just in order to see. Consequently, it does not seek the leisure of tarrying observantly, but rather seeks restlessness and the excitement of continual novelty and changing encounters. In not tarrying, curiosity is concerned with the constant possibility of distraction. . . . Both this not tarrying in the environment and this distraction by new possibilities are constitutive items for curiosity; and, upon these is founded the third essential characteristic of this phenomenon, which we will call the character of never-dwelling-anywhere [*Aufenthaltslosigkeit*].[21]

As Heidegger suggests, the character of "never-dwelling-anywhere" points to the relationship between the "curious" and the "distracted" gaze, for both succumb to the restlessness and banality of the merely novel ("what one 'must' have read or seen"). In his later writings on poetry and language in the 1930s and 1940s, Heidegger specifically links the most "distracted" cultural activities to the "everyday" phenomena of mass culture—the cinema, the illustrated press, and television.[22] Rehearsing a mode of perception that Heidegger calls "amazed to the point of not understanding," these mass cultural practices produce the world as image, as picture, as purely subjective experience. As he explains in his 1938 essay "The Age of the World Picture,"

> The fundamental event of the modern age is the conquest of the world as picture. The word "picture" [*Bild*] now means the structured image [*Gebild*] that is the creature of man's producing which represents and sets before. In such producing, man contends for the position in which he can be that particular being who gives the measure and draws up the guidelines for everything that is.[23]

Heidegger's assessment of mass culture would seem to anticipate the feminist critique of representation for securing the male viewer in a position of mastery over the visual field. But where the feminist critique insists on the manner in which the *woman* is made into an object for the pleasure of the male gaze, Heidegger's analysis suggests how it is *man* himself who experiences becoming and then being an image, who is made to yield his existence for another's use.[24] In an early section of *Being and Time*, for example, Heidegger writes,

> *Dasein*'s everyday possibilities of Being are for the Others to dispose of as they please. These Others, moreover, are not definite Others. On the contrary, any Other can represent them. . . . In this inconspicuousness and unascertainability, the real dictatorship of the "they" is unfolded. We take pleasure and enjoy ourselves as *they* take pleasure; we read, see, and judge about literature and art as *they* see and judge; likewise, we shrink back from the "great mass" as *they* shrink back; we find "shocking" what *they* find shocking. . . . Overnight, everything that is primordial gets glossed over as something that has long been well known. Everything gained by a struggle becomes just something to be manipulated. Every secret loses its force.[25]

According to Heidegger, the subject ought to distance himself from the tyranny of the "they"—from that seductive force of "distraction" which remains the preserve of others. In his view, only painting and poetry afford such distancing, since both artistic forms demand a leisurely "contemplation" that not only provokes reflection but also allows for a repossession of self (*Eigentlichkeit*). If Heidegger clearly refuses the kind of mastery he associates with a mass-produced visual culture, he also resists its effects of depersonalization and loss; in other words, contemplation becomes a means of compensating for powerlessness, a way of overcoming the radical otherness of the self in a more detached and, hence, more intellectually mediated aesthetic experience.

This brief analysis suggests how Heidegger retains the familiar distinctions between art and mass culture and the structures of contemplation and distraction associated with each. Significantly, however, "distraction" comes to figure in Heidegger's writings both as a perceptual response to mass culture and as the originary structure of experience—the splitting and division of the subject in language. In view of this apparently paradoxical "double meaning" of distraction, it is crucial to raise the following questions: What is the relationship between the "alienation" of mass culture and the "dissociation" of the subject in language? And does this alienation or dissociation have something to do with sexual difference?

As Derrida has suggested, Heidegger employs the concept of distraction to address the role of sexual duality in the constitution of modern experience.[26] This is not to say that Heidegger recognizes sexual duality as constitutive of different experiences in the modern world; on the contrary, he sees duality as concealing a neutrality and even a certain asexuality in our experience of being-in-the-world (our experience of being-there as marked by the term *Da-sein*). In a close reading of a series of lectures Heidegger delivered at the University of Marburg in 1928, Derrida details and defends Heidegger's attempt to "neutralize" the issue of sexual duality; in Derrida's view, it is only by neutralizing questions of sexuality and experience that Heidegger avoids the binary logic inherent in anthropology, biology, and psychology.

Derrida points out that in his Marburg lectures, Heidegger is quite careful to pass from the masculine to the neutral term when defining the theme of his analysis: "For the being which constitutes the theme of this analysis," Heidegger writes, "we have not chosen the heading 'man' (*der Mensch*) but the neutral heading '*das Dasein*.' "[27] Heidegger's neutralization of the question of being, Derrida further remarks, also carries over to his postulation of a certain neutrality or asexuality of experience (das Dasein). Again, as Heidegger writes, "the neutrality signifies also that the Dasein is neither one of the two sexes."[28] For both Heidegger and Derrida, the neutrality of Dasein or our experience of being-in-the-world does not mark a negativity but instead marks a positivity or powerfulness (*Mächtigkeit*). As Derrida puts it, "neutrality does not de-sexualize, rather to the contrary: it does not use ontological negativity with regard to sexuality itself (which it would instead liberate), but with regard to the mark of difference and, more strictly, to sexual duality."[29]

For Derrida, as for Heidegger, sexual difference is not a property of biology or something that originally exists in human beings. Nevertheless, because the question of "sexuality itself" comes to displace the concept of experience in the writings of both theorists, the historical and social construction of gender is effectively elided. Heidegger, for example, denies sexual difference a determining role in his analysis of experience because sexual duality marks a fundamental negativity (woman as nonman). At the same time, however, sexuality itself is said to retain a "neutral" signification (woman as the same as man) since it allows sexuality to emerge as multiplication, dissemination, even liberation. The subject whose sexuality is, in fact, liberated in the passage from the masculine (der Mensch) to the neutral (das Dasein) is suggested by the interpretive gesture that must repress the feminine term to achieve "neutrality." If, in this way, Heidegger's ontology avoids binary logic, it also effaces the feminine as a term within language and as a social position for women that is symbolically constructed and historically lived.

This is not to imply, however, that femininity as it relates to *male* identity is completely effaced in Heidegger's ontology. Heidegger's description of mass cultural dissociation (where the "I" is forced to yield his existence to the "they") leads him to argue for a repossession of self in contemplation—a repossession that will alone restore mastery under the conditions of pervasive powerlessness. If Heidegger's ontology represents a response to modernity and to the loss of cultural mastery, it would seem that something quite specific precipitated this loss: namely, the emergence of a mass cultural audience and the presence of others previously excluded from mass cultural reception. In this regard, it is symptomatic that Heidegger sees division both as constitutive of subjectivity and as debasing to cultural experience. Indeed, his plea for a "neutralization" of sexuality and experience would seem to be a plea to get beyond the difficulties of gender more generally: to dissolve the other that inhabits the self and, equally, to repress the other that contends for access to culture in the modern age.

PERCEPTION, MASS CULTURE, AND DISTRACTION:
WALTER BENJAMIN AND SIEGFRIED KRACAUER

> Benjamin recalled his sexual awakening when, en route to the synagogue on the Jew-
> ish New Year's Day, he became lost on the city streets. . . . [He writes:] "While I was
> wandering thus, I was suddenly and simultaneously overcome, on the one hand, by
> the thought 'Too late, time was up long ago, you'll never get there'—and, on the
> other, by a sense of the insignificance of all this, of the benefits of letting things take
> what course they would; and these two streams of consciousness converged irre-
> sistibly in an immense pleasure that filled me with blasphemous indifference toward
> the service, but exalted the street in which I stood as if it had already intimated to me
> the services of procurement it was later to render to my awakened drive."[30]

Few theorists have addressed Walter Benjamin's fascination with the city and the
street as it reveals assumptions about sexuality and sexual difference.[31] Indeed, it is
not sexual politics but politics in general that remains the central topic of debate
in Benjamin criticism. As one commentator puts it, "The Left has been . . . concerned to defend [Benjamin's] legacy from mystical appropriations of it, the Right
to establish its distance from any orthodox canon of historical materialism."[32]

If we are to believe those theorists who claim to position themselves on neither
the Left nor the Right of this debate, Benjamin's writings owe less to Marxism and
to mysticism than they do to ontological phenomenology. In his introductory essay
in *Reflections,* for example, Peter Demetz argues that Benjamin's "hermeneutical
urge" to read cities and social institutions as if they were sacred texts reveals his al-
legiance to Heideggerian philosophy or the "turn to language which alone communicates what we can philosophically know."[33] In much the same manner, Hannah Arendt maintains that Benjamin was as keenly aware as Heidegger of "the
break in tradition and loss of authority which occurred in his lifetime" and that
both theorists discovered strikingly similar ways of responding to the past and the
present. Benjamin's remarkable feeling for language and for history, she continues,
confirms that he had more in common with ontological thought than "he did with
the dialectical subtleties of his Marxist friends."[34]

Benjamin's reflection on language and history reveals the profoundly phenomenological dimension to his thinking (and it is to Arendt's and Demetz's credit to
have pointed this out). Nevertheless, this phenomenological dimension should not
be confused with Heideggerian philosophy, for it is Benjamin's attempt to combine
phenomenology with social theory that establishes his strongest intellectual affinities: not with Heidegger or ontological phenomenology, but with Siegfried Kracauer and critical theory.

As colleagues and collaborators, Benjamin and Kracauer are among the first
Weimar intellectuals to think seriously about the perceptual as well as the political
effects of mass-produced art on subjectivity and experience. In contrast to Heidegger, who tends to dismiss mass culture as thoroughly vacuous and degraded,
Benjamin and Kracauer insist on the perceptual possibilities of photography and
film and go so far as to claim that mass culture alone responds to the changed re-

ality of technological and industrial society. Drawing on the phenomenology of Georg Simmel,[35] Benjamin and Kracauer consider the entire urban panorama—moving from photography to film to the city and the street—in an effort to discern how all aspects of modernity register the historical process in which an absorbed or concentrated gaze has been replaced by a more distracted mode of looking. While claiming to describe psychic and economic changes as these reveal structural changes of a general historical nature, Benjamin and Kracauer at the same time elaborate a theory of subjectivity that builds on a very specific theory of sexuality and sexual difference.

In his essay "Some Motifs in Baudelaire," for example, Benjamin argues that "the experience of shock" has transformed the spatiotemporal register of sense perception. As he explains, modern modes of production and technology have submitted the human sensorium to a "complex kind of training." To cope with the rapid succession of ever-increasing stimuli, tactile senses have been trained in abruptness and optic senses have been trained to deal with distraction.

> The invention of the match around the middle of the nineteenth century brought forth a number of innovations which have one thing in common: one abrupt movement of the hand triggers a process of many steps. . . . One case in point is the telephone, where the lifting of a receiver has taken the place of a steady movement that used to be required to crank the older models. . . . Tactile experiences of this kind were joined by optic ones, such as are supplied by advertising pages of a newspaper or the traffic of a big city. Moving through this traffic involves the individual in a series of shocks and collisions. . . . Whereas Poe's passersby cast glances in all directions which still appeared to be aimless, today's pedestrians are obliged to do so in order to orient themselves to traffic signals.[36]

It is well known that Benjamin's response to these changing perceptual relations remains fundamentally ambivalent. In some instances, he argues that the modern experience of distraction and shock revealed in techniques of photography and film provide for a deepening of perception, extending the range of the "optical unconscious."[37] In other instances, however, he maintains that shock experience reduces the play of the imagination, inducing a fragmented perception that drains memory of its content.[38] Benjamin's ambivalence toward mass cultural distraction is perhaps most strikingly articulated in his essays on Baudelaire. Furthermore, the manner in which he expresses his ambivalence reveals how he often projected his own fear of and fascination with mass culture onto the figure of woman (in particular, the prostitute) and onto Baudelaire's description of the big-city crowd.

"As regards Baudelaire," Benjamin writes, "the masses were anything but external to him; indeed, it is easy to trace in his work a defensive reaction to their attraction and allure."[39] Benjamin defends his preference for Baudelaire's poetry by stressing that, in contrast to such conservative philosophers as Bergson, Baudelaire did not consider the poet to have privileged access to structures of experience and memory. Instead, like Benjamin himself, Baudelaire understood the need to direct attention to the metropolitan masses, for they alone came to experience modernity in the form of shock perception. As Benjamin acknowledges, if the metropolitan masses had a privileged relationship to modern experience, the spectacle of the masses also inspired fear and dread among the most sympathetic of observers. Poe and Engels, as Benjamin documents, found the big-city crowds "barbaric," a vortex of confusion inspiring fear, revulsion, even horror. And when Benjamin explains that it was precisely this image of the big-city crowd that became decisive for Baudelaire, he reveals how his own reaction to the spectacle of mass culture involves elements of attraction and dread, fascination and horror.

In Baudelaire's sonnet "A une passante," for example, Benjamin detects Baudelaire's attraction to a "figure that fascinates," an unknown woman mysteriously carried along by the crowd who comes to represent "the object of love which only a city dweller experiences."[40] That this figure becomes an object, however, anticipates the crowd's equally menacing aspect. The "distracted" gaze that has lost the ability to look in return—a crucial aspect of what Benjamin calls the "aura"—serves to describe a kind of looking that inspires as much fear as fascination in the poet.

> The deeper the remoteness which a glance has to overcome, the stronger will be the spell that is apt to emanate from the gaze. In eyes that look at us with mirrorlike blankness, the remoteness remains complete. . . . When such eyes come alive, it is with self-protective wariness of a wild animal hunting for prey. (Thus the eye of the whore scrutinizing passersby is at the same time on its guard against the police. Baudelaire found the physiognomic type bred by this kind of life delineated in Constantin Guy's numerous drawings of prostitutes. "Her eyes, like those of a wild animal, are fixed on the distant horizon; they have the restlessness of a wild animal . . . but also the animal's sudden tense vigilance.")[41]

To cope with this experience of shock, Benjamin explains, Baudelaire adopted one of two strategies: either he would assume an "attitude of combat" and battle the crowd or he would adopt the posture of the old women he describes in the cycle "Les Petites vieilles," who stand apart from the crowd, unable to keep its pace, no longer participating with their thoughts in the present.[42] Benjamin thus assigns to the figure of woman in Baudelaire's poetry both the threatening character of distraction and the contained repose of distance. Nevertheless, at the conclusion of his essay, Benjamin recalls how Baudelaire imagined himself betrayed by the old women and suggests how this left him with only one option.

> To impress the crowd's meanness upon himself, [Baudelaire] envisaged the day on which even the lost women, the outcasts, would be ready to advocate a well-ordered life, condemn libertinism, and reject everything except money. Having been betrayed by these last allies of his, Baudelaire battled the crowd—with the impotent rage of someone fighting the rain or wind. This is the nature of something lived through (*Erlebnis*) to which Baudelaire has given the weight of an experience (*Erfahrung*). He indicated the price for which the sensation of the modern age might be had: the destruction of aura in the experience of shock.[43]

When read from the perspective of Benjamin's own critical ambivalence toward mass culture, these remarks concerning the "price" Baudelaire paid for his battle with the crowd acquire a special meaning. Benjamin, too, could not stand apart from the spectacle of mass culture but was determined to struggle with its contradictory meanings and effects. However compelling Benjamin's ambivalent relation to mass culture remains, it is important to recognize how this ambivalence came to be expressed through reference to the metaphorical figure of woman (a figure that stands as much for modernity as it does for the continually renewed search for a lost plenitude).

In essays on the cinema and mass culture that he wrote in the 1920s, Kracauer not only anticipated Benjamin's analysis of modernity by several years but also elaborated a similar theory of historical changes in structures of perception and experience. In his 1927 essay, "Cult of Distraction" (Kult der Zerstreuung), for example, Kracauer maintains that distraction in the cinema models itself on the rationalization of labor more generally and thus reveals how processes of abstraction have come to permeate forms of perception, representation, and experience. Kracauer therefore argues against those artists and intellectuals who condemn the cinema as a vacuous or superficial "distraction," explaining that such condemnation fails to understand that distraction involves a complete restructuring and a different logic in social reality.

> One says the Berliners are addicted to distraction (*zerstreuungssüchtig*); this accusation is petit-bourgeois. Certainly the addiction is stronger here than in the provinces, but stronger and more apparent here is also the tension of the working masses—a basically formal tension that fills their day without making it fulfilling. . . . This emphasis on the external has the advantage of being sincere. Through it, truth is not threatened. Truth is threatened only by the naive affirmation of cultural values that have become unreal and by the careless misuse of concepts such as personality, inwardness, tragedy and so on, terms which themselves refer to lofty ideas but which have lost most of their scope along with their supporting foundations due to social changes.[44]

Kracauer's insistence on the "sincerity" of the commitment to distraction is not a simple endorsement of alienation in cinematic reception or industrial modes of labor. In fact, even though Kracauer criticizes artists and intellectuals for attempting to preserve outmoded aesthetic values, he explains that distraction in the cinema carries with it a contradictory "double meaning." On the one hand, Kracauer argues that cinematic distraction has potentially progressive effects, since it translates modes of industrial labor into a sensory, perceptual discourse that allows spectators to recognize the need for collective action under the changed conditions of modern social reality: "In the pure externality of the cinema, the audience meets itself, and the discontinuous sequence of splendid sense impressions reveals to them their own daily reality. Were this reality to remain hidden from them, they could neither attack nor change it."[45] On the other hand, Kracauer insists that cinematic distraction contains reactionary tendencies, since it rationalizes perception to such an extent that spectators fail to recognize forms of exploitation and therefore lose the ability to act: "The production and mindless consumption of abstract, ornamental patterns distract from the necessity to change the present order. Reason is impeded when the masses into which it should penetrate yield to emotions provided by the godless, mythological cult."[46]

Significantly, however, when Kracauer discerns the most reactionary tendencies of mass cultural reception, he refers less to an emotional involvement that impedes reason and more to a rationalized response that impedes involvement. In his 1931 essay, "Girls and Crisis," for example, Kracauer suggests how mass culture has adopted the capitalist goals of streamlining and administration to mask contradiction and promote uncritical consumption. Choosing the American dance troupe the Tiller Girls to represent this trend, he writes,

> In that postwar era, in which prosperity appeared limitless and which could scarcely conceive of unemployment, the Girls were artificially manufactured in the USA and exported to Europe by the dozens. Not only were they American products; at the same time they demonstrated the greatness of American production. . . . When they formed an undulating snake, they radiantly illustrated the virtues of the conveyor belt; when they tapped their feet in fast tempo, it sounded like, *business, business;* when they kicked their legs with mathematic precision, they joyously affirmed the progress of rationalization; and when they kept repeating the same movements without ever interrupting their routine, one envisioned an uninterrupted chain of autos gliding from the factories into the world, and believed that the blessings of prosperity had no end.[47]

Kracauer's description of the abstraction and fragmentation of the female body in the service of capitalist expansion attests to his awareness of the construction of woman in mass culture as spectacle, as object of desire and endless exchange. Yet it is clear that he is less interested in the cultural construction of woman than he is in the effects of rationalization on the mass cultural spectator. Kracauer suggests, for example, that the structures of seeing that the mass ornament develops to ensure its readability depend on images of artificially manufactured women. And while these images serve to reassure the mass cultural spectator, they also function to "distract" or divert attention away from the irrationality at the basis of a capitalist social order. Kracauer thus implies a correspondence between the untrustworthiness of the image and the vulnerability of the mass cultural spectator, since both run the risks he associates with femininity—the risks of passivity, uniformity, and uncritical consumption.

A somewhat different reading of mass culture and spectatorship emerges from Kracauer's series of sketches "The Little Shop Girls Go to the Movies" (1927).[48] Although he continues to associate the most dubious aspects of mass culture with passivity and femininity (for example, when he refers to the vacuity of the *Tippmamsells* or the "stupid little hearts" of the shop girls), his analysis also reveals that modes of spectatorship and representation in Weimar were not always based on rationalized models. In the eighth sketch in the series, for example, Kracauer begins his analysis of film melodrama by describing a symptomatic narrative. A young woman, left in poverty by her father's suicide, is subsequently abandoned by her fiancé, who is concerned with promoting his career as a lieutenant and avoiding any hint of poverty or indecency. To support herself, the young woman takes a job under an assumed name as a dancer on the stage. After many years, the lieutenant and the woman meet again, only now the lieutenant wants to put things right and suggests marriage. But, as Kracauer explains, "the unselfish dancer poisons herself in order to force her lover, through her death, to think only of his career."[49] Following this narrative description, Kracauer offers a critique of the sentimentality in film melodrama in which he implies a correspondence between the figure of woman in melodrama and the female spectator: "There are many people who sacrifice themselves nobly, because they are too lazy to rebel. Many tears are shed because to cry is sometimes easier than to think. The stronger the position of power in society, the more tragically act the weak and stupid."[50] At the conclusion of this critique, Kracauer adds a somewhat enigmatic remark: "Clandestinely the little shop girls wipe their eyes and powder their noses before the lights come up."[51]

Despite its patronizing tone, Kracauer's analysis clearly contests the view that all cinematic practices require a rationalized or distracted attention; the little shop girls may be momentarily distracted from everyday life, but they are clearly in a state of concentration at the movies. Indeed, it is Kracauer himself who is distracted by the presence of women in the cinema; shifting his gaze restlessly from audience to image, he looks at women in the act of looking rather than focusing his attention exclusively on the screen. It should be recalled that Kracauer holds distraction in the cinema to be reactionary only when spectators passively consume abstract, ornamental patterns and fail to recognize the loss of individual mastery under the changed conditions of modern social reality. While the emotional response of the little shop girls may reveal an acknowledgment of a loss of social mastery, their concentrated gaze involves a perceptual activity that is neither passive nor entirely distracted. In an effort to resolve this apparent paradox, Kracauer concludes that when spectators acknowledge their loss of mastery, they often lose the ability to act.

Although Kracauer fails to consider his earlier argument about the recognition of powerlessness as positively enabling social action, his discussion of female spectatorship provides us with a starting point from which to challenge the view of the cinema and perceptual response in Weimar as thoroughly streamlined, rationalized, and distracted. In other words, even though Kracauer refers to the little shop girls and film melodrama in a disparaging manner, his analysis nonetheless suggests the existence of a mode of spectatorship and form of representation that failed to keep pace with rationalized models in the realm of leisure. Following from Kracauer's observations, we may suspect that women's relationship to modernity was entirely different from what was commonly projected onto the figure of woman during the Weimar period. Indeed, it would seem that women's relationship to modernity and mass culture has all too frequently been confused with male desire, and with male perceptions of gender difference.

MEN'S MODERNISM VERSUS WOMEN'S MODERNITY: WEIMAR WOMEN AT WORK AND AT THE MOVIES

It is one thing to claim that modernity has transformed the structure of experience, but it is quite another to conclude that various phenomena of modernity, such as film, photography, and mass culture, have transformed experience so profoundly that they admit only one form of perception or one kind of experience: the form constitutive of the male spectator or subject.

However, it would be difficult to deny the similarities between early assessments of perception and representation in Weimar and contemporary theories of the cinema and spectatorship. The writings of Heidegger, Benjamin, and Kracauer serve in many ways to corroborate what Christian Metz has described as the inherently masculine economy of film technology and spectatorship, where the cinema exists as a male prerogative and vision remains a masculine privilege. More precisely, the implicit reliance on male identity in early theories of perception would seem to confirm Mary Ann Doane's argument about the nonidentity of woman in theories of representation and spectatorship: the overpresence of woman as object or metaphor and her nonexistence as subject within a phallocentric discourse.

But unless we want to dispense with the possibility of understanding female spectatorship altogether, it is crucial to challenge the assumption that cinematic vision is inherently masculine or that the cinema and mass culture are synonymous with the further repression and exclusion of women. As I have suggested, the almost obsessive attempt to preserve male authority in Weimar reveals a parallel effort to distance a mass cultural audience perceived as threatening, as other, and as female. The presence of women in the modern city—on the streets, in industry, in the arts, and in the cinema—obviously distracted the attention of male intellectuals, who aimed to efface or at least to contain the power of the female gaze.[52] And while this strategy of containment certainly testifies to the tenacity of male desire, it also points to a threat that was neither purely imaginary nor metaphorical. In other words, mass culture and the cinema in Weimar cannot be aligned simply with the further exclusion of women, since both domains, given their economic interests, were in many ways responsive to women's demands for a greater share in German cultural life.

The growing visibility of women in Weimar in fact helps explain the defensive reaction toward woman in the discourses of artists and intellectuals: their attempt to distance and thereby master the threat perceived as too close, too present, too overwhelming. While this defensive reaction can be explained in psychic terms (the threat of castration, the trauma inspired by the female body), it can be explained in historical and economic terms as well. For example, German law prohibited women from attending public meetings or joining political organizations until 1908.[53] Even after women were granted the right to assemble, the very act of a woman attending a public gathering was considered scandalous, even immoral. Nevertheless, the cultural sanction against women's right to assemble was not heeded by the promoters of mass cultural entertainment, who sought to capitalize on changes in women's legal status and thus to profit from the economic potential of female audiences. The cinema, in particular, became one of the few places in German cultural life that afforded women a prominent position and privileged access, and the growing visibility of women at the movies did not go unnoticed by those who held mass culture responsible for exacerbating the decay of standards brought about by technology and industrial rationalization.

Of course, it was not only the presence of women at the movies but also their visibility in traditionally male spheres of labor that provoked resentment and contributed to the perception that women had made enormous strides toward reaching economic parity with men during the Weimar years. (This latter perception may indeed account for the attempt by media institutions to cater to female audiences, since women were now considered to have disposable incomes of their own.) The intensive rationalization of industry after 1925, for instance, made the hiring of cheap, unskilled labor possible—and women were a readily available source. While women never came close to replacing men in industry (and never achieved anything like economic parity in the workplace), the very fact of an industrial female labor force was nevertheless considered a powerful challenge to traditional divisions of male and female labor. As the historian Renate Bridenthal explains, "The picture of women streaming into assembly-line jobs while men were pounding the pavement looking for work [gives] a superficially persuasive but fundamentally misleading impression. Contrary to the commonly held assumption, loudly voiced during the Depression, women were not displacing men. Rather, they were themselves displaced, moving out of agriculture and home industry into factories where they were more visible as a workforce and thus more likely to provoke resentment."[54]

The presence of women in places they had never been before (notably, in industry and in the cinema) explains the perceived threat of woman registered in various discourses during the Weimar years. And while it would be a mistake to assume that either the workplace or the cinema was entirely liberating for women, it would also be wrong to confuse male perceptions of woman with women's perception, for to do so would be to mistake male desire for female subjectivity.

To theorize female subjectivity in Weimar requires that we revise notions about perception and spectatorship in the cinema and explore the ways in which modernity was experienced differently by women during the 1920s. The female spectator's rapt attention in the cinema, for example, suggests that women were indeed situated differently from men with respect to the image and to structures of looking. In psychic terms alone, we may say that women did not share the male fear of the female body and thus did not retain the same investment in aesthetic distance and detachment. Although the female spectator's particular passion for perceiving was commonly disparaged and set against the male spectator's more objective, detached, and hence more mediated gaze, it is obvious that women's closeness to the image can only be conceived as a "deficiency" within a masculine epistemology. In other words, women's absorption in the image can only be considered regressive or dangerous if representation itself is assumed to be so thoroughly masculine that it admits only one kind of vision or perceptual response. The threat of losing oneself in mass culture, it should be recalled, was central to Heidegger's claim that the loss of self is inseparable from the specter of losing oneself to others. Since it would be difficult to equate this sense of self with female subjectivity, it becomes crucial to discern the psychic and historical determinants of women's experience in Weimar—their experience of mass culture and of everyday life as well.

Here the writings of Benjamin, Kracauer, and Heidegger prove useful in revising notions about spectatorship and perception in Weimar. In spite of their almost exclusive attention to male spectatorship and identity, all three theorists aim to account for the ways in which sense perception is neither natural nor biological but the result of a long process of differentiation within human history. Each theorist succeeds to a certain degree, even as each only partially manages to account historically for his own experience of this process. Benjamin's analysis of changes in perception, for example, clearly underscores the ways in which technology and capitalism have transformed vision and experience. Furthermore, Benjamin focuses his attention on the metropolitan masses since, in his view, the masses alone have a privileged relation to industrial modes of labor and thus to changes in perception and experience. While Benjamin insists on the historical nature of subjectivity and experience, his apparently gender-neutral concept of "the masses" nevertheless elides any discussion of female subjectivity, proposing that all forms of perception are modeled on industrial modes of labor and reveal the extent to which an absorbed or concentrated gaze has been replaced by a distracted and defensive way of looking. However, Benjamin's approach to questions of perception and experience can still be appropriated for an analysis of female subjectivity in Weimar, since his strategy of tracing possibilities for engagement in the cinema reveals as much about the parameters of perceptual responses to modernity as it does about different social experiences: that is to say, about experiences of cultural and economic change that were not accompanied by fundamental changes in the cultural definition of labor.

The years between 1916 and 1929, for example, are commonly described as years of intensive and rapid transition in the employment patterns of German women. The historian Tim Mason explains that "older types of work, many of them of a pre-industrial kind, persisted alongside a proliferation of new opportunities in commerce, administration and industry, and in the 1920s, women had a remarkably wide range of roles in the economy."[55] But, as Mason goes on to point out, this apparently remarkable range of roles served merely to reflect in an accentuated form the unequal development of German capitalism as a whole: the tensions within a social and economic structure in which technically advanced industrial monopolies existed side-by-side with peasant farms and economically precarious corner shops. For women seeking employment outside the home, this usually meant that job possibilities were limited to the least modern sectors of the economy: shops, bars, cafés, or the workshops of husbands, fathers, or other male relatives. The vast majority of women in Weimar, moreover, lived on unearned income, or pensions, or the earnings of children or husbands: the vast majority of women, in other words, did not work outside the home at all.[56]

The economic crises in Germany in the 1920s merely exacerbated the already precarious definition of women's work in the industrial and domestic spheres. Women who kept their jobs in industry, for instance, typically suffered cutbacks in unemployment insurance, received lower compensation due to an original wage differential, and in many cases were more likely to find employment in uninsured home industry or temporary jobs.[57] After 1925, when the demand for unskilled, underpaid female labor actually increased, women's household tasks similarly increased. The historian Atina Grossmann points out that inflation and depression particularly affected lower-middle- and working-class women, who not only fell victim to unemployment but also endured physical and emotional stress, since most of them had two additional jobs: housework and child care. "On a material level," Grossmann explains, "social reproduction such as health care and food production was reprivatized into individual households" as a result of governmental cutbacks in social welfare. Furthermore, on an emotional level, "women were called upon to stabilize the family in a turbulent time, to soothe the tensions of unemployment, and to mediate the conflicts supposedly caused by increased competition for jobs between men and women."[58] Given the multiple demands placed on female labor during the 1920s, it is hardly surprising that women often experienced modernity as merely intensifying traditionally defined gender roles and responsibilities.

The positioning of women's work between modernity and tradition may also account for what Kracauer recognized as the female spectator's very different mode of attention in the cinema. The sensory deprivation of household labor, where women were called on to manage an ever more precarious family existence, may indeed explain women's particular passion for the cinema: their desire to escape the monotony of routine in the heightened experience of film viewing. Kracauer's analysis certainly suggests that female viewers were capable of maintaining a high degree of perceptual activity (managing turns in narrative development as well as shifts in point of view), even while they were intensely involved with the images on the screen. And although Kracauer implies that the absorbed attention of the little shop girls in the cinema has nothing to do with contemplation (given his view that they are merely "swept away" by the image and lack the capacity to reflect on its meaning), a contemplative aesthetic may actually account for women's emotional and highly concentrated gaze, precisely because it afforded the kind of heightened sensory experience that simultaneously responded to and compensated for women's experiences of everyday life.

Once we understand the appeal of contemplation in this way, it becomes possible to appropriate certain tenets of Heideggerian phenomenology for a more precise conceptualization of female spectatorship. Heidegger's critique of epistemology for holding vision alone to confirm knowledge and subjectivity, for example, is especially useful for revising clichés about gendered spectatorship. The female spectator's concentrated attention in the cinema cannot be understood in terms of vision alone, since modes of looking—even contemplative modes of looking—only become meaningful when we attend to the historical determinants of subjectivity and experience. Male or female spectatorship, in other words, cannot be theorized apart from questions of gender and experience, for perceptual response is constructed as much in history as it is by positioning and address within individual films.

NOTES

1. Klaus Theweleit, *Männerphantasien: Frauen, Fluten, Körper, Geschichte*, vol. 1 (Frankfurt: Verlag Roter Stern, 1977), 586 fn. 88. This book is also available in English translation. See Theweleit, *Male Fantasies: Women, Floods, Bodies, History*, vol. 1, trans. Stephen Conway (Minneapolis: University of Minnesota Press, 1987).

2. Peter Gay, *Weimar Culture: The Outsider as Insider* (New York: Harper and Row, 1970), 129.

3. For an extremely illuminating discussion of modernity and film culture in Weimar, see Anton Kaes, Introduction, in *Kino-Debatte: Texte zum Verhältnis von Literatur und Film, 1909–1929*, ed. Anton Kaes (Tübingen: Max Niemeyer Verlag, 1978). A slightly modified version of this introduction is available in English translation as "The Debate About Cinema: Charting a Controversy (1909–1929)," trans. David J. Levin, *New German Critique*, no. 40 (1987): 7–33.

4. Harold Nicolson, "The Charm of Berlin," *Der Querschnitt* (May 1929) (originally in English), reprinted in *Der Querschnitt: Das Magazin der aktuellen Ewigkeitswerte, 1924–1933* (Berlin: Ullstein Verlag, 1980), 261–263.

5. Carl Zuckmayer, *Als wär's ein Stück von mir* (1966), 311–314, reprinted in translation as *A Part of Myself*, trans. Richard and Clara Winston (New York: Harcourt Brace Jovanovich, 1970), 217.

6. On the feminist movement in turn-of-the-century Germany, see Richard J. Evans, *Comrades and Sisters: Feminism, Socialism and Pacifism in Europe 1870–1945* (New York: St. Martin's Press, 1987); Richard J. Evans, *The Feminist Movement in Germany 1894–1933*, vol. 6 (London: Sage Studies in Twentieth-Century History, 1976); Jean Quataert, *Reluctant Feminists in German Social Democracy, 1885–1917* (Princeton: Princeton University Press, 1979); Werner Thönnessen, *The Emancipation of Women: The Rise and Fall of the Women's Movement in German Social Democracy 1863–1933*, trans. Joris de Bres (London: Pluto, 1976).

7. See, for example, Miriam Hansen, "Early Silent Cinema: Whose Public Sphere?" *New German Critique*, no. 29 (1983): 147–184; Tania Modleski, "The Terror of Pleasure: The

Contemporary Horror Film and Postmodern Theory," in *Studies in Entertainment: Critical Approaches to Mass Culture*, ed. Tania Modleski, Theories of Contemporary Culture, vol. 7 (Bloomington: Indiana University Press, 1986), 155–166; Andreas Huyssen, "Mass Culture as Woman: Modernism's Other," also in Modleski, *Studies in Entertainment*, 188–207; and my "Mass Culture and Feminine: The 'Place' of Television in Film Studies," *Cinema Journal* 25, no. 3 (1986):5–21.

8. Egon Friedell, "Prolog vor dem Film," in *Blätter des deutschen Theaters* 2 (1912); reprinted in Kaes, *Kino-Debatte*, 43.

9. Bruno Schönlank, "Kino," in *Deutsche Arbeiterdichtung 1910–1933*, ed. Günter Heintz (Stuttgart, 1974), 293–294.

10. Christian Metz, *The Imaginary Signifier: Psychoanalysis and Cinema*, trans. Celia Britton, Annwyl Williams, Ben Brewster, and Alfred Guzzetti (London: Macmillan, 1982).

11. Metz, "The Passion for Perceiving," in Metz, *The Imaginary Signifier*, 56–60.

12. Mary Ann Doane, "Film and the Masquerade: Theorizing the Female Spectator," *Screen* 23, no. 3–4 (1982): 87.

13. Ibid., 78.

14. Mary Ann Doane, "Woman's Stake: Filming the Female Body," *October* 17 (Summer 1981): 23.

15. Sigmund Freud, *Civilization and Its Discontents*, trans. James Strachey (New York: Norton, 1962), 46–47.

16. Mary Ann Doane, " ' . . . when the direction of the force acting on the body is changed': The Moving Image," *Wide Angle* 7, no. 1–2 (1985): 42–58.

17. The impact of Heidegger's and Benjamin's writings on theories of postmodernism is a case in point, but even Kracauer's early writings have recently gained the attention of scholars interested in defining a resolutely historical approach to questions of mass culture, modernity, and perceptual response. The renewed interest in Kracauer's early work will certainly be facilitated by the English translation of several groundbreaking essays by Kracauer in *The Mass Ornament: Weimar Essays*, ed. Thomas Y. Levin (Cambridge: Harvard University Press, 1995).

18. Jacques Derrida, "Geschlecht: Différence sexuelle, différence ontologique," *L'Herne* (September 1983):419–430. I am indebted to Natasa Durovicová for her astute translation of this essay. All translations of this essay that follow are hers.

19. Gay, *Weimar Culture*, 82.

20. Hans Georg Gadamer, "Heidegger's Later Philosophy," in *Essays in Philosophical Hermeneutics*, trans. David E. Linge (Berkeley and Los Angeles: University of California Press, 1976), 214–215.

21. Martin Heidegger, *Being and Time*, trans. John Macquarrie and Edward Robinson (New York: Harper and Row, 1962), 216–217.

22. See, for example, Heidegger's series of essays collected in *Poetry, Language, Thought*, trans. Alfred Hofstader (New York: Harper and Row, 1972). Heidegger was perhaps most explicit in his condemnation of mass culture in his 1955 lecture entitled "Memorial Address." This address is available in English in *Discourse on Thinking*, trans. John M. Anderson and E. Hans Freund (New York: Harper and Row, 1966), 43–47.

23. Martin Heidegger, "The Age of the World Picture," in *The Question Concerning Technology*, trans. William Lovitt (New York: Harper and Row, 1974), 134. "Die Zeit des Weltbildes" was first given as a lecture at Freiburg University in June 1938.

24. Alice Jardine also makes this point in relation to Heidegger, Benjamin, and Barthes. See her interesting and important discussion of these three theorists in *Gynesis: Configurations of Woman and Modernity* (Ithaca, N.Y.: Cornell University Press, 1985), 73–75.

25. Heidegger, *Being and Time*, 164–165.

26. Derrida, "Geschlecht."

27. Quoted in Derrida, "Geschlecht," 421.

28. Quoted in Derrida, "Geschlecht," 422.

29. Derrida, "Geschlecht," 423.

30. Susan Buck-Morss, "Benjamin's Passagen-Werk: Redeeming Mass Culture for the Revolution," *New German Critique*, no. 29 (Spring–Summer 1983): 223 fn. 27.

31. Notable exceptions, however, would include Heide Schlüpmann's discussion of early German film theory in her essay "Kinosucht," *Frauen und Film* 33 (October 1982): 45–52; and Christine Buci-Gluckmann's essay on Benjamin and allegory, "Catastrophic Utopia: The Feminine as Allegory of the Modern," *Representations* 14 (Spring 1986): 220–229.

32. Ronald Taylor, *Aesthetics and Politics: Debates Between Ernst Bloch, Georg Lukács, Bertolt Brecht, Walter Benjamin, Theodor Adorno,* ed. Ronald Taylor (London: New Left Books, 1977), 200.

33. Peter Demetz, Introduction to Benjamin's *Reflections: Essays, Aphorisms, Autobiographical Writings,* trans. Edmund Jephcott (New York and London: Harcourt Brace Jovanovich, 1978), xxi.

34. Hannah Arendt, Introduction to Benjamin's *Illuminations,* trans. Harry Zohn (New York: Schocken Books, 1969), 46.

35. A founding text of critical theory is indeed Georg Simmel's "Die Grossstadt und das Geistesleben," in *Die Grossstadt: Jahrbuch der Gehe-Stiftung* (Dresden, 1903), 187–206, reprinted in translation as "The Metropolis and Mental Life," in *The Sociology of Georg Simmel,* ed. Kurt H. Wolff (New York: Free Press, 1950), 409–424. Although far less central to the development of critical theory, Simmel's writings on sexuality and the woman's questions are of great interest. See the essays collected under the title *Georg Simmel: On Women, Sexuality, and Love,* trans. Guy Oakes (New Haven: Yale University Press, 1984).

36. Walter Benjamin, "Über einige Motive bei Baudelaire," *Gesammelte Schriften* (hereafter cited as *GS*), vol. 1, pt. 2, ed. Rolf Tiedemann and Hermann Schweppenhäuser (Frankfurt am Main: Suhrkamp, 1974), 630. This essay is available in English translation. See "Some Motifs in Baudelaire," in *Charles Baudelaire: A Lyric Poet in the Era of High Capitalism,* trans. Harry Zohn (London: New Left Books, 1973), 105–154.

37. As Benjamin suggests through Baudelaire's example, "In his 'Salon de 1895,' Baudelaire lets the landscape pass in review, concluding with this admission: 'I long for the return of the dioramas whose enormous, crude magic subjects me to the spell of a useful illusion. I prefer looking at the backdrop paintings of the stage where I find my favorite dreams treated with consummate skill and tragic concision. Those things, so completely false, are for that reason much closer to the truth, whereas the majority of our landscape painters are liars precisely because they fail to lie.' " Benjamin, "Über einige Motive bei Baudelaire," 650; English translation, 151. See also "Das Kunstwerk im Zeitalter seiner technischen Reproduzierbarkeit," *GS,* vol. 1, pt. 2, first version, 431–469; second version, 471–508. The second version of this essay is available in English translation in Benjamin's *Illuminations,* 217–251.

38. Benjamin, "Über einige Motive bei Baudelaire," 644; English translation, 146.

39. Ibid., 620–621; English translation, 122.

40. Ibid., 623; English translation, 125.

41. Ibid., 649; English translation, 150–151.

42. Ibid., 622; English translation, 123.

43. Ibid., 652–653; English translation, 154.

44. Siegfried Kracauer, "Kult der Zerstreuung," in *Das Ornament der Masse* (Frankfurt am Main: Suhrkamp, 1977), 313–314. This essay has recently been made available in English translation. See "Cult of Distraction: On Berlin's Picture Palaces," trans. Thomas Y. Levin, *New German Critique*, no. 40 (1987): 91–96.

45. Kracauer, "Kult der Zerstreuung," 315.

46. Siegfried Kracauer, "Das Ornament der Masse," in *Das Ornament der Masse*. This essay has been reprinted in English translation as "The Mass Ornament," trans. Jack Zipes and Barbara Correll, *New German Critique*, no. 5 (1975): 67–76.

47. Siegfried Kracauer, "Girls und Krise," *Frankfurter Zeitung* (27 May 1931); quoted in Karsten Witte, "Introduction to Siegfried Kracauer's 'The Mass Ornament,' " *New German Critique*, no. 5 (1975): 63–64.

48. Siegfried Kracauer, "Die kleinen Ladenmädchen gehen ins Kino," in *Das Ornament der Masse*, 279–294.

49. Ibid., 291–292.

50. Ibid., 292.

51. Ibid., 292–293.

52. A number of theorists have recently attempted to retrieve the concept of distraction for a theory of the female spectator. See, for example, the special issue on Weimar film theory in *New German Critique*, no. 40 (1987), edited by David Bathrick, Thomas Elsaesser, and Miriam Hansen. However, I have endeavored to show that although distraction was often associated with a female figure or the female gaze, it was the male critic who was in fact most distracted in the cinema, particularly by the presence of women in the audience. The intensity of the female gaze, as registered in the writings of male critics, has also led me to theorize female spectatorship in relation to the concept of contemplation. In associating a contemplative aesthetic with female spectatorship, I aim to challenge the assumption that contemplating distraction was the sole prerogative of male intellectual audiences in Weimar. Meaghan Morris makes a similar point in her book *Upward Mobility*, and poses what I believe to be a crucial question about women and modernity. "In this project," she writes, "I prefer to study . . . the everyday, the so-called banal, the supposedly un- or non-experimental, asking not, 'why does it fall short of modernism?' but: 'how do classical theories of modernism fall short of women's modernity?' " See Meaghan Morris, *Upward Mobility* (Bloomington: Indiana University Press, forthcoming).

53. For a discussion of the legal status of women in turn-of-the-century Germany, see Quataert, *Reluctant Feminists in German Social Democracy.*

54. Renate Bridenthal, "Beyond *Kinder, Küche, Kirche:* Weimar Women at Work," *Central European History* 6, no. 2 (June 1973): 158. This essay has also been reprinted, with additions from another author. See Renate Bridenthal and Claudia Koonz, "Beyond *Kinder, Küche, Kirche:* Weimar Women in Politics and Work," in *Liberating Women's History: Theoretical and Critical Essays*, ed. Berenice A. Carroll (Champaign: University of Illinois Press, 1976), 301–329.

55. Tim Mason, "Women in Germany, 1925–1940: Family, Welfare and Work," *History Workshop: A Journal of Socialist Historians* 1 (1976): 78.

56. Ibid., 77–79.

57. Atina Grossmann, "Abortion and Economic Crisis: The 1931 Campaign Against Paragraph 218 in Germany," *New German Critique*, no. 14 (1978), 119–138.

58. Atina Grossmann, "The New Woman and the Rationalization of Sexuality in Weimar Germany," in *Powers of Desire: The Politics of Sexuality*, ed. Ann Snitow, Christine Stansell, and Sharon Thompson (New York: Monthly Review Press, 1983), 157.

THREE

Female Flanerie and the *Symphony of the City*

Anke Gleber

Following the course of modernity in the nineteenth and twentieth centuries involves, among other things, tracing the footsteps of the flaneur as he strolls in the streets of nineteenth-century Paris, appears in Charles Baudelaire's metropolitan poems, and structures Walter Benjamin's perspective in his project of the Paris Arcades. An overlooked yet pivotal figure of modernity, the flaneur both defines and is defined by his perception of the outside world. He experiences city streets as interiors; he views traffic, advertising, displays, and the world of commodities as *Denkbilder*, as images that evoke reflection. Both a product of modernity and its seismograph, in the cities of modernity he represents the *man* of the streets. If, according to Benjamin, flanerie manifests itself as a form of sensory experience shaped by the exterior "shocks" of modernity and corresponding to the conditions of modern perception, for Siegfried Kracauer it names the experience of "distraction" found in Weimar culture.[1] By way of flanerie—a mode of movement that is at the same time a process of reflection and a manner of walking with an attendant presence of mind and close attention to images—the flaneur transcends modern alienation through an epistemological process of intensive perception. He is at once a dreamer, a historian, and an artist of modernity, a character, a reader, and an author who transforms his observations into literary, or more precisely, latently filmic texts. Collecting scenes and impressions, he relates them through stories and histories of the city and its streets. Surrounded by visual stimuli and relying on the encompassing power of his perception, the flaneur moves freely in the streets, solely intent on pursuing this seemingly unique and individual experience of reality.

What is of interest to me here is that, within the domains of literature, culture, and public life, this unbounded, unrestricted pursuit of perception has been mainly ascribed to *men*. It is no accident, for example, that Heinrich Heine and Ludwig Börne, writing of their times in *Briefe aus Berlin* (Letters from Berlin) and

Schilderungen aus Paris (Depictions from Paris), respectively, take their point of departure from their own physical and tangible presence as men in the city: they evoke and facilitate their flaneuristic reflections by observing a contemporary public in the streets. In his exemplary tale of scopophilia and physiology, *Des Vetters Eckfenster* (The Cousin's Corner Window), E. T. A. Hoffmann initiates a male protagonist into the "principles of the art of looking." In *Das öde Haus* (The Deserted House), his narrator abandons himself to what he calls "my old inclination . . . to stroll the streets by myself and delight in every copper engraving on display, in every notice [*affiche*], or to look at the figures approaching me." Such unabashed and unadulterated pleasure in the sights, views, and images of the street seems reserved to an experience of *male* spectators. Both moving through and perceiving public spaces emerges as a uniquely gendered practice, (almost) exclusively associated with male authors and protagonists.

If this art of taking a walk takes many shapes throughout the nineteenth and twentieth centuries—symbolist forms, impressionist paths, and surrealist sensitivities—all these excursions and experiments are reserved for male perception and authorship, as is apparent from the following series of texts. Baudelaire perceives the streets and passersby of Paris in "A une passante" and "Paysage" (Landscape) as cityscapes in their own right that bring with them their own aesthetics. Edouard Dujardin, an impressionist author and bourgeois dandy of the 1880s, records the various aspects of the city, rendering its exteriors, sights, and light effects in the sensitive nuances of a seeing-as-reading-as-writing that predates the mode of "interior monologue." After the turn of the century, Louis Aragon passes through the decaying arcades of Paris in the 1920s, experiencing the city in ever-increasing intensity and in an accelerated manner, as a veritable medium of surrealist intoxication. Aragon attempts to fix these sensations in an *écriture automatique* closely modeled on and imprinted by the labyrinths of the "passages," the capitalist commodity arcades.

Every one of this succession of flaneurs shares a fascination with images as icons of a modern mythology and an intoxication with the light and structures of the city. Every one of them, however, can indulge this experience of the street only by first freely roaming, unimpeded, unintimidated, as a male spectator moving in a space reserved for the eyes of male pedestrians. In their intense pursuit of subjectivity and perception, these flaneurs and their gazes are restricted neither by insecurity, convention, modesty, anxiety, or assault nor by barriers erected through the controlling or commodifying presence of an other. The possibility of a female flanerie, however, would seem to be absent from the cities of modernity. When Benjamin announces *Die Wiederkehr des Flaneurs*, the return of the flaneur, in 1929, he fails to acknowledge his awareness of the numerous women he encounters every day in the streets of Berlin and Paris.[2] While the Berlin architect August Endell describes *Die Schönheit der grossen Stadt* (The Beauty of the Big City, 1908) in great and minute detail, women walkers remain absent from his closely watched streets. Kracauer, an eminent critic and observer of Weimar culture and public spaces, also moves through his reflections of *Strassen in Berlin und anderswo* (Streets in Berlin and Elsewhere, 1930) without registering the women he encounters in these public spaces as equal elements of and stimuli to the Denkbilder of his society. Benjamin's friend Franz Hessel, deriving and formulating an aesthetic project in his *Spazieren in Berlin* (Walking in Berlin, 1929), explicitly cautions against walking with women, claiming that they are a potentially distracting influence on the flaneur's solitary wanderings.[3]

This conspicuous absence and predominant oversight within male culture moves this female historian and critic of flanerie to search for the traces of an alternate form of flanerie, one that might eventually inscribe the presence and potential of a female flaneur in the history of perception. The following scenes from literary and filmic texts may suggest ways to rethink the status of a female flaneur in the streets of the city. These speculations on an absence seek to conjure an appearance, to assist us in reconsidering female scopophilia in movement or in moving images, and to theorize about the presence of women in public spaces, the female spectator, and a gendered definition of "modernity." In so doing, they hope to sketch a concept of female flanerie that may in turn help to reshape the way we think about the spaces of modernity.

I

The female flaneur has been an absent figure in the public sphere of modernity, in its media and texts, and in its literatures and cities. Even when she is noticed, her presence in the streets is marked as a marginal one. From the very first step she takes, her experience is limited and circumscribed. This is why female flanerie has no more been considered than has its expression in language—and in a concept of its own—been sayable. In its German usage, the term *flaneuse* bears associations of the "typical" female, of "necessarily" menial occupations such as those of the *Friseuse* (female hairdresser) or *Masseuse* (female massage worker), the latter two carrying contingent, sexually suggestive, and discriminatory connotations. Since "flaneuse" comes with this dubious baggage, since it invites unwanted, unwarranted associations, we will try to circumvent it wherever possible. Alternatively, another name for the "female flaneur" or "woman walker," as Meaghan Morris has suggested,[4] has not yet inscribed her presence in any visible or speakable form into the texts or language of flanerie. As a potential form of female existence, the female flaneur has not been noted as an image that the canonical authors of flanerie would expect to come across in the streets or as a concept that would give the female flaneur a figure and a term of her own. In the texts, theories, and versions of flanerie mentioned above, we do not and cannot expect to encounter a "flaneuse" in the street. The female flaneur has remained absent from debates over the status of the image and the perception of modernity.

The question of the presence and representation of women in the streets, however, is neither an academic nor an accidental and marginal one. On the contrary, it suggests a pivotal constellation that may help to articulate questions concerning the prevailing structures of power and domination in Western society as a direct function of the (gendered) distribution of leisure, time, and status, that is to say, the economic, psychological, and physical autonomy and self-assurance of that society's subjects. Since the nineteenth century, flanerie, the phenomenon that Benjamin theorizes and Baudelaire celebrates, has not only been the privilege of a bourgeois, educated, white, and affluent middle class, it has, above all, remained a privilege of male society. During the same period that their male contemporaries discovered the space of the city as flaneurs and travelers, experienced urban spaces constituted by ever new and changing stimuli, and approached them with innovative technologies of perception, such as the medium of photography and a mobilized gaze, women's voices speak of a different approach to and involvement with this modernity. These women struggle foremost against the very secluded position that excludes them from the options and developments reserved for men. Rather than celebrate their indulgence in multiple scopic possibilities, women have long wished for admission to the coveted realms of the spectacle, a right-of-way into the new spaces of flanerie and to an experience of the images of modernity. Only when chaperoned by companions, disguised in men's clothes, or covered by other means of subterfuge, was this entrance even partially and tentatively possible, as a trial and exception. George Sand's efforts to overcome these obstacles give vivid evidence of the difficulties and prohibitions facing women of her era. Sand realized that she could never fully approach and appreciate the outside world so long as she remained a woman who, in habit and behavior, adhered to contemporary conventions of femininity. Instead, she enters the world as a female flaneur in disguise, functionally outfitted for that purpose in male clothes, pants and boots. She immediately revels in the first moments of this escape from the constrictions of a culturally constructed "femininity" that used to control and restrict her every attire and attitude.

> With those little iron-shod heels, I was solid on the pavement. I flew from one end of Paris to another. It seemed to me that I could go around the world. And then, my clothes feared nothing. I ran out in every kind of weather, I came home at every sort of hour, I sat in the pit at the theatre. No one paid attention to me, and no one guessed at my disguise. . . . No one knew me, no one looked at me, no one found fault with me; I was an atom lost in that immense crowd.[5]

The fiction of male identity—constructed here through its exterior trappings—grants Sand the temporary entrance into a realm of considerable, if relative, freedom, opening up a seemingly unlimited, previously utopian mobility as well as the promise of omnipresent adventure.

The realities of many more women's lives during this period, however, were to remain determined and limited by rather different material pressures and psychological factors. This tendency is evident in the public spaces of the nineteenth century and can be traced in its texts. In another document, Jules Michelet testifies in his treatise *La Femme* (1858–1860) to the myriad spatial impediments and obstacles to women's liberty and mobility.

> How many irritations for the single woman! She can hardly ever go out in the evening; she would be taken for a prostitute. There are a thousand places where only men are to be seen and if she needs to go there on business, the men are amazed, and laugh like fools. For example, should she find herself delayed at the other end of Paris and hungry, she will not dare to enter into a restaurant. She would constitute an event; she would be a spectacle: All eyes would be constantly fixed on her, and she would overhear uncomplimentary and bold conjectures.[6]

Many of these obstacles would remain in women's way long into the twentieth century. In texts and films from Weimar Germany, idle women are depicted and regarded as prostitutes, and even feminists as late as the 1970s still hesitate to enter nocturnal streets and restaurants on their own.[7] While the nominal and official presence of women in public seemed to grow gradually, it was only with the end of the nineteenth century that (the bourgeois) woman was permitted by society's conventions to walk its streets freely. As Anne Friedberg notes in her search for the origins of female flanerie, "The female *flaneur* was not possible until a woman could wander the city on her own, a freedom linked to the privilege of shopping alone. [. . .] It was not until the closing decades of the century that the department store became a safe haven for unchaperoned women. [. . .] The great stores may have been the *flaneur*'s last coup, but they were the *flaneuse*'s first."[8] However, the territories of such preliminary and rudimentary forms of flanerie—the preoccupied strolling and shopping of a female consumer—have to be regarded, in view of the vast terrain of existing real city spaces, as decidedly circumscribed and distinctly derivative. Limited excursions of shopping in a prescribed ghetto of consumption amount to little more than secondhand distraction, never approximating the flaneur's wide-reaching mode of perception, unimpeded by aims, purposes, and schedules. The conflation of shopping and strolling noted by Friedberg necessarily relativizes what initially appears as a first instance of the "empowered gaze of the *flaneuse*."[9] Reduced in its potential to the purposefully limited and capitalistically promoted license to shop, the early "department store flaneuses" who "roam" the interiors of capitalist consumption represent little more than a bourgeois variant of domesticized flanerie. They replicate forms of female presence that proletarian women had long since presented in the streets before them. Women workers and housewives had always already entered the streets without ever becoming flaneuses in their own right. Instead, the street presented itself to them as a space of transition en route to functional purposes: they would face the street in doing the shopping rather than "going" shopping, in running errands rather than jogging their imagination, in picking up their children rather than experiencing free-floating impressions, in making their ways straight to the workplace, not idling without ever arriving.

The public presence and exterior excursions of these working women are commonly bound by functions that do not allow for the flaneur's leisure of "getting lost" or his impulse of "losing himself" in the spectacle of the street. Beyond the immediate sphere of their duties, proletarian women like agrarian wives in effect live "outside" the city, regardless of where they actually work, as they are limited to households that remain preindustrial and formative of their imagination in this way. By projecting all their endeavors in compensation for such confinement into their domestic interiors, women are—unwillingly—made complicitous with their exclusion from exteriority as well as from new ways of technology, production, and perception.[10] This very confinement excludes women from being exposed to the shocks and images of the street and bars them from developing any immediate sensory relationship to the phenomena of modernity as they are being registered in the street.

Other, less domestic manifestations of female presence in the street, such as the figures of the prostitute or the bag lady, only further underline the disempowered status of female subjects in the public sphere. The overall absence of a female flaneur is the result of a social distribution of power that prescribes the exclusion of women from public presence.[11] Because of the precarious presence of women in the street, the question To whom do the streets "belong"? pertains more to women than to underprivileged male subjects' class, race, or age. May the street belong to the leisure or the working class of society, to its dandies or demonstrators, pedestrians or flaneurs: the free and unimpeded movement of women undergoes additional peril under any of these constellations. The street does not "belong" to women. They cannot take possession of walking it freely without also expecting to be impeded by public judgments or conventions that cover and prescribe their images, effectively rendering them objects of the gaze. The female flaneur is considered to be absent, "invisible"; she is not presumed to have a presence in the street.[12]

A few critics, however, have taken steps to approach this assumed absence of the female flaneur, formulating a tentative presence of women in the street from specific angles and for diverse territories. Griselda Pollock, a feminist art historian, elaborates the specific restrictions to which women's status, gaze, and image were subjected in the public sphere: "They did not have the right to look, to stare, scrutinize or watch."[13] While women were positioned as the passively receptive objects and images to a publicly active and male gaze, their desire for a freedom of movement can still be read in numerous women's texts of the nineteenth century, such as those of adventurous female travelers and explorers who would risk the pursuit of their socially sanctioned scopophilia.[14] In going one step further, Pollock virtually maps the very real participation of women onto the spaces of modernity. She revisits the work of female impressionist artists who were present and at work—as painters who happened to be women—in the same locations that circumscribe the formative places and movements of impressionism: "The key markers in this mythic territory are leisure, consumption, the spectacle and money. And we can reconstruct [. . .] a map of impressionist territory which stretches from the new boulevards via Gare St. Lazare out on the suburban train to La Grenouillere, Bougival or Argenteuil."[15] It turns out to be the mere presence in the same urban spaces that creates impressionable minds and transformed women artists such as Berthe Morisot and Mary Cassatt into "painters of modern life," as Baudelaire called these flaneurs, artists of either gender or origin. While the woman stroller is as evidently present on metropolitan pavements as her male contemporaries, she requires an additional measure of physical and psychological confidence: the initial courage to step out, face the threat of assault, or erase her latent misrecognition as a prostitute, in short, to undergo the constant encounter and annoyance of being made into and treated as an object. Despite the persistent, real, and material limitations on women's access to the street, the very presence of women in public spaces indicates their insistent desire and determination to locate an experience of the city on their own.

The precarious and acute status of this quest—however unchronicled and unacknowledged its struggles may have gone in our cultural memory—can be framed by the following statements from two women a century apart. On January 2, 1879, the artist Marie Bashkirtseff notes in her diary her experiences with the streets of Paris: "What I long for is the freedom of going about alone, [. . .] of walking about old streets at night."[16] More than a century later, a headline from the *Oxford Mail* on November 9, 1979, announces that the state of things for women in the street has not changed: "Any woman walking alone after dark *invites* trouble."[17] In regarding women's images and their relation to public space, recent feminist sociology has suggested tendencies toward a "basic asymmetry" in the gendered distribution of physical and psychological power, resulting in unequal and inimical constellations that render women the more likely victims of rape, assault, intimidation, and other forms of harassment. Such latent and manifest factors must, as Shirley Ardener declares, necessarily have "a bearing on how women use space [. . .] and must be considered when the question of women's use of space is discussed."[18]

Women's specific use of space has historically been marked by anxieties and limitations that make them go about their daily matters in a more cautious fashion than men, assuming fewer, less expansive spaces to be open to their gaze and presence at any time. Restricted to the home, limited to functional forays into the public, forced to forgo the lure of aimless strolling without a specific purpose or destination, women are unable to indulge their full fascination with the metropolis, especially at night, when any excursion in the city may mean, beyond hidden revelations in the street, the more manifest dangers of attack. This epistemological awareness is fundamentally inscribed as an anxiety into women's experience of public spaces and remains a scarcely changing constant, a continuing "containment of women"[19] that curtails their access to and movement in the street. The concomitant politics of a "women's movement" must be understood in its extended, literal implications, lifting the term "movement" from the status of mere metaphor to a factor that is to be taken seriously in its immediate materiality.[20] When Adrienne Rich investigates the factors that determine the dominant socialization of heterosexual women in patriarchal societies, the material conditions of appearance and movement largely determine women's diminished existence. She asserts that the prescription of female movement is exercised as a pivotal measure by patriarchal societies that have always, in one form or another, attempted to restrict women's rights and ways in order to control and contain them in secluded, subdued positions.

> Characteristics of male power include the power of men: [. . .] to confine [women] physically and prevent their movement [by means of rape as terrorism, keeping women off the streets; purdah; foot-binding, atrophying a woman's athletic capabilities; haute couture, "feminine" dress codes; the veil; sexual harassment on the streets].[21]

These physical and material obstacles are reinforced by means of a psychological containment that often comes in internalized forms of (self-)control. It works to impede women's mobility, restrict their gaze, censure their public presence, and stylize women's images into displays. Gertrud Koch describes the status of female images as the "desired objects of male voyeurism" and suggests that the subjects behind these objects "themselves had to hide their own desires behind their veils, the bars on their boudoir windows, their expensive and time-consuming makeup rituals."[22] While the history of this inequality in the distribution of power and positioning of women on the other side of the gaze prevails, these relations between the subjects of looking and the objects that are being looked at, between the spectator's subjectivity and a woman's status as image and object, have come to be gendered and are no longer easily reciprocal or reversible. Confronted with social environs in which they cannot be present as invisible or undisturbed observers, even as they themselves are made the "natural" objects of observation, women are at once excluded from both public presence and spectatorship.[23] This constellation lets the absence of female flanerie appear not as any individual lack or incapacitation but as a crucial blind spot of society that converges to illuminate the limitations that conventions impose on women's lives.[24]

While the most obvious and explicit restrictions to women's movement have been removed so as to integrate women in the pursuit of specific business functions and adjust their traditional roles to a changing economy, their status as an overdetermined image continues to carry these same socially restrictive and restricting expectations into the present.[25] Men still habitually "check out" and evaluate women's images in a way that continues to make women's presence in public spaces a precarious and volatile one. Despite women's formal equality and democratic rights, the uncommented, uninhibited, and unobserved presence of a female person in the streets is in no way acknowledged as a self-evident right. The female flaneur still runs into a degree of scrutiny, attention, evaluation, judgment, and prejudice and forms of surveillance, suspicion, and harassment that her male predecessors and contemporaries do not expect to encounter. Even a self-confident and feminist flaneur in contemporary Berlin describes a self-consciousness in the streets that forces her to delineate her urban experience by deliberations and strategies of survival.

> Cities are no longer forbidden spaces. . . . But in the streets, we continue to move strategically, always alerted to having to justify our presence. We learn self-assertion, we practice . . . the aim-oriented walk which is to demonstrate that we are protected and bound: at least bound by an agenda, on our ways to a secure location, to a job, to a clearly defined aim—and that we are not just loitering around.[26]

Pollock reinforces this point when she observes the following situation for women in the streets of modernity: "The spaces of femininity still regulate women's lives—from running the gauntlet of intrusive looks by men on the streets to surviving deadly sexual assaults. In rape trials, women on the street are assumed to be 'asking for it.' "[27]

The public realities of women's lives still necessitate navigating an obstacle course between their theoretically assured rights and the practical liberties that they can really hope to assume. Their ways and movements in the street remain oriented along and organized by "invisible fences,"[28] contained by imaginary but socially sanctioned boundaries that redistrict and restrict their "social maps" even after the most "concrete" restrictions of female roles have been removed.[29] Even acutely aware and critical female subjects have not been able significantly to change the terms on which their images will be perceived in the street, the codes and judgments of a culture that perceives them as objects and images. As long as a woman's movement in the street involves facing more forms of intrusion, surveillance, and violence and requires more self-determination and self-confidence than a man's, female flanerie does not really come into its own. As long as the empowered position of the male gaze prevails, females are unable to move at will.

II

Within these considerations, the period of Weimar Germany figures as a formative time for both the formulation of a new feminist consciousness and the formidable obstacles that continue to face women in the streets to this day. Weimar Germany can be regarded as a pivotal age in these developments, as an age that witnessed an avant-garde women's movement in Berlin confronts the patriarchal relics of Wilhelminian society, a dynamics that yielded an open moment of modernity that is apt to illuminate the very contradictions that both orient and impede women's movement.[30] Signs of the female flaneur are to be found after all, arising from the times of Weimar modernity after centuries of male flanerie. Veritable female flaneurs are already present, even if they have been overlooked in the scenes and sites of the metropolis. A document from modern scopophilia, recording the city of modernity with the most advanced medium of its times, provides a promising point of departure in search of the ostensibly absent female flaneur.[31] For we may find traces of the female flaneur, signs of a female public presence, in the first significant filmic production that takes as its focus a reflection of the metropolis itself.

Walter Ruttmann's *Berlin, Symphony of the City* (1927), a city film from the times of the Weimar *Kino-Debatte* (cinema debate), shows an era that is passionately engaged in and defines itself through the cinema and its new discourse. Although Ruttmann's metropolitan symphony is not a production of "feminist" modernism, it does present multiple images of New Women on the screens and streets of modernity, elucidating and illuminating, in a first step, the many facets of women's presence in modern spaces. One scene in particular provides a striking commentary on the question of the female flaneur, highlighting the predicaments that a woman-as-streetwalker may encounter. It presents the appearance of a woman who literally "walks" the boulevards of Berlin and turns a street corner in *Symphony of the City* to focus her gaze on a man through a shop window. Her positioning in public and assumption of an active gaze provides a critical turning point for the urban woman as spectator, as her behavior can be regarded as one of the first visually recorded manifestations of the long-absent female flaneur. In previous criticism of the film by (male) critics, this woman walker has commonly been considered as a professional one, a woman who goes after her business as a "streetwalker." In 1947, Kracauer describes these street scenes of the film and comes to the following conclusion: "The many prostitutes among the passers-by also indicate that society has lost its balance."[32] By 1982, William Uricchio's perception of these very scenes in his analysis of the film has not moved far from this reading: "After several shots whose common element involves streetwalkers as a subject, a specific mating instance is presented. A prostitute and potential customer pass one another on the street."[33] In juxtaposing these two accounts with the recent description of this same scene by a female critic, however, one observes a striking case of gendered spectatorship. Whereas Uricchio repeats Kracauer's view of a scene of prostitution, Sabine Hake sees a different action taking place: "The camera almost seems omnipresent [. . .] following several young women on the streets by themselves: one as she is being picked up, [. . .] another as she waits impatiently at a corner, and yet another as she window shops on elegant Kurfürstendamm."[34]

The striking discrepancies in judging and naming these women might well provoke another look at the function and scenes of the female image in *Berlin, Symphony of the City*. A new reading of this metropolitan text might indeed discover a literal, female streetwalker, a new figure of subjectivity free of any professional purposes other than her own processes of walking, seeing, and, potentially, recording these actions: a *femme flaneur*. As the critical reception of the female image in *Symphony of the City* reveals, however, any woman walking the streets on her own, even in the presumably emancipatory age of Weimar Germany,[35] has to first justify, assume, and establish her stance of flanerie. When a woman signals the flaneur's aimless and purposeless drifting along the streets, she risks being perceived as a "streetwalker," as the object of a male gaze not usually characterized by the flaneur's disinterested attitude.[36]

One of the earliest scenes of the film sets the stage for this mise-en-scène of the female image. After the camera establishes the metropolis in spatial terms—trains, tracks, and telephone poles—it continues its sequence of abstract, architectural, and inanimate shots in panning forward and around a corner, past a shoemaker's store—a foundational site of production for the film's ensuing fetishism—and coming to rest on the first "human" figures that the camera singles out. Following its logic of the male gaze, it finds a group of five women mannequins, standing arranged behind a window, all frozen into a static pose to exhibit their attire, a slip, the one item of underwear that barely covers their puppet bodies. It is apparent from this scene what the intended object on display is, that the one item of apparel attracts the gaze less to this showcase than to the overall assemblage of female figures. The next shot hints at a partial consequence of this display—the image status of female existence—as it cuts to the stark picture of water running under a bridge, a bridgepost erected as the marker of future death, a proleptic image of the drowning suicide that is to come as a woman's self-destructive act at the dramatic center of the film.

Symphony of the City revisits similar locations in many instances, focusing on window shots and the display of women's bodies as images. One of these scenes presents a full frontal view of mannequins' plastic surfaces, as we see in mirrored reflections on the women's motionless bodies inscribed, virtually imprinted, the store signs as markers of ownership. These women's artificial and simulated bodies are clearly inscribed, through the reflection of light, as both properties on display and as circulating commodities on the market.[37] However, their own gazes do not seem to be present in this scene, as their complete figures and faces have no part in this picture. While the women are *all* parts, they also in one way remain quasi-impartial and almost resistant to their display as an image. In what seems the mere quote of a fashion pose, they raise only symbolically, in a possible gesture of irony, their twisted plastic hands. A man is seen strolling by this display, maybe a flaneur, with the sufficient leisure and visual desire to pause in front of the window, contemplating the display for a moment, considering it, dismissing it, walking on.

Similar scenes follow this prototypical situation of a public display and evaluation of women's images. On the runway of a fashion show—presenting the small-scale model of an artificial "street"—women circulate within the confines of their modeled and modeling walk, a form of movement that sells—in more than an exterior sense—women's bodies and images. The fashion scene is preceded by the film's most desperate act, the drama of a woman's suicide, a woman whose jump from a bridge takes place at just that location and position which links it to the previous exhibition scene with the foreshadowing water shot. A narrative of women's lives is suggested that seems to connect their existence and demise in the city to the ways in which their images are exhibited and exploited in this society. The film pursues an implicit logic from the first scenes with women as models, instruments, and coat hangers of capitalism, images on display as well as commodities for sale, to the crucial cluster of street scenes where a leisurely strolling woman is perceived as nothing but a marketable image that presumably takes possession of her entire body and persona. The woman in the street is herself foremost an image by social and cultural definition, a commodity trying to sell herself in more than just one sense. In a closer look at this scene, however, we discover that this presumed prostitute presence does in fact collapse and thus hide a multitude of individual women walkers. Indeed, any scrutiny that is more attentive to women's presence finds that these scenes are not all sites of prostitution but are instead comprised of at least four distinct instances of female figures, fashions, and habits in the street.

The first of these women is introduced as she looks out over the street, seemingly surveying the scene. She is shown in profile with a gray hat that leaves an open space next to her view for the spectator's own gaze to take in the long-shot of a street scene surrounding her image. This attentive character is not seen again, neither by herself nor as a companion to any of the men to follow in this sequence. Her striking image is but a glimpse of a potential female flaneur and her scrutiny of the city, as the symphony cuts from her gaze immediately to that of yet another "other," the image of a black man surrounded by a small group of pedestrians. Along with this sequence of visual suspects on the Weimar scene, the camera proceeds to capture the image of another woman who walks by slowly and wears a different hat with a band. She is introduced already in the company of a man when she appears on the scene, with no markers of a commercial transaction or solicitation defining their association. Independently of her two predecessors in the street, a third woman strolls by on the far edge of the sidewalk. She sports a white hat and a curious gaze that she directs with admitted interest on her fellow pedestrians in the crowd. No other signals allow us to define her specular intensity as either professional interest or aimless flanerie, leisure or prostitution. Completing this sequence is a fourth woman in a black hat whose swaying walk has continuously elicited clichés from male spectators to whose minds her sensual flexibility has suggested nothing if not the "coquettish," self-advertising stroll that they imagine of a prostitute. This female image is the instantly suspect one who turns the corner and gazes back at another, male, pedestrian, using the 90-degree angle through the shop window as much as a reflective mirror than as a looking-glass front, a transparent surface of specularity. Her interested gaze is commonly interpreted as so provocative that it presumably causes the man to retrace his steps and return around the corner to join her. Yet as we review this scene more closely without attaching immediate labels of prostitution to the woman with the active gaze, we find the woman with the black hat in fact walking off by herself after all. It is perhaps even a different man who subsequently walks by with another woman at the other side of the window, a couple that through blind repetition and conventional viewing has come to be regarded as a successful transaction in "streetwalking." In reality, however, the scene proves itself open to a new presence of women in the street, requiring an even closer analysis that reveals an instance that confounds rather than confirms preconceived notions of women walking and watching in the streets.

On closer inspection, *Berlin, Symphony of the City* represents many facets of the status of women in the modern city. Their walking down the street opens a space for the female flaneur, develops the presumably nonexistent, improbable, and un-canny presence of a woman in the street as in a photograph, that is to say, renders it visible as a more complex spectacle and presence than conventions have per-mitted us to see and say. In this film, women shop, stroll, go to work, sit in cafés, and observe the crowd. However, even these manifest images of public women are contained by male interpretations that consider progressive women as prostitutes. Looking upon—and down on—the female figure in public places as a professional "streetwalker" only repeats, replicates, and prescribes the clichéd image of women walking in the street, women who are indeed very real participants in a public spectacle to be acknowledged as perceptive as well as consumptive presences. The previously limited roles of women in the streets, circumscribed en route to de-partment stores and workplaces, for purposes of shopping and working only, are juxtaposed and directly related to an interpretation that collapses a variety of filmic figures into the one of the prostitute, a public type that reduces women to a hardly aimless presence, a mere commodity and vehicle for the purposes of sell-ing. By way of selling herself, the figure represents an inverted function of both "shopping" and "working," the two accepted female activities in the public sphere.

From the nineteenth century onward to Benjamin and his contemporaries, the historical spectators and participants of this *Symphony of the City*, the prostitute rep-resents the only current, perceivable, and conceivable form of female presence in the street. The ensuing typification of this figure into a veritable allegory of the city and female counterpart of the flaneur is nothing if not the inscription of a male fantasy onto a female type who—a "streetwalker" out of need, not by leisure—does not frequent the streets to share her subjective experience with the male pedestrian but rather is defined by a very immediate objectification and com-modification in her own body. Unlike the male flaneur and bearer of the gaze, the prostitute as his presumed female equivalent is rather the image and object of this gaze. Not free to drift along the streets, she is driven into and down the streets by pressing economic motives. She does not pursue her own sensory experience but rather seeks to divest herself of this very experience by gainful means. "[That] the image of the whore [is] the most significant female image in the *Passagen-Werk*"[38] remains a blind spot in the enlightening perception of a long line of male critics and flaneurs.

The absence of a genuine female flaneur typifies the history of male flanerie in its indifference toward female experience if prostitution can indeed be considered, as Susan Buck-Morss suggests it was, "the female version of flanerie."[39] The work of prostitutes, however, is in no way the equivalent to a freely chosen form of flanerie. The prostitute in general is neither flaneuse nor nymphomaniac, and does not have the streets at her disposal any more than she commands the use of her own body. She does not represent the new image of a self-determined female subject of the streets any more than the shopping flaneuse who has been mobilized by bourgeois consumption, or the bag lady who has been expelled into the streets and consumed by the system. Within the public facets of female lives, these women form nothing if not the cynically distorted female images of consumption and flanerie in an age of capitalist and sexist exploitation.[40] In the scene succeeding the one of the strolling woman, a number of women are presented, ostensibly, as counterimages: perfected models strutting the runways, bourgeois ladies decorating the sidewalks, and female tableaus sitting displayed at café tables, captured frequently in the moment of restoring their made-up facades.

These exhibited images illustrate the extent to which even in the presumably liberated age of the 1920s, "the spaces of femininity are defined by a different organization of the look."[41] Gertrud Koch describes the dynamics that contain women's own images as well as their access to the images of others: "The aim of the sanction against going alone to pubs, etc. is to remove women from the voyeuristic gaze of men, whereas the implicit cinema prohibition denies the voyeuristic gaze to woman herself." With no images of female moviegoers presented in *Berlin, Symphony of the City*, the film's instance of a female spectator as walking woman presents a specular process that approximates the "spectatrix's" filmic viewing.[42] In strolling, this femme flaneur fixes her gaze on the other pedestrians and takes in the spectacle of the street through the frame of a shop window. Despite this woman's singular courage, however, the prevailing scopic dynamics remain multiplied against the female pedestrian in the street, as the critical reception of this figure and her "provocative" behavior has shown. As conventions of women's images and public presence continue to objectify her, the uneasiness experienced by the female flaneur has to be regarded as far more than an isolated incident of individual paranoia or exaggerated insecurity. Her precarious status expresses an epistemological condition of female existence within the gendered dynamics of the gaze that Koch elucidates as a feminist critic of film and specularity: "Being looked at, I become the object of the Other who casts his judgment at me with his glance. Every woman knows this situation which Sartre describes as an ontological one: the domination through the appraising gaze which degrades into an object the one looked at, and subordinates her."[43] From the perspective of woman, Sartre's "ontology" does indeed describe a male epistemological position rather than an "objective" philosophical one. This view of the world marks its own blindness quite strikingly when Sartre exemplifies his definition of the Other via his perception of a *woman* in the street: "Cette femme que je vois venir vers moi [et autres passants] sont pour moi des objets, cela n'est pas douteux."[44] No less doubtful, however, is the consequence that many women who are faced with such massive scrutiny and daily objectification—and not only through a male philosopher's gaze—find themselves lacking the self-evident self-confidence that is traditionally exercised by and attributed to their male contemporaries. Women's scopophilia, along with the potential for female flanerie, has become subjected to so many historical restrictions that they may withdraw from the public sphere altogether, no longer willing or even capable of further exposing themselves to the dominant gaze of daily evaluation. A potential female flaneur may disassociate herself from an exterior world that is largely defined by the male gaze, and withdraw into domestic interiors. She may also embrace the cult of women's own bodies and appearance, assume her culturally sanctioned presence as a man's companion, or retreat into the shelter of friends and families instead of pursuing a flanerie of her own.[45]

The female flaneur's desire for her own exploration of the world ends where it encounters its limits in male pedestrians and fantasies, assaulting, annoying, disturbing, and perpetually evaluating her in the street. Woman's socially prescribed status as an image formulates an epistemological position defined by powers that overshadow her potential as an observer. Prevailing definitions of modernity reveal their gendered bias if one considers them in light of the gaze and the case of the missing flaneuse. It seems no accident that it was a recent feminist critic who would explicitly name the sense of ominous discontent that Georg Simmel had described in the early years of this century for the interiors of public transportation.[46] As Ulrike Scholvin explains, the cause of this modern anxiety lies, more than in the experience of mere anonymity as such, in a realization that is known to every woman about the extent to which a person's image and appearance is exposed to a ceaseless barrage of visual judgments within a narrow space: "It is probably less anxiety-provoking to see oneself [herself] than to realize in the eye of the Other that one is being seen by *him*."[47] This anxiety, most common to a woman's experience, prevails even in the absence of a male gaze as she continues to be a specular object to other women who have themselves internalized the criteria of male evaluation. This pivotal predicament of women's image becomes apparent in the film's scenes of shop windows where females appear only in display cases and as window dolls. Woman's epistemological status is one of constant display, exhibition, and exposition as the object of male desire and, beyond that gaze, as object to the internalized gaze of female competition that renders women objects of their own self-censorship. Wherever woman goes and looks, she finds her image surrounded by a (self-)critical gaze that subordinates and subjects her image value to permanent specular evaluation, valorization, and assessment. As Buck-Morss explains: "[Women] make themselves objects. Even with no one looking, and even without a display case, viewing oneself as constantly being viewed inhibits freedom."[48] The female shoppers and strollers gazing into the windows of *Symphony of the City* demonstrate how a potential flaneuse may come to direct her gaze on herself and her own image instead, as a construction that stands in competition with that of other female images that surround her reflection in the window. A woman's gaze consequently loses its potential for attentive autonomy toward the exterior world, as she turns to invest it rather into the image value of her own appearance.

The filmic image of the male flaneur, reflected in the glass and superimposed on the female androids in the window, also reveals the destination of the female shopping flaneuses who pursue the perfection of their own images along the criteria of the male gaze. While department store strollers and window-shoppers are predominantly women, they have not assumed the purpose-free gaze of the flaneur. Shopping malls likewise have become centers of female self-consciousness rather than feminist self-confidence as their spaces are filled with normative images of femininity, presenting only a virtual reality that does not allow for the flaneur's roaming scopophilia and free orientation in the modern public sphere.[49] Ruttmann's *Symphony of the City* provides an early echo to this prevailing predicament, in scenes that position women gazing into the display windows of apparel stores. The woman confronted with these shop windows finds her real reflection in this mirror contrasted to, that is, compared and judged in relation to, the mannequins' images of a socially sanctioned "ideal" appearance that is arranged and on display in the shop windows. Through the window, the shopper's gaze meets the scrutiny of saleswomen who are styled in the fashion of the mannequins and trained in the sale of their images. Subjected to this exchange of values, the woman as buyer and as appearance before the window is rendered at once an object of the gaze emitted by the sellers as well as by other shoppers for images. A competitive exchange of the gaze prevails whereby each of its female participants evaluates the other woman's image in the context of the store's images, in connection to its commodities, in the context of the store's ambience, and in comparison and competition to her own value as an image. A woman's gaze into the shop window reveals foremost its own disappearance, as her image is refracted in infinite reflections of its own object status, before her gaze ever has a chance of meeting (with) the exterior world. In this way, the potential for female flanerie is fractured and thus broken through its infinite refractions into commodity mirrorings. The only way out of this labyrinth, this mirror cabinet of mutually reflecting image values, seems to be a woman's—even if voluntaristic—decision to pursue a flanerie of and on her own, despite the odds and obstacles, to approach and redeem the exterior world in her own ways and on her own terms. In the existing reality of aggression, competition, and comparison, under the specular laws of the market remains only the refusal, as one feminist critic has postulated, "to dissociate under the [controlling] gaze of the Other. A woman's possible utopian gaze may transcend her own image only if she becomes an active spectator in her own right, "if she succeeds in holding her ground before this gaze as the subject of a self-confidence against which the *Other* freezes into the object." This act of perception, with its implicit dynamics of reversing the existing objectification, presents a first step toward resisting woman's exclusive status as an image and may free up a space for her own gaze onto an exterior world of new sights and views.[50]

This space, however, suggestive of an all-round observation and free-floating flanerie, has already been prefigured in another realm: the scopophilia of the cinema. The film's window, with its frames through which the stroller sees her own objectification—and beyond if she dares—is replicated in the frame of the camera yet extended on the images of an entire world. The cinema releases the female participant and spectator in these scenes of her exclusion from the world and of her reduction to a mere image. The sites and spheres of female flanerie have been inscribed into the medium of film from its earliest times. With its exploration of the images of reality, cinema takes as its focus and premise these prevailing constructions of power and the gaze, and in this reflection opens up reservoirs of unclaimed territory by allowing an institutionalized act of perception in which even a woman is free to partake in and engage her scopophilia. In so doing, the spectatrix in the movie theater approximates a prototype of the female flaneur, a moving spectator in the streets. Early cinema can be seen as one of the first public places in which this new freedom and position of the gaze was available for, accessible to, and exercised by women who had before been excluded from scopic pleasure. Like very few other spaces of mainly stationary, limited, and select visual pleasure that had traditionally been accessible to women—the housewife's gaze from the windows out of her interior, the shopper's gaze into the interiors of the department store—the mediated gaze through the eye of the camera, despite its industrial and institutional production, grants the female spectator a relatively uncontrollable gaze by rendering and recording the reality provided by its moving pictures. Max Horkheimer and Theodor W. Adorno theorize this context.

> In spite of the films which are intended to complete her integration, the housewife finds in the darkness of the movie theater a place of refuge where she can sit for a few hours with nobody watching, just as she used to look out of the window when there were still homes and rest in the evening.[51]

In the cinema's enclosed, private, and privileged realms, its spaces specifically constructed and expressly set aside for the purpose of looking, female scopophilia finds one of its first and open hideaways. Consequently, an initial censorship against women who go to the cinema emerges, a prohibition that characteristically, as Koch points out, "applies most strongly to the women who go alone."[52] The particular lure of the cinema's closed interiors, in combination with the promise of increased scopic stimuli, exerts an irresistible fascination on the female spectator who has been largely excluded from the streets. The darkened space of the cinema removes her from the gaze of others while at the same time allowing her own gaze unrestricted and accelerated access to all the shocks and impressions of modernity, approximating and even exceeding the experience of the street. It is this onset of the cinema that finally liberates women's rights to indulge their scopic desires, as Heide Schlüpmann emphasizes: "the cinema finally accepted women as social and cultural beings outside their familial ties."[53] While the move of women toward the liberating movies encountered significant initial resistance, they nevertheless embraced the new medium as a catalyst that gave way to their first legitimate and protected form of access to spectacle and perception.

> While the bourgeois theatergoer continued to reject [the movies], his wife already spent her free time in the cinema. For women, the cinema as a rule meant the only pleasure they would enjoy outside the house on their own, and at the same time also more than entertainment; they brought into the cinema the claim, not delivered by the theater, "to see themselves."[54]

The contested participation of women in *Symphony of the City* coincides with the popular arrival of cinema in the 1920s, a time when women enter a world of images that has long been denied to them in the streets. Simultaneous with their new gaze at the world on the screens, they can see for themselves and be seen by themselves in the city, the public sphere of Weimar Germany. Via the form of flanerie that film presents its spectators, stationary yet infinitely mobile in an imaginary way, the cinema transmits images of exterior reality even to the presence of women and allows them to begin to relate to the world as unimpeded, invisible, respectable flaneurs in their own right. On the screens and streets of modernity, the arrival of female flanerie extends and responds to prevailing questions about the female spectator. With spectatorship an analogy and apparent synonym for flanerie, with urban streets a realm intrinsically related to scopophilia on the screens, the female flaneur can become a prototype for gendered spectatorship in the cinema. The flaneur pursues what is akin to a cinematic gaze, enacting a modern perspective that at once performs the activities of the spectator (with his eyes), of the camera (with his mind as a medium of recording), and of the director (with his writing and reordering the collected images into a text of what he—or she—has seen). The eventual appearance of an ostensibly invisible female flaneur, as in *Berlin, Symphony of the City,* is therefore able to confirm female spectatorship in many ways. In response to pivotal inquiries in feminist film theory—"Why Women Go to Men's Films"—it would be helpful to acknowledge that there also are and have long been female flaneurs in modernity, women with an active desire for a specularity of their own in response to public spaces and images. To establish such a genuine "prefilmic" disposition in the streets would go far to concede woman's scopophilia, a specular desire that exceeds and predates her becoming subject to the codified images of prevailing forms of dominant cinema. The film of the street is not merely the medium of "men's films."

To be able to speak of a female flaneur would offer the new figure of a resistant gaze, an alternative approach, and a subject position that stands in opposition to women's traditional and prevailing subsistence as an image on the screens and in the streets. The figure of the female flaneur goes beyond woman's cultural construction as an image, wherein she exists primarily to be looked at and offered as a valuable visual commodity to the male spectator as consumer.[55] This figure may also help to reformulate theories of spectatorship that organize the gaze entirely along gender lines, that posit an active male spectator who seems to be in control of female images. Recognizing a female flaneur would enable women to trace an active gaze of their own to a preexisting tradition of female spectatorship in the public sphere, to an already actively looking female figure who can return the gaze directed to her. At first sight, the conventional assumptions of woman as image, man as bearer of the gaze dominate the specular scene of the city and its *Symphony,* with women walking the streets only so as to be looked at, displayed to, and checked out by the male gaze. Within this context, the discovery of a female flaneur would help to inscribe a model of resistance for women, one that would establish wide possibilities and open new spaces for their own gaze. A stance of female flanerie allows us to formulate a position that would offer an alternative to woman's status as an image, to override her cultural "to-be-looked-at-ness." The female flaneur would provide an antidote, a new approach and paradigm that might destabilize the dominance of the male gaze and counter it with another gaze. After the long history of male flanerie and the privileged male spectatorial position it involves vis-à-vis the image, we should wish to extend and elaborate on all theories of women's spectatorship and visual authorship, whether they involve the perception of modernity in the cinema or in the city, on the screen or in the street. In allowing for a potential flanerie by woman walkers and bearers of the gaze, we could introduce an important perspective into the cultural construction of women's images and toward women's authorship of their images of the world. It is time to reconsider concepts of the image for and from the perspective of the female subject as a flaneur, that is, as a camera, spectator, and director of a text of her own.

NOTES

1. Siegfried Kracauer, "Kult der Zerstreuung," in *Das Ornament der Masse* (Frankfurt am Main: Suhrkamp, 1977), 311–320.

2. See Walter Benjamin's essay on Franz Hessel's writings in the Weimar Republic, "Die Wiederkehr des Flaneurs," *Die literarische Welt*, October 4, 1929.

3. A "second return of the flaneur" under the auspices of the New Subjectivity in German literature and film since the 1970s, a movement characterized by a radically subjective turn toward the objective reality of exteriority, is also mainly discussed in terms of its male authors and directors.

4. See Meaghan Morris, "How to Do Things with Shopping Centers," Milwaukee Working Papers 1 (Fall 1988).

5. George Sand, quoted by Janet Wolff, "The Invisible *Flaneuse*: Women and the Literature of Modernity," in *The Problems of Modernity: Adorno and Benjamin*, ed. Andrew Benjamin (London: Routledge, 1991), 148.

6. Quoted by Griselda Pollock, *Vision and Difference: Femininity, Feminism and Histories of Art* (London: Routledge, 1988), 69.

7. See Verena Stefan, *Häutungen* (Shedding) (Munich: Frauenoffensive, 1975).

8. Anne Friedberg, "*Les Flaneurs du Mal(l)*: Cinema and the Postmodern Condition," *PMLA* 106, no. 3 (May 1991): 421.

9. Ibid., 422.

10. See Gertrud Koch, "Von der weiblichen Sinnlichkeit und ihrer Lust und Unlust am Kino: Mutmassungen über vergangene Freuden und neue Hoffnungen," in *Überwindung der Sprachlosigkeit*, ed. Gabriele Dietze (Darmstadt: Luchterhand, 1979), 116–138.

11. Susan Buck-Morss, "The Flaneur, the Sandwichman and the Whore: The Politics of Loitering," *New German Critique*, no. 39 (1986):119. Buck-Morss also touches on the question on ownership of the street, p. 114.

12. See Wolff's study on the "impossibility" of female flanerie, "The Invisible *Flaneuse*." As she argues, women might disavow altogether a modernity with its emphasis on the "public world of work, politics and city life," a world that appears to privilege the experience of

men. Yet the challenge to the prevailing "separation of 'public' and 'private' spheres of activity" replicates the exclusion of women from spheres and spaces of modernity that were potentially accessible to women after all. Validating women's interior activities at the expense of their presence in modernity's exteriors does not challenge the perception that women did not, or were not able to, participate in the "public" of male experience. The conclusion that "the solitary and independent life of the flaneur was not open to women" implies a resignation that is not too distinct from the restrictions under critique, statements that the flaneuse "was rendered *impossible* by the sexual divisions of the nineteenth century" once more exclude women from a significant realm of experience. Perpetuating the thesis of a "missing flaneuse" may too quickly foreclose our attention to instances of female flanerie and narrow the focus of a debate on women's presence in public spaces.

13. Pollock scrutinizes the specific social and historical circumstances of female lives that condition this exclusion of female flanerie, modifying the notion of an "invisible flaneuse" into the more cautious observation that there was not *supposed* to be a female flaneur, and that not *many* women managed or dared to exceed such prevailing prohibitions. As one example, Pollock cites Marie Bashkirtseff, in her attempts to live in Paris on her own terms, a quest for independence that suggests a woman's existing and prevailing desire for female flanerie. Her vivid description of the struggles that this desire encounters indeed typifies the restrictive circumstances of the century in which she lives as a woman: "What I long for is the freedom of going about alone, of coming and going, [. . .] of stopping and looking at the artistic shops, [. . .] of walking about the old streets at night; that's what I long for; and that's the freedom without which one cannot become a real artist. Do you imagine that I get much good from what I see, chaperoned as I am, and when, in order to go to the Louvre, I must wait for my carriage, my lady companion, my family?" Pollock, *Vision and Difference*, 70.

14. See other women writers and female travelers of the nineteenth century, especially women such as Johanna Schopenhauer, Fanny Lewald, and Emma von Niendorf, who traveled to Paris, the city of the 1830 and 1848 revolutions.

15. Pollock, *Vision and Difference*, 52.

16. Quoted in Pollock, *Vision and Difference*, 70.

17. Shirley Ardener quotes this piece of contemporary evidence in her sociological study, "Ground Rules and Social Maps for Women: An Introduction," in *Women and Space: Ground Rules and Social Maps*, ed. Shirley Ardener (London: Oxford University Women's Studies Committee, 1981), 33; my emphasis.

18. Ibid., 29.

19. Pollock, *Vision and Difference*, 63.

20. Also see Ardener's statement: "Foot-binding, tight corsetting, hobble skirts, high heels, all effectively impede women's freedom of movement." *Women and Space*, 28.

21. See Adrienne Rich, "Compulsory Heterosexuality and Lesbian Existence," in *Powers of Desire: The Politics of Sexuality*, ed. Ann Snitow, Christine Stansell, and Sharon Thompson (New York: Monthly Review Press, 1983), 177–205. In her groundbreaking essay, Rich exposes and defamiliarizes a number of "natural facts" of female existence as socially constructed factors that oppress and literally impede women's movement with crippling consequences. By extension, these material and physical restrictions ultimately result in the "horizontal segregation of women in employment" and the "enforced economic dependence of wives," all aimed at restricting women's movement and reach in an extended and immediate sense.

22. Gertrud Koch, "Why Women Go to Men's Films," in *Feminist Aesthetics*, ed. Gisela Ecker, trans. Harriet Anderson (Boston: Beacon, 1985), 108 ff. To the extent that these fac-

tors describe and prescribe women's point of view and access to public space, they are neither "abstract nor exclusively personal, but ideologically and historically construed." Because of their historical seclusion and lack of mobility, women have remained in particular
ways within these prescribed "spaces of femininity," rendered the "product of a lived sense
of social locatedness, mobility and visibility, in the social relations of seeing and being seen."

23. In a society organized around and dominated by the male gaze, "any presence of
women" remains and continues to be "sexualized." There is no representation of the female image that is neutral to and removed from issues of gender and power. For these and
similar formulations, see the survey of related arguments in feminist film theory in *New Vo-
cabularies in Film Semiotics: Structuralism, Post-Structuralism and Beyond*, ed. Robert Stam, Robert
Burgoyne, and Sandy Flitterman-Lewis (London: Routledge, 1992), 176.

24. Ulrike Scholvin, a feminist critic in contemporary Berlin, situates this problematic
production of the female image by a male gaze that does not reflect the desires or subjectivity of its object in the following way: "The cities into which we carry our projections in
order to lose ourselves in them are blocked with images that our wishes have not produced."
See her *Döblins Metropolen: Über reale und imaginäre Städte und die Travestie der Wünsche* (Wein-
heim: Beltz, 1985), 8.

25. Cf. the popular success of one recent investigation, Naomi Wolf, *The Beauty Myth:
How Images of Beauty Are Used Against Women* (New York: Doubleday, 1991). Wolf's critique
continues an ongoing line of feminist reflections on the normative codings that govern and
concern many aspects of the female image: Wendy Chapkis, *Beauty Secrets: Women and the Pol-
itics of Appearance* (Boston: South End, 1986); Robin Tolmach-Lakoff and Raquel Scherr,
Face Value: The Politics of Beauty (London: Routledge, 1984); Nancy C. Baker, *The Beauty Trap:
Exploring Woman's Greatest Obsession* (New York: Franklin Watts, 1984); Lisa Schoenfielder and
Barb Wisser, *Shadow on a Tightrope: Writing by Women on Fat Oppression* (Iowa City: Aunt Lute
Book Company, 1983); Kim Chenin, *The Obsession: Reflections on the Tyranny of Slenderness*
(New York: Harper and Row, 1981); and Susie Orbach, *Fat Is a Feminist Issue* (Middlesex:
Hamlyn, 1979).

26. Scholvin, *Döblins Metropolen*, 7 ff.

27. Pollock, *Vision and Difference*, 89.

28. Ardener, *Women and Space*, 12.

29. Susan Buck-Morss, a current critic of this "politics of loitering," speaks for women
who have begun to read and uncover these invisible confines of the system, contemporary
feminists who may be in a position to declare that "the politics of this close connection between the debasement of women sexually and their presence in public space [is] clear." See
"The Flaneur, the Sandwichman and the Whore," 119.

30. See Patrice Petro's study of women and the Weimar public sphere, *Joyless Streets:
Women and Melodramatic Representation in Weimar Germany* (Princeton: Princeton University
Press, 1989).

31. Anne Friedberg suggests the same expansion of women's space in rethinking
Wolff's deliberations via a new scrutiny of the texts of modernity: "Someone [. . .] who
wants to produce a feminist sociology that would include women's experience should also
turn to literary texts by female 'modernists.' " Friedberg, "Les Flaneurs du Mal(l)," 430.

32. Siegfried Kracauer, *From Caligari to Hitler: A Psychological History of the German Film*
(Princeton: Princeton University Press, 1947), 186.

33. William Uricchio, "Ruttmann's *Berlin* and the City Film to 1930," Ph.D. dissertao-
tion, New York University, 1982, 209.

34. Sabine Hake, unpublished manuscript, generously provided by the author.

35. See Atina Grossmann, "The New Woman and the Rationalization of Sexuality in Weimar Germany," in Snitow, Stansell, and Thompson, *Powers of Desire*, 153–171.

36. Buck-Morss, "The Flaneur, the Sandwichman and the Whore," 119.

37. See Luce Irigaray, "Women on the Market," in *This Sex Which Is Not One*, trans. Catherine Porter (Ithaca: Cornell University Press, 1985).

38. Buck-Morss, "The Flaneur, the Sandwichman and the Whore," 122, 119.

39. Ibid., 120.

40. Ibid., 119.

41. Pollock, *Vision and Difference*, 84. Koch describes this dynamics between the looker and the objects of his look in the following way: "Woman is subjugated to the dominant gaze before she can even begin to measure herself against man, to measure her gaze against his. All she can do is look demurely at the ground, to strip her expression of all meaning in order to deny and avoid the aggression of his gaze, or to take refuge behind the mask which conceals the gaze." This cultural strategy is especially apparent in the restriction governing women's entry into privileged spaces of seeing, such as pubs and cinemas, where they must be accompanied by others, mainly men. See Koch, "Why Women Go to Men's Films," 109.

42. See the special issue of *Camera Obscura* (1989): 20–21 on "The Spectatrix," ed. Janet Bergstrom and Mary Ann Doane, for reflections on and approaches to the female spectator.

43. Koch, "Von der weiblichen Sinnlichkeit und ihrer Lust und Unlust am Kino," 125.

44. Jean-Paul Sartre, *L'Être et le Néant: Essai d'ontologie phénomènologique* (Paris: Gallimard, 1957), 310.

45. See the resigning conclusion to Verena Stefan's autobiographical account, *Häutungen*.

46. Georg Simmel, "Die Grosstädte und das Geistesleben," in *Die Grosstadt: Vorträge und Aufsätze* (Dresden: Jahrbuch der Gehe-Stiftung, 1903), 227–242.

47. Scholvin, *Döblins Metropolen* 66, my emphasis.

48. Buck-Morss, "The Flaneur, the Sandwichman and the Whore," 125. Also see John Berger, *Ways of Seeing* (New York: Penguin, 1977).

49. "In the shopping mall, the *flaneuse* may have found a space to roam [. . .] like the *flaneur*, with the privilege of just looking-but what is it she sees?" Friedberg, "Les Flaneurs du Mal(l)," 429.

50. Scholvin, *Döblins Metropolen*, 66.

51. Max Horkheimer and Theodor W. Adorno, *Dialectic of Enlightenment*, trans. John Cumming (New York: Herder and Herder, 1972), 139.

52. Koch, "Why Women Go to Men's Films," 108. Attempts at censoring the female gaze follow the logic of restricting women's movement and perception through the "traditional sanction against unaccompanied women in public meeting-places like pubs, streets, stations, etc. [in order to protect them] as a man's private property from the gaze of other men."

53. Heide Schlüpmann, *Die Unheimlichkeit des Blicks: Das Drama des frühen deutschen Kinos* (Frankfurt: Stroemfeld/Roter Stern, 1990), 13.

54. Ibid., 16.

55. Mulvey's remarks on the gendered construction of dominant cinema apply to the cultural dynamics of public spaces as well: the "socially established interpretation of sexual difference [. . .] controls images, erotic ways of looking, and spectacle." In "Visual Pleasure and Narrative Cinema,"*Screen* 16, no. 3 (1975): 6.

FOUR

The Conspiracy of Women: Images of City Life in the Work of Jeanne Mammen

Annelie Lütgens

Born in Berlin in 1890 and raised in Paris, Jeanne Mammen was forced to return to Germany during World War I as a stranger. As a result of the outbreak of the war in 1914, the affluent Mammen family had lost its entire fortune. From that point on, Jeanne and her two older sisters had to support themselves. The eldest learned stenography and typing, the two younger sisters, Maria Louise and Gertrud Johanna, called Jeanne, attempted to support themselves by making use of the art education they had received in Paris and Brussels. Compared with the great European cultural center of their childhood, Berlin seemed conservative and provincial.

> The streets were dark, without light or shops, . . . the houses plump and pompous, everything buttoned up and frosty, highly respectable, . . . the military stiff, the *Herren* snobby and obnoxious. Even the bohemians in the Café des Westens were refined, ordering their drinks from Herr Oba with a friendly distance. They crawled before money, those who didn't have any were treated like dirt.[1]

Such distance from her new environment and her social situation manifested itself in Mammen's art in the 1920s. Unlike those German artists of her generation who had become political through war and revolution, developing their socially aware art from dada and expressionism, Mammen became a critical contemporary through the experience of her new social situation and the exposures to a city she found cold and repulsive. Combined with her natural tendency to be a loner, this experiential background was the basis of her solitary situation as an artist in the Berlin of the 1920s.

The social descent from young bourgeois artist to unemployed graphic designer was aggravated by the culture shock that resulted from the involuntary move from Paris to Berlin. Mammen's observation, "I never really made my peace with Berlin," made at age eighty-five, demonstrates how deeply this change of cultural environment had affected the young artist. In her work, Mammen never makes reference to the November Group or dada. In her "Short Report" of 1974, the postwar years come up solely in the context of the "English hunger blockade" and "inflation." Her memory of these years clearly centers around material hardship, not politicization.

Earning a living in illustration and fashion design was by no means an easy task in wartime and the postwar years of turmoil and inflation. Only a few of Mammen's illustrations are known from this time. In 1916 the *Kunstgewerbeblatt* exhibited a few pieces she did while a student in Brussels.[2] In 1917 the Mammen sisters illustrated two volumes of gloomy trivial stories by Paul Schlüter, *The Poison in Women* and *The Blonde Sphinx*, edited by the publishers of *Lustige Blätter.*[3] This satirical journal—founded in 1886—had sponsored a series of books during World War I which they marketed as follows: "They are a welcome gift in these hard times . . . a carefree reading matter . . . ideal as distraction in shelters, camps, military hospitals, etc."[4] Apparently, Schlüter's book sold well, since the second editions appeared as early as 1918. His "strange tales" are reminiscent of Edgar Allan Poe's and Gustav Meyrink's short stories in that they perpetuate the image of woman as demonic femme fatale: a mermaid becomes the fatal destiny of a marine officer; a doctor, deluded to believe that his wife's blood contains the "female poison," drains her arteries until she dies. Jeanne Mammen's symbolist illustrative style successfully underscored the "mysterious" atmosphere of these texts. Obviously, the artist was not in a position to be choosy about her assignments.

Up until that point, Mammen's artistic development had remained almost untouched by the avant-garde movements of the early twentieth century. At the beginning of the 1920s, her style and sensibility still followed turn-of-the-century models. Out of the disillusioned, distanced position toward her new environment, Mammen developed a dispassionate narrative style that took on more and more verist traits toward the end of the decade. This distinguishes her from her male German colleagues, whose verism was rooted in expressionism and the experiences of war and revolution.

By the late 1920s, Mammen had finally established herself as a graphic artist. In 1930, the renowned private art gallery Gurlitt mounted her first solo exhibition and for the first time, introduced her to the Berlin public not only as illustrator but as painter as well. This recognition of the by now forty-year-old artist occurred during the highly politicized and crisis-ridden final phase of the Weimar Republic. With the crash of the New York Stock Exchange, the relative stabilization of the German economy that had been accomplished by foreign loans and investments came to a sudden end. The dark sides of economic prosperity and the half-hearted democracy had not escaped Mammen's attention. Only now did she do what many of her artist colleagues had already done during the 1918 revolution; she became politically involved, and joined the Communist party. No longer did she know the common people in the streets only from the perspective of a well-trained observer; now she met them as their equal: impoverished and looking for work. This experience, however, did not automatically translate into proletarian-revolutionary themes in her work. Mammen's social criticism expresses itself in her representation of human relationships. The scenes she depicts in her water-colors and drawings are primarily set in the world of entertainment of the newly rich and the petit bourgeois. She partakes in the feelings and emotions of her fel-low human beings. Her representations of the middle class, to which she herself belongs, express an acute awareness of the deterioration of its values and illustrate its vain attempts to bring together aspirations toward personal advancement with individual claims to happiness; Mammen's images reflect her contemporaries' growing sense of alienation as well as their uneasiness with the increasing com-modification of human relationships. That Jeanne Mammen's illustrations reveal exactly those societal structures that they perpetuate, given that they themselves are part of mass entertainment, marks the ambivalence of her work.

Mammen's experience in Berlin in the 1920s was not unlike that of many other women who had come to this young metropolis to seek fame and fortune. The mag-azines and satirical papers publishing Mammen's illustrations beginning in 1924 were very much part of what Siegfried Kracauer had termed *Angestelltenkultur*. Mod-ernized after World War I, with the help of American dollars, Berlin had become the center of German economy, employing masses of people in trade, banking, transportation, and industry. Nearly half of them were women, mostly single, who had left their families behind in the provinces. Their aspirations can be summed up in two words: making money. The golden glitter of consumer articles triumphed, and the new method of installment purchasing allowed some dreams to come true more quickly than before. Revues and bars tempted with their neon colors. With the loss of family ties, consumption and cultural diversion gained a higher level of ac-ceptance than before, and the expanding consumer products and entertainment in-dustries were surrogates for empty interpersonal relationships. People were sup-posed to and wanted to forget: the frustrating realities of their lives, competition in the workplace, the fear of being fired, and the dependence on the boss. This act of forgetting had a name: the weekend. Once a week one tried to be the man of the world or the elegant woman, because six days a week at the office, in the store, and in the factory, one was just a number among many others. Advertising and mass media discovered female employees as a new target group, creating the New Woman with her short hair and short skirt; thin, sporty, and cool.[5] This pattern very effectively combined the characteristics of lesbian subculture—men's haircut, mon-ocle, tie, tailored suit—and the American model of the Girl and the vamp, which were a remake of the turn-of-the-century *femme enfante* and the femme fatale.

Armed with a sharp eye trained in the observation of city life in Paris and Brus-sels and a style of drawing reminiscent of Degas, Toulouse-Lautrec, and Steinlen, Mammen traveled through the wealthy west and poor east of the city, through pubs, seedy bars, and dance halls, the pleasure centers of the rich, the demimonde, and the underworld. Her own freedom of action is almost on a level with that available to pioneering male city artists like Manet and his followers.[6] Small, nondescript,

Figure 4.1. Jeanne Mammen in Berlin in the 1920s. Reprinted courtesy of VG Bild-Kunst, Bonn. © Jeanne Mammen Gesellschaft, Berlin.

dressed in an old raincoat, wearing a beret over her short-cut hair, with a drawing pencil in one hand and a cigarette in the other—we can imagine her in this way—Mammen enjoyed the freedom to be overlooked (fig. 4.1).[7] She herself, however, never overlooked women. They are the focal point of her metropolitan tales.

WORKING GIRLS

The "clean" occupation of office work opened up acceptable career opportunities for women from upper-class backgrounds who would have refused a job in the traditional urban female workplace: behind or in front of the counter in dubious establishments providing entertainment and/or prostitution. Mammen's scenes from the world of pleasure show this traditional occupation of women in the public and semipublic spheres of the city. In the 1920s, the strict borderlines between housework and the morally questionable public sphere became blurred. With the enormous rise in the numbers of young working women in offices and stores, the sexual harassment increased enormously; at the same time, it became socially more acceptable for women to work in or visit bars and dance halls alone. Sexual exchange was still a part of public life, but it was no longer exclusively prostitutes who saw the public as potential customers. To add to the confusion, prostitutes could no longer be easily distinguished from other women.[8] That could be one reason behind the publication of the famous *Führer durch das lasterhafte Berlin* (1930), which provided the interested city visitor with descriptions of places of sexual exchange according to time of day and social class.

> The Tauentzien is most definitively an afternoon street. It is most intensely alive between 5 o'clock tea and dinner. . . . Beautiful women once again stroll along the Tauentzien, before they disappear for their 5 o'clock tea and afternoon dance. . . . Men, hurrying toward their afternoon *jeu*, review the lineup of mundane beauties one last time, examine the flirtatious youth, and, in passing, fight a few visual duels. Yet acquaintances are made, perfected, that characteristically Berlin genre of street acquaintances that is bound by no obligation.[9]

The ambivalence of the women promenading on the boulevards is evident in Mammen's drawings and watercolors. They are masters at the game of being observers wishing to be observed. What is one to think, for example, of the three women she depicts in the magazine *Ulk* of 26 July 1929? They are wearing tight-fitting, widely cut out afternoon dresses, fur coats; their hats are pulled down over their foreheads. One is puffing on a long cigarette holder. Where do the elegant clothing and the hardened faces come from? From fishing for men or overtime at the office? Or both? Or are their faces rather a metaphor for survival in the city, as Bernard von Brentano remarked in 1926.

> It is impossible in such a big city, populated with so many people and filled with so many events, to live alone without possessing a hard and resistant surface that repels water like a glass wall that would otherwise rip holes in umbrellas. There is only one answer to the question What are those people doing? They are fighting for survival.[10]

In Mammen's work, women are allies in this struggle. They work as barmaids, cloakroom girls, hairdressers, beauticians, or sales girls. When among themselves, one can sense a nearly conspiratorial spirit of alliance, underlined with erotic tones. For example, *You Have Beautiful Hands* (1929) depicts a scene from a cosmetic salon. The relationship between customer and manicurist is one of trust and intimacy as suggested by the two women's concentration, their glances, and the touch of their hands.

The central compositional strategy with which Mammen distances her protagonists from their metropolitan backdrop does not differentiate between working

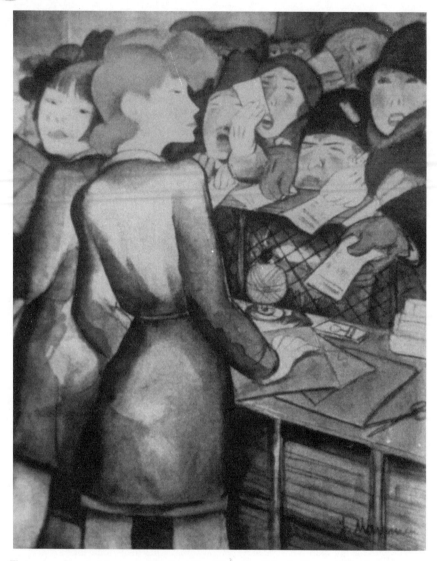

Figure 4.2. Jeanne Mammen, *Vor dem Gitter-Hinter dem Gitter* (In Front of the Grate—Behind the Grate) (1930). Reprinted courtesy of VG Bild-Kunst, Bonn. © Jeanne Mammen Gesellschaft, Berlin.

women and "working girls." The *public* has the same meaning for the two prostitutes standing on the empty streets at night before the well-lit windowpanes[11] as it does for the young women working in the wrapping department of a large store. *Customers: In Front of the Grate—Behind the Grate* from 1930 depicts the sales girls caged in behind a counter, surrounded by customers waving their claim checks (fig. 4.2).[12]

Figure 4.3. Jeanne Mammen, *Nutten* (Hookers) (1930). Reprinted courtesy of VG Bild-Kunst, Bonn. © Jeanne Mammen Gesellschaft, Berlin.

The two women stand closely together: one turns to the left, exposing her *Bubikopf* hairstyle that frames her round face; the other faces the crowd head-on.[13] We can see her expressionless profile buried under a bright red twist of hair. As in *Nutten*, the silhouettes overlap, dividing the direction of their gazes between profile and en-face views (fig. 4.3).[14] Together they don't miss a thing—be it on the street or in the store. Even the (male) viewer is addressed as potential customer through their outward glance.

COUPLES, PEDESTRIANS

The centerfold of *Ulk* magazine from 18 October 1929 is a full-page watercolor by Jeanne Mammen. It depicts a boulevard in Berlin at night, most likely the Kurfürstendamm (fig. 4.4). A tightly packed crowd is shuffling past a busy café.[15] At the top of the composition, the geometric forms of the light buildings rise up in front of a dark sky. Store windows and a double-decker bus complete the urban scene. In the left foreground, between the street and the people in the café, a mass of pedestrians move diagonally from right to left, led by a young woman looking over her shoulder. Her glance guides us into the scene. At the top left, between the sky, the buildings, and the café crowd, the street masses disappear. The people stroll by, alone or in pairs, and glance at those sitting in the café or at those approaching. One is staring into the space. They are common folks, tourists. Their nearly caricaturelike vanity seems ridiculous. The same holds true for the café guests, smoking, drinking pearl wine out of straws, making snide comments about the passersby, smugly enjoying the action. Cafés, pedestrians, and the cityscape create triangular forms that touch and intersect in the upper third of the picture. The directions of the bus, the showroom windows, and especially the angle of the pedestrians move the viewer's eyes to the left center of the composition. In the montage technique developed by the futurists and dadaists, artists reacted to the simultaneity and fracturing of urban impressions, where no single center of the composition existed. This broken perspective was accepted as real, as Elias Canetti recalled: "The horrible confusion with which one is confronted in the drawings by George Grosz, was not exaggerated; in Berlin it was natural."[16] In comparison with Grosz's 1918 ink drawing *Friedrichstrasse*, the people and houses in Mammen's work seem well ordered.[17] The difference in approach lies on yet another level; in Grosz's work the slanted fronts of the buildings, the architectural and billboard fragments, and the stylized people are tightly embedded in a chaotic network of lines and slashes creating a closed, simultaneously perceived, (dis)harmonious urban vision. Mammen maintains the contours of her figures, emphasizing them further through her use of light. Her protagonists remain in a state of suspension between type and individual. Beyond that, she places a female couple in the center of the crowd. Here as well as everywhere else where she shows two women as social or erotic allies, Mammen unifies their contours, isolating them from the surrounding crowd. For the dealers, beggars, whores, and murderers emerging from Grosz's pen, the city is a natural habitat, the marketplace, the survival ground. Mammen's pedestrians, in contrast, fill the cityscape, but remain strangers to it. For them, it is just an after-hours pleasure. Those sitting, walking, gazing, seeing, and being seen appear to be under the impression that the entire scene, the entire electric evening glow, has been created as a backdrop just for them. The lights, the cafés, the traffic, the im-

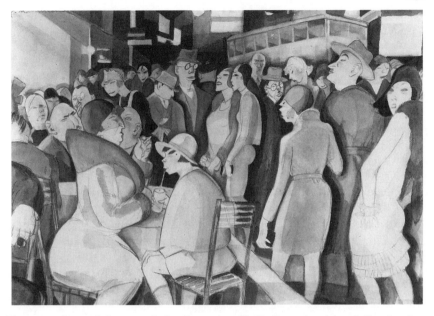

Figure 4.4. Jeanne Mammen, *Berliner Strassenszene* (Berlin Streetscene) (1929). Reprinted courtesy of VG Bild-Kunst, Bonn. © Jeanne Mammen Gesellschaft, Berlin.

material glow of the buildings create their own "celebration of life, that sparks anew every evening, (but) serves only to conceal the dehumanization of life, the metamorphosis of man and objects into consumer products."[18] They find themselves mirrored in the crowds, elevated above everyday routine. That is the reason behind their openly exhibited arrogance.

GIRLFRIENDS

In her images of urban couples, Jeanne Mammen depicted the hunger for money and the representation of status symbols as a particular aspect of the relationship between man and woman.[19] In the lower classes, the artist shows people desperately clinging to each other in an effort to save themselves from "going to the dogs."[20] Communication, understanding, tenderness, not to mention partnership, are completely absent. These are things Mammen reserves for the relationships between women. The often-recurring girlfriends motif in the 1920s (not only in the work of Jeanne Mammen but also in that of, for example, Rudolf Schlichter, Christian Schad, Richard Ziegler, and Tamara de Lempicka) appears to encompass a type of hope or utopia—an alternative to the estrangement of the sexes. In her 1923 essay collection *Wir Frauen*, the philosopher Leonore Kühn characterizes the contemporary woman as follows:

She must conquer, confirm, and achieve everything anew—under such circumstances, only a girlfriend can prove helpful, the naturally like-minded, possibly more
experienced one can assist in carving a path through the wood. . . . In many ways the
need to be loved, tenderness and understanding, the need for spiritual investigation—areas that would otherwise be the domain of a man—have today become the
greatest areas of support by a girlfriend.[21]

The revue song sung in a duet by Marlene Dietrich and Margo Lion entitled "My
Best Girlfriend" addresses the erotic application of female companionship: "Before there was the houseboy / but that was yesterday / and instead of houseboys
/ I have a housegirl today."[22] Vicki Baum deals ironically with this trend in her
story "People of Today":[23] Ypsi, a young lady, wants more than anything else in
the world to be up-to-date and talks her best girlfriend into outfitting herself as lesbian with crewcut, monocle, and horsewhip.

In 1931–1932, Jeanne Mammen produced her last illustrations of the Weimar
period: eight lithographs for Pierre Louÿs's *Bilitis*, an homage to lesbianism that,
although full of personal commitment, also allows for a certain critical look at female relationships.[24] With the falling away of taboos and the emergence of a new
openness in sexual questions, public interest in everything nonconventional grew.
Whereas at the turn of the century, homosexual men and women in Berlin had
been forced into secret locations and meeting places to avoid legal retribution, the
1920s experienced the growth of a fertile subculture that also drew a large
voyeuristic public. In 1930, the social scientist Curt Moreck had published his
Führer durch das lasterhafte Berlin. This "immoral city guide" acknowledged the
tremendous popular interest in metropolitan nightlife, introducing its visitors to
the erotic playgrounds of high society, the demimonde, and the underground, including the numerous gay bars in Berlin. In literary circles, it was considered styl-
ish to frequent establishments like the Eldorado where stage stars such as Marlene
Dietrich, Claire Waldoff, or Anita Berber could be found. Painters such as Otto
Dix and Christian Schad documented the atmosphere of dance halls and bars in
their works. The illustrations in Moreck's guidebook, however, also came from
Jeanne Mammen. While Schad depicted the meeting places of the homosexuals,
Mammen's illustrations represent the ladies' clubs. In his description of the locales
of lesbian subculture, Moreck's description almost literally follows the 1928 publication of Margarethe Roelling's *Berlin's Lesbian Women.*[25] The author provides an
overview of the best-known women's bars and clubs—the social strata represented
among its visitors, the main forms of entertainment, and the celebrations and activities arranged by them. Throughout her text, Roelling emphasizes that lesbian
women as well as homosexual men continued to be discriminated against, despite
modern tolerance and the fact that female homosexuality was not prosecuted by
law. The argument that underlies her text is that it is for that reason that lesbian
women make every effort not to draw attention to themselves in their daily lives,
limiting their public appearances together to specific bars where they would remain among themselves. Roelling's sympathetic report is clearly written to gener-

ate understanding in the reader. Unlike Moreck's guide, its goal is to educate rather than cater to the sensationalist cravings of a heterosexual audience.

In this context, Mammen's 1926 watercolor *Como,* published in the journal *Junggeselle,* provokes a comparison with Otto Dix's 1927 watercolor *Eldorado.*[26] The wine restaurant Como, decorated in red and purple, was frequented by homosexuals of both sexes. Warm hues of red, purple, and violet consequently dominate Mammen's representation. In the foreground, a virile, heavy older woman in simple dress is sitting at a table. She casts a friendly glance at a slender effeminate man with short lacquer-black hair, dressed in women's clothes, wearing heavy makeup, and drawing on a cigarette extension in a "ladylike" fashion. All other guests, men as well as women, are enveloped in the shadowy atmosphere of the "purple night," as a contemporary song characterized the world of the Others. Dix's depiction of the scene, in turn, is harsh and garish: a blue and red curtain marks the specificity of the locale; what dominates the scenery, however, are the large expanses of the carmine carpet and the orange wall. Three figures stand isolated in the room that betrays none of the intimately social atmosphere. At the bar is a broad-shouldered transvestite, wearing a large patterned Charleston dress that ends right above his/her knee, clad with female fashion accessories like a necklace, earrings, fan, and high heels. Given his voluminous upper body, his short neck and squarish head, this attire gives him a ludicrous appearance. Condescendingly, he looks over the slender young man who approaches him at the bar, also wearing a short dress. He has also attracted the attention of the bartender, who has a sly smile on his/her face. The aggressive coloring supports the sense of isolation, the need for self-representation and human contact that dominates Dix's illustration. The seemingly perverted world of *Eldorado* is governed by the same laws as all other entertainment establishments. Mammen's depiction, however, is similar to other documents of lesbian subculture in the Weimar period in that it creates a harmonious counterworld that is different from the discriminating environment, a world of beauty and elegance shaped by lifestyles that celebrate societal exclusion as exclusive. Mammen's perspective on homosexual love differs from that of Dix or Schad in that it is not that of an uninvolved spectator. Her numerous illustrations of metropolitan subculture reveal and transcend the unique personal perspective of the marginalized lesbian woman and artist.

Rarely does Mammen depict two female companions outside of their social ambience. Where she does, she sensitively and poignantly transforms the women's social background into body language, outward appearance, and the strain in adjusting to the fashionable stereotypes. *Boring Dolls* is the title of a watercolor from 1929, showing two bored, blasé young women casually leaning on each other (fig. 4.5).[27] Their costume jewelry, plain yet elegant clothes, and fashionable Garçonne hairstyles display a "touch of accepted affluence."[28] One is smoking a cigarette, the other is leaning on the crossed legs of her girlfriend. Behind them sits a doll in a clown's costume with very noticeable, strangely made-up, and nearly half-closed eyes. The doll caricatures the characteristic outfit of the flapper. "The essence of

Figure 4.5. Jeanne Mammen, *Langweilige Puppen* (Boring Dolls) (1929). Reprinted courtesy of VG Bild-Kunst, Bonn. © Jeanne Mammen Gesellschaft, Berlin.

being blasé is a callousness to the variety of things," wrote Georg Simmel in 1903.[29] The title blurs the difference between painted doll and painted doll–like women.

A WOMAN ARTIST IN THE MAN'S DOMAIN

The late 1920s saw the transformation of the unemployed graphic artist Jeanne Mammen into a successful illustrator featured by the renowned Gallery Gurlitt in a solo exhibition in 1930. Evidently, the fascination with the New Woman, as reflected in the media and the social sciences, generated more interest in those women artists whose works could be considered to document advanced levels of female emancipation and assertiveness. Consequently, Mammen's art was received as proof for the equality of artistic talent in men and women. In the context of the "woman question," it was interpreted as follows:

> The grotesque is its trait, the decadent that is condemning itself. All souls are some-what decayed and putrid, gnawed on by the worm of want and greed. The women glance sideways out of slanted eyes at their prey; the men are either consumed by their bellies or eaten up by desire. . . . The bitter taste in your mouth never disap-pears. There is always something sadistic about it: the woman's revenge? Revenge for the century-long repression of the spirit?[30]

Critics missed in her work what was expected of a woman of talent, namely, the representation of "the positive orientation of human nature."[31] Consequently, Mammen's artistic style was identified as "masculine," and the artist was men-tioned in conjunction with Grosz, Dix, and Toulouse-Lautrec.

Mammen's work of the 1920s does in fact show the influence of Toulouse-Lautrec (1864–1901) on more than one level. The atmosphere of the Belle Époque, which so significantly marked her early years and whose last tremors in Paris and Brussels she captured in her sketchbooks, had fundamentally shaped her vision. With this training, she subsequently found her artistic subjects in the hectic met-ropolitan life of her time: the cafés, bars, the demimonde, the worlds of fashion and entertainment, the dives, joints, and red zones at the margins of this urban so-ciety. Like Lautrec, Mammen is more interested in the work of chansonnettes, revue girls, street performers, and prostitutes than in that of the industrial prole-tariat. Her sympathies with the downsides of bourgeois society are not only an ex-pression of *bohème*, but are connected with her own subjective experience of (sex-ual) difference. As an old woman, she still describes this sensation of difference.

> I don't have many friends. In a way, all people are foreign to me, because I can't get myself to understand them. I am so terribly different from everyone else. . . . It's a sensation of sadness and wonder, I feel completely foreign. I have a lot of fun, but it doesn't touch me. I feel I don't belong.[32]

This distance is at the basis of the sobriety and sharp observation of Mammen's metropolitan terrain. Toulouse-Lautrec paints with a sharp brushstroke, using large surfaces of subdued colors. In her watercolors, Mammen uses a similar technique. The scenes are often nervous, the contouring lines drawn several times. The watercolor, mostly various shades of gray, permeates the drawing and lends it volume. Yet the penciled lines envelop the body, almost setting it in motion. With Lautrec, Mammen also shares Japanese influences, as the facial features of the two girlfriends in *Boring Dolls* clearly demonstrate. She employs what might be called an aesthetics of exotic typology, whenever she wishes to draw attention to the difference of lesbian couples. Parallels between the works of Lautrec and Mammen also exist with regard to their rendition of woman in a patriarchal society. Because of his misshapen body, Lautrec had been effectively expelled from the male entourage of his social circles. From early childhood on, the sympathies of the aristocratic painter on Montmartre remained with the washerwomen, the drunks, and the most exploited—the whores. In his series of lithographs, *Elles,* he depicts the lesbian relationships between the inhabitants of a bordello in a factual way, without a voyeuristic gaze. Mammen takes this perspective yet a step further: in her illustrations, the exploited themselves become exploiters who, in the street, in cafés, in the theater, shamelessly calculate the effects of their physical attractiveness. For them, happiness is finding a wealthy john; affection is found only in homosexual relationships. When Lautrec draws couples, juxtaposing the woman with her impish, wilted beauty with a foolish male, he not only follows the aesthetic taste of his time, he also casts a critical glance at the relationship between the sexes. Mammen's glance comes from a similar direction but is sober rather than cold, sympathetic, yet devoid of false sentiment.

Despite stylistic parallels, considerably fewer connections can be established between Mammen's work and that of her contemporary George Grosz. As I mentioned earlier, Mammen's verism of the late 1920s, unlike that of her German colleagues, did not develop out of expressionism, war, revolution, and dada. By the mid-1910s, Mammen continued to emulate the work of Toulouse-Lautrec and Steinlen, whereas Grosz, three years her junior and a "profound misanthrope" after World War I, had already fully developed his graffitilike style of drawing.[33] Between 1919 and 1924, when Grosz's critical societal analysis in drawings like *The Flop* or *The Bat,* published in left-wing satirical journals, promoted the struggle against the bourgeoisie, Mammen was busy drawing fashion sketches and film posters to survive inflation-struck Berlin. Only toward the end of the decade did the artist's experiences dictate harder brushstrokes. In the spare sketches, primarily defined by penciled outlines, she depicts scenes from everyday life. Her caricatures, however, are not as aggressive as Grosz's pen-and-ink drawings of the late 1920s and early 1930s. After his combative phase, however, Grosz became increasingly disillusioned. His drawings were no longer published in communist journals, but rather in bourgeois publications like *Der Querschnitt* or *Simplicissimus,* which also published Mammen's work. They had become less analytical and more observant of his subject, the philistine and the petit bourgeois. It is here where Mammen and Grosz meet. Still, George Grosz's work is more compelling when it is at its most negative. Through the societal analysis in works from the early 1920s, such as *The Communists Are Down and Foreign Currency Is Up* (1920) or *5 A.M.*, he created valid pictorial formulations of a politically and propagandistically defined art form, revealing the crass class differences through a technique of physiognomical exaggeration and montagelike combination. Even the most critical works by Mammen do not measure up to this standard. Unlike Grosz's, her work is not based on hatred but on disillusionment. To publish in bourgeois humorous or fashion journals meant, after all, that she affirmed existing social conditions, and adapted to market constraints to escape the most serious economic difficulties. In that respect, Mammen differed little from her contemporaries who week after week contemplated her illustrations in the magazines, projecting their own desires onto them. If it is true that Grosz developed from "misanthropy to class struggle" and from "class struggle to moralism,"[34] it must also be true that Jeanne Mammen's political and social engagement was morally legitimate from the beginning. The admiration of beauty and elegance displayed by her artificial silk girls, their mad chase after status symbols and social mobility, are depicted with criticism *and* sympathy. Even the bourgeois couples that she frequently caricatured are represented as conceited and self-indulgent rather than despicable or threatening. In this context, Mammen's style is much closer to that of her *Simplicissimus* colleague Karl Arnold. Until 1934, Mammen published her sketches in *Simplicissimus* and *Querschnitt*. However, she no longer depicted the mundane world of amusement, but rather unemployed workers in front of shop windows, organizing food supplies, or watching street vendors—minute observations of everyday life during the economic crisis.

At the moment that the crisis had destroyed people's hopes for a secure existence and the danger of fascism had become more and more imminent, Mammen was willing to lend an ear to proclamations like *Art Is Endangered*. Written by George Grosz and Wieland Herzfelde as early as 1925, the text proclaimed that "today's artist, unless he wants to be an idler, an antiquated dud, has but two choices: technique or class struggle."[35] By "technique," Grosz and Herzfelde meant the field of applied arts, like architecture, design, or advertising, a field no longer of importance to Mammen. Rather, her work developed in a different direction, namely, one in which the artist became "the observer and critic of our times . . . submerging himself in the army of the oppressed."[36] When Mammen finally joined the Communist party in the early 1930s, Georg Grosz, who had left the party in 1923, was getting ready for exile in the United States. Mammen, however, remained in Germany during the Nazi regime. Once again undercover as an unemployed graphic artist, she secretively began to paint in a consciously "degenerate" style, embarking on a dialogue with the cubism of Picasso's *Guernica* that is without comparison in German art of the "inner emigration."

Nevertheless, her watercolors and drawings from the 1920s find the greatest echo with her public today. This could be because the art and culture of this decade are fascinating documents of the dream of a new world, and because these years—their rocky beginnings notwithstanding—were among the happiest in

Mammen's life. The style and themes of her illustrations are an essential part of urban art of our century and exemplify, to this day, our vision of Berlin in the 1920s.

Translated by Katharina von Ankum

NOTES

1. Jeanne Mammen in an interview with Hans Thiemann, in *Jeanne Mammen, 1890–1976*, Bildende Kunst in Berlin 5 (Stuttgart–Bad Cannstatt: Edition Contz, 1978), 143–144.

2. Fritz Hellwag, M. L. Folcardy, and Jeanne Mammen, in *Kunstgewerbeblatt*, n.f., 27, no. 10 (July 1916): 181.

3. Paul Schüler, *Das Gift im Weibe: Seltsame Geschichten* (Berlin, Verlag Lustige Blätter, 1917); Willy Rath, *Die blonde Sphinx: Tragikomische Sachen* (Berlin: Verlag Lustige Blätter, 1917).

4. Following an advertisement in *Lustige Blätter* 32, no. 30 (1918).

5. See Katharina Sykora, Annette Dorgerloh, Doris Noell-Rumpeltes, and Ada Raev, eds., *Die neue Frau: Herausforderung für die Bildmedien der Zwanziger Jahre* (Marburg: Jonas Verlag, 1993).

6. T. J. Clark, *Painting of Modern Life: Paris in the Art of Manet and His Followers* (New York: Knopf, 1985); Griselda Pollock, "Modernity and Spaces of Femininity," in *Vision and Difference: Femininity, Feminism and the Histories of Art* (London: Thames and Hudson, 1988).

7. Annelie Lütgens, *"Nur ein paar Augen sein . . . ": Jeanne Mammen, eine Künstlerin in ihrer Zeit* (Berlin: Erich Reimer, 1991), 205–206.

8. Sykora et al., *Die neue Frau*, 130.

9. Curt Moreck, *Führer durch das lasterhafte Berlin* (Leipzig: Verlag moderner Stadtführer, 1930), 26–28.

10. Bernard von Brentano, *Wo in Europa ist Berlin: Bilder aus den zwanziger Jahren* (Frankfurt am Main: Suhrkamp, 1981), 97 ff.

11. *Nutten* (1930), lithograph, 46.5 × 35 cm, Jeanne-Mammen-Gesellschaft, Berlin, in *Simplicissimus*, 35.27, 29, September 29, 1930, 317.

12. Jeanne Mammen, *Vor dem Gitter-hinter dem Gitter, Jugend* (1930).

13. *Jugend*, 35.15 (1930), 218. Erich Kästner describes a similar scene in his poem "Warenhaus": "The crowd is pushing / down stairs and hallways / to see what's for sale. / And the crowd comes to a halt, / in order to dig through piles of merchandise and buy, / before it moves on. / And the crowd rolls on / from the display table to the cashier, / where the register is ringing. / And then the crowds of people wait in line / in front of the grate, where the transactions take place. / But the wrappers / whose ears they yell into, are standing there yawning / or pull faces. / And they think proudly and bitterly, "Thank God for the grate / that separated us from that nice audience!"

14. Jeanne Mammen, *Nutten* (1930), lithograph 46.5 x 35 cm.

15. Jeanne Mammen, *Berliner Strassenszene*, watercolor, reproduced in *Ulk* 58.42 (1929). Collection Marvin and Janet Fishman, Milwaukee, Wisconsin.

16. Elias Canetti, *Die Fackel im Ohr: Lebensgeschichte, 1921–1931* (Frankfurt am Main: Fischer, [1980] 1982), 279.

17. *Friedrichstrasse*, folio 1 from the series *Ecce homo*, 1922–1923.

18. Ernst Bloch, *Erbschaft dieser Zeit* (1935) (Frankfurt am Main: Suhrkamp, 1981), 216.

19. Lütgens, "*Nur ein paar Augen sein,*" 51–52.

20. Ibid., 53–54.

21. Quoted in *Eldorado: Homosexuelle Frauen und Männer in Berlin, 1850–1950* (Berlin: Berlin-Museum, 1984), 136.

22. Quoted in Charles Higham, *Marlene, ein Mythos-ein Leben* (Reinbek: Rowohlt, 1978), 52.

23. Vicki Baum, "Leute von heute" (1927), in *Die Dame: Ein deutsches Journal für den verwöhnten Geschmack, 1912–1943,* ed. Christian Ferber (Frankfurt am Main: Ullstein, 1980), 165–167.

24. Jeanne Mammen, *Langweilige Puppen,* watercolor reproduced in *Jugend* 34.35 (1929), 558. Collection Marvin and Janet Fishman, Milwaukee, Wisconsin. Lütgens, "*Nur ein paar Augen sein,*" 70–75; Hildegard Reinhard, "Die Lieder der Bilitis," in *Jeanne Mammen: Köpfe und Szenen, 1920–1933* (Emden: Kunsthalle Emden and Stiftung Henri Nannen, 1991), 55–74; Katharina Sykora, "Jeanne Mammen," *Woman's Art Journal* (Fall/Winter 1988–1989): 28–31.

25. The cover illustration of the 1982 reprint is by Jeanne Mammen. See Adele Meyer, *Lila Nächte: Die Damenclubs der Zwanziger Jahre* (Köln: Zitronenpresse, 1981).

26. *Como,* edited in *Der Junggeselle,* 39 (1926); see Lütgens, "Nur ein paar Augen sein," Otto Dix, *Eldorado,* watercolor, 56 x 39 cm, 1927, Berlinische Galerie, Berlin.

27. *Jugend,* 34.35 (1929): 558, entitled "Plauderei," in *Art in Germany 1909–1936: From Expressionism to Resistance, the Marvin and Janet Fishman Collection,* ed. Reinhold Heller (Munich: Prestel, 1990), 184.

28. Ibid.

29. Georg Simmel, "Die Grosstädte und das Geistesleben," in *Das Individuum und die Freiheit* (Berlin: Wagenbach, 1984), 196.

30. Max Deri in *BZ am Mittag,* 21 October 1930.

31. *Art in Germany,* 184.

32. Hans Kinkel, "Begegnung mit Jeanne Mammen," in *Jeanne Mammen 1890–1976,* ed. Jeanne Mammen Gesellschaft in cooperation with Berlinische Galerie (Stuttgart: Cantz Verlag, 1978), 94.

33. Uwe M. Schneede, "Hubbuch, Grosz, Nerlinger," in *Karl Hubbuch* (Karlsruhe: Badischer Kunstverein, 1981), 39.

34. Uwe M. Schneede, *George Grosz: Der Künstler in seiner Gesellschaft* (Köln: Dumont, [1975] 1984), 146.

35. *Künstlerschriften der 20er Jahre: Dokumente und Manifeste aus der Weimarer Republik,* ed. Uwe M. Schneede (Köln: Dumont, [1979] 1986), 154.

36. *Künstlerschriften,* 154.

FIVE

The Misogynist Machine: Images of Technology in the Work of Hannah Höch

Maria Makela

Of all the issues confronting Germans in the 1920s, the question of technology and its proper role in modern society was among the most hotly debated. The topic was of special concern to residents of major cities, who, more frequently than those in the provinces, repeatedly encountered new technologies both at home and in the workplace. Indeed, just as the assembly line, scientific management, and new standards of speed, efficiency, and productivity fundamentally transformed German economic life after World War I, so, too, did the introduction of appliances like the vacuum cleaner and the washing machine forever change housework. Even the most intimate aspects of life were modernized in the 1920s, including human sexuality, which was irrevocably changed by the discussion and dissemination of birth control devices.

Not surprisingly, Germans registered their reactions to this complex of issues frequently and vociferously. From differing perspectives, literary texts of every sort addressed modern technology and its functions in postwar German society, be they manifestos like the 1919 founding statement of the Bauhaus, books like Oswald Spengler's 1923 *Decline of the West,* or the countless articles about German industry in the popular press of the period. Works of art and other images likewise reflect the debate about technology, from Moholy-Nagy's spray-gunned canvases and Marcel Breuer's tubular steel chairs to Fritz Lang's 1927 film *Metropolis* and the photographs of skyscrapers in the illustrated press.

Historians of the period have analyzed this multifaceted discourse at length and have recently begun to consider the differences in male and female responses to the mechanization and rationalization of urban life. Atina Grossmann, for example, has argued that women were even more sensitive than men to the technological "advances" of the 1920s, for unlike their fathers, brothers, and husbands, they actively engaged with them both in the workplace and at home. Those women who could afford the new time-saving household appliances bought them as soon as possible, while those who could not internalized the concepts of automated efficiency they had learned in the factories and implemented them in the home as a means of managing both wage work and housework. Even women's bodies were now scientifically managed by the new Sex Reform movement, which aimed to help the female juggler of the double burden accommodate wage labor and active sexuality with birth control, sexual technique, and a properly small nuclear family. Small wonder that Weimar Germany's "thoroughly rationalized female," as Grossmann describes her, experienced the crisis of modernization more intensely than did men.[1]

The artist Hannah Höch did not have a full-time job on an assembly line, nor did she have a husband or family at home to care for. Yet in the late 1910s and early 1920s she not only supported herself and her lover with her salary as a handiwork designer, she simultaneously produced prodigious amounts of artwork and maintained her own apartment in Berlin by adhering to a rigorous and exhausting schedule. The recipient of two abortions that she would rather not have had, she, too, was profoundly affected by Sex Reform and its scientific management of the body. Perhaps not surprisingly, Höch also appears to have been far more sensitive to the phenomena of technology and rationalization than her male colleagues in Berlin.

By comparing a select few of Höch's photocollages to works by contemporaneous Berlin artists, I will argue that Höch became aware of the deleterious effects of technology sooner than did most of her male colleagues,[2] and that she then uniquely inflected the debate on the issue in her artwork.[3] In contrast to John Heartfield and George Grosz, whose photocollages, prints, and drawings critiqued big business, industry, and the phenomenon of rationalization for exploiting the working class, Höch typically censured technology for its effects on *women*. I will further suggest that Höch could take this position not only because she was herself a "thoroughly rationalized female" but also because certain other aspects of her professional and, especially, private life sensitized her to the downside of an overly "rational" and technological world. Indeed, I will argue that Höch's private affairs shed a novel light on those of her works that address technology, and it is my emphasis on biography that differentiates my approach from the most recent accounts of Höch's art.[4]

Born in 1889 to a middle-class family living in the town of Gotha in Thuringia, Höch was the eldest of five children. When she moved to Berlin in 1912 to pursue a career in the arts, she first enrolled at the Kunstgewerbeschule Charlottenburg (Applied Art School of Charlottenburg) and then transferred in 1915 to the Unterrichtsanstalt des königlichen Kunstgewerbemuseums (School of the Royal Museum of the Applied Arts) after her schooling had been interrupted by the outbreak of the war. Her choice of applied rather than fine art schools was not surprising, since official policy at the time barred women from attending the Royal Academy. To be sure, Höch might have enrolled at one of the many private fine art schools for women, as Käthe Kollwitz and Paula Modersohn-Becker had done before her. They attended the Zeichen- und Malschule des Vereins der Künstlerinnen (Drawing and Painting School of the Association of Women Artists) in Berlin, a school that employed moonlighting male academicians as teachers of the drawing, painting, and graphics classes.[5] But Höch's parents, though generally supportive of their daughter's artistic aspirations, were nevertheless anxious that she learn some marketable skills, and like so many of her female colleagues in similar situations, Höch acquiesced to their wishes.[6]

As part of her training in the applied arts, Höch studied calligraphy and pattern design, and excelled at both. Not only did she become an accomplished calligrapher, employed, for one, by the city of Charlottenburg to design elaborately scripted and decorated certificates of honor for its employees, she also developed a reputation for her embroidery and fabric patterns, numerous of which were published in the prestigious handiwork journal *Stickerei- und Spitzenrundschau* (Embroidery and Lace Review).[7] It was probably this wide-ranging expertise in design that landed Höch a job at Ullstein Verlag, Germany's preeminent publisher of the picture magazine.[8] From 1916 to 1926 she worked three days a week in Ullstein's handicrafts department, sketching patterns for and then making embroidered and lace cloths in various techniques.[9] Between 1922 and 1925, *Die Dame* alone featured at least twelve of Höch's designs, and before she left Ullstein in 1926 many more were likely published here and in other Ullstein journals such as *Die praktische Berlinerin*.[10]

With this background in small-scale, precision design, Höch was unusually well positioned to capitalize on the delicate medium of photocollage when she first encountered it while vacationing in August 1918 on a small island in the Ostsee. There, in the homes and businesses of local residents, she and her lover, Raoul Hausmann, were impressed by some oleolithographs portraying German soldiers. In each case, the bodies of the soldiers were identical, but photographic portrait heads of the men away at war were seamlessly montaged atop these generic uniformed torsos. Realizing the potential of this popular form of photocollage, Höch and Hausmann immediately began to experiment with the technique by clipping photographs from Ullstein magazines, newspapers, advertising brochures, and other illustrated sources and then recombining them in new, often unsettling ways.[11] Such unexpected juxtapositions were meant to shock viewers out of complacency and force them to question conventional assumptions about the media and its construction of "reality." That is, photocollage was deconstructive in that it used mass media images to question the very language with which mainstream ideology was articulated.[12]

Among the many popular beliefs that early twentieth-century photocollage challenged was the notion of the creative artist, and it is here that the issue of technology comes into play. Because photocollagists merely appropriated preexisting photographic reproductions, their self-concept was that of a technician less personally engaged in the creative process than those artists for whom the unique, individual gesture was paramount. As Höch later put it, "We regarded ourselves as engineers, we maintained that we were building things, we said we put our works together like fitters."[13] Indeed, traditional painting and sculpture were now anathema to most of the Berlin photocollagists, who posited a new model for postwar Germany based in the impersonal cut of the knife or scissor and, more generally, in the rational, unsentimental functioning of the machine.

If the technique of photocollage reflected the Berlin avant-garde's initial enthusiasm for the pragmatism of a technological culture, initially so did the subjects of their work. Placards at the First International Dada Fair in 1920 announced the death of traditional art and the birth of a new "machine" art, and many of the exhibited works championed technology and/or America, which now came to be seen as synonymous with the unsentimental rationality of machines.[14] Höch's *Cut with the Kitchen Knife Dada through the Last Weimar Beer Belly Cultural Epoch of Germany* (fig. 5.1), discussed in more detail below, prominently displayed images of machines, machine parts, and American skyscrapers, while the catalog cover reproduced a photocollage that celebrated the American entertainment industry and the advanced technology that made that industry possible. Titled *Life and Times in the Universal City at Five Past Noon* (1919; fig. 5.2), this now-lost collaborative work by Grosz and Heartfield featured popular American phrases like " 'CHEER, BOYS CHEER!' " and "SON OF A GUN" amid fragments of film strips, views of skyscrapers, and photographs of Hollywood actors such as Rudolph Valentino and Lillian Gish. The fast-paced tempo of the film industry specifically and of modern American life more generally—especially at "five past noon," when workers rush from their offices and factories for lunch—found its analogue in the work's animated pictorial format, which frankly celebrated America's dynamism.[15]

Yet as the 1920s progressed and the artists witnessed mechanization firsthand, the star of technology and of America began to dim. While many of the erstwhile dadaists continued to work with photocollage, the subject matter, if not the technique, of their work now often implied a more critical stance toward technology. Particularly sobering were the effects of rationalization, the catchall term used to describe the innovations of the Americans Frederick Taylor and Henry Ford. Already in the first decade of the century Taylor had popularized a process of labor discipline and workshop organization based on supposedly scientific studies of human efficiency and incentive systems. By timing basic work actions, he devised wage scales based on piecework. Ford reorganized the entire productive process by implementing standardization and the assembly line. When German manufacturers adopted these practices in the mid-1920s, productivity did indeed increase, but only at the expense of skilled workers now forced to perform monotonous tasks on the assembly line or fired to make way for more "efficient" machines.[16]

Heartfield referred to this in *Rationalization Marches. A Spectre Goes Round Europe* (fig 5.3), a photomontage published in 1927 in the Communist paper *Der Knüppel*.[17] Heartfield's "spectre" is a dehumanized figure whose limbs are mechanical elements and whose body is a wage–cost analysis sheet. His stopwatch head, a reference to Taylor's timing of basic work actions, ticks away as he races through

Figure 5.1. Hannah Höch, *Schnitt mit dem Küchenmesser Dada durch die letzte Weimarer Bierbauchkulturepoche Deutschlands* (Cut with the Kitchen Knife Dada through the Last Weimar Beer Belly Cultural Epoch of Germany) (1919–20). Reprinted courtesy of the Staatliche Museen zu Berlin, Stiftung Preussischer Kulturbesitz, Nationalgalerie, Berlin.

Europe clutching the Social Democratic newspaper *Vorwärts* in his hands. Like the many contemporaneous bourgeois papers that championed American efficiency as the solution to Germany's economic problems,[18] *Vorwärts* here proclaims that rationalization is among "the most important prerequisites of economic growth." In contrast to the chaotic pictorial structure of *Life and Times in the Universal City*, the

Figure 5.2. John Heartfield and George Grosz, *Leben und Treiben in Universal-City, 12 Uhr 5 mittags* (Life and Times in the Universal City at Five Past Noon) (1919). Copyright © Artists Rights Society (ARS), New York/VG Bild-Kunst, Bonn. © 1996 Estate of George Grosz/Licensed by VAGA, New York, New York.

formal clarity of *Rationalization Marches* renders Heartfield's critique of technology and Americanization unmistakable. Indeed, Heartfield and his colleagues George Grosz, Otto Dix, and Georg Scholz were but a few of many Berlin artists who, from the mid-1920s on, explicitly or implicitly denounced in their work a mechanized, industrial, capitalist society that oppresses the working class.

Like her male colleagues, Hannah Höch was at first enthusiastic about and then increasingly critical of technology. Yet rather than shape the discourse around issues of class, Höch typically cast the debate in light of gender issues, examining in her work the relationship between modern technology and Weimar Germany's New Woman. *Cut with the Kitchen Knife* of 1919–1920 is of special note here. One of her largest and most important works, this photocollage portrays a teeming, phantasmagoric zoo in which crossbred men, women, and animals twist and turn, leap and lunge, and animate the shallow space they inhabit through the centrifugal force of their collective dance. Höch once said that she wanted this cast of hundreds to represent a cross section of the turbulent times in which she then

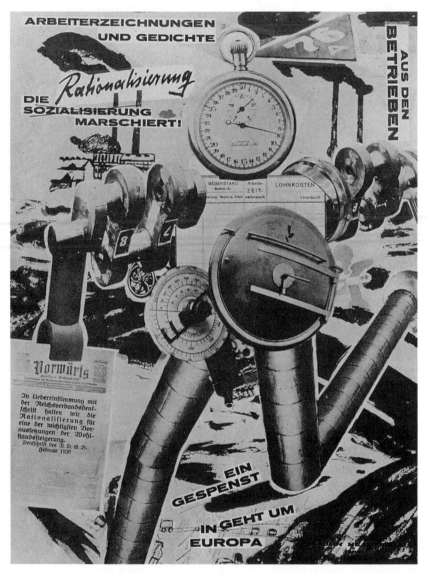

Figure 5.3. John Heartfield, *Die Rationalisierung marschiert. Ein Gespenst geht um in Europa* (Rationalization Marches. A Spectre Goes Round Europe) (1927), *Der Knüppel* no. 2 (February 1927), 5. Copyright © 1996 Artists Rights Society (ARS), New York/VG Bild-Kunst, Bonn.

lived,[19] and, in fact, the collage is a virtual encyclopedia of every important political, military, and cultural figure in early Weimar era Germany. While representatives of the now-defunct Empire, the military, and the moderate government of
the Republic fill the "anti-dada" corner at the upper right, Lenin, Karl Marx, the
Communist leader Karl Radek, and other radicals consort with the dadaists. The
meanings of this complex work are as heterogeneous as its cast of characters, but
fundamental to any reading is its statement on the interrelationship of women and
technology.[20]

In fact, images of technology predominate, most notably of mechanical objects
that facilitate movement. Be they merely component parts of machines (tires, ball
bearings, spoked wheels, and cogwheels) or fully assembled machines (cars, trucks,
and trains), these objects animate the work both formally and conceptually. Of the
many figures in *Cut with the Kitchen Knife*, it is the women who also function in this
way. Although men are in the majority, they are either stationary or merely lend
their heads to agile, active female bodies like the ice skater beside the automobile
at the lower left edge of the photocollage. She was featured in *Berliner Illustrirte
Zeitung (BIZ)* together with her skating partner, also portrayed in *Cut with the Kitchen
Knife* behind the phrase "Komm" at the top center. The popular contemporary
dancer Sant M'hesa is seen behind the spoked wheel in the upper right quadrant
of the picture; at the bottom center edge the actress Pola Negri is represented in
her role as Carmen. The only woman with a male body is the actress Asta Nielsen
at the right lower edge of the picture, just above the word "Dadaisten."
Significantly, Nielsen was celebrated at this time for playing the role of Hamlet, in
which she spawned the popular women's hairstyle of the 1920s known as the *Bubikopf* (pageboy). Even those women who are motionless in *Cut with the Kitchen Kni*
were celebrated in the popular press of the period for their physical energy. Th
two swim-suited figures to the left of the phrases "Die grosse" and "dada" in t
bottom right quadrant of the picture, for example, were German divers p
tographed after winning a diving competition. Indeed, the center of the ph
collage is occupied by a double image of female and mechanical movement.
rounded by an area of blank space that highlights her figure, the child-d
Niddi Impekoven pirouettes gracefully while playfully tossing above her th
of the artist Käthe Kollwitz. Repeatedly featured in *BIZ* and other contem
illustrated journals and newspapers, the petite Impekoven seems here to h   )
motion the oversized ball bearing below her.[21]

Such images of energetic, active women were thoroughly familiar to a viewing
public in early Weimar Germany. For not only were women of the Republic far
more likely to hold a job outside the home than were women of their mother's
generation, they were also more likely to participate regularly in sports. With
health reformers placing a new emphasis on physical fitness in the postwar period,
women of all classes became far more involved with athletics, and contemporary
magazines repeatedly featured active, sporty females like the divers and ice skaters
in *Cut with the Kitchen Knife*. Images of technology were equally widespread in the

early Weimar period, when illustrated periodicals published photographs of and articles on technological wonders like American skyscrapers. Hannah Höch thus knew that her viewing public would likely recognize New York's Wall Street at the lower left corner of *Cut with the Kitchen Knife,* as well as the New York Times building to the left of the two female divers and New York's Pennsylvania Hotel at top center.[22] This skycraper particularly fascinated Germans. *BIZ* alone featured the hotel several times between 1919 and 1921, describing with awe its twenty-seven elevators, its eight hundred kilometers of electrical wiring, and its two thousand rooms, each with attached bath.[23]

Still, *Cut with the Kitchen Knife* is not merely an upbeat restatement of the contemporaneous dialogue about athletic women and technology. Rather, it interweaves these strands of debate into a fabric that is specifically political in texture. In this regard, both the full title of the work and the newspaper fragment at the bottom right corner of the photomontage are key. This fragment—a map of Europe that Höch clipped from a November 1919 issue of *BIZ*—identifies those countries where women could already or would soon be able to vote, including Germany, which granted women suffrage when the Republic was founded.[24] Almost all German women welcomed their new responsibility enthusiastically, and although there was little consensus on a common women's platform, the women's press of the period repeatedly published articles in 1919 and 1920 that celebrated the important role women would now play in shaping the new postwar Germany.[25]

Höch, too, was optimistic at this time. Not only did she include the *BIZ* voting map in her monumental photocollage, she placed it at the lower right corner where she normally signed her work and included a small self-portrait head at the top left corner of the map. Because the title of the photocollage also refers to women's work (*Cut with the Kitchen Knife*), the image as a whole suggests that the bourgeois, patriarchal, "beer belly" epoch in Germany had come to an end precisely because German women could now participate in the political process. Together with the dynamism of technology, energetic, active women would bring this era to a close.

Six months later Höch constructed the relationship of women and technology rather differently. In *The Pretty Girl* of 1919–1920 (fig. 5.4), a female bather sits on an I-beam, resting a parasol on one shoulder. Like Niddi Impekoven in *Cut with the Kitchen Knife,* she is surrounded by signs of technology, which, however, now seem not liberating but constricting. A tire and a crankshaft pen her in at the left and right, while BMW insignia crowd in from behind. Above, a hand holds a watch, the 1920s sign of Taylorism. This bather is, in fact, so dominated by the technological world around her that she is part mechanical herself, her head having been replaced by an incandescent lightbulb topped by a lace bow.

The inclusion of this lightbulb has prompted readings of *The Pretty Girl* as a celebration of the "enlightened" New Woman of Weimar Germany. Yet such an interpretation does not take into account the figure emerging from within the tire at

Figure 5.4. Hannah Höch, *Das schöne Mädchen* (The Pretty Girl) (1919–20). Private Collection.

the left, which Höch snipped from an August 1920 issue of *BIZ*.[26] Here the American boxer Jim Jeffries is shown in the ring with Jack Johnson, who Höch then used to land a punch on her female bather. Boxing, of course, was immensely popular in Weimar Germany. *BIZ*, for example, regularly published detailed articles on the sport or on the lives of famous boxers. The Dadaists, too, were wildly enthusiastic about boxing. Not only did they themselves box, they considered the activity an apt metaphor of the dadaist enterprise. As Raoul Hausmann once put it, dada is a "punch in the eye."[27] In *The Pretty Girl*, the boxer seems to "knock some sense" into a woman who has let technology get the better of her, and has lost not only her head in the process but her dynamism as well. Unlike her active female counterparts in *Cut with the Kitchen Knife*, this empty-headed bather merely sits, displaying her body to the viewer. Tellingly, Höch titled the work *Das schöne Mädchen*, or *The Pretty Girl*, a description that infantilizes this adult woman who neither thinks nor acts and is therefore merely an object.

If *The Pretty Girl* counters the optimistic discourse on Weimar Germany's New Woman and on technology, an untitled photocollage from 1921 does so even more decisively (fig. 5.5). In this work a woman stands atop a ball bearing of the type represented in *Cut with the Kitchen Knife*, but here nestled in an open case bearing the abbreviations "Deu," "Waf," and "Muni" (Deutsche, Waffen, and Munitionen), clear references to the German munitions industry. From the right outside edge of the image a man leans in toward the posing woman, seemingly to point at or tickle her. The three round circles behind the woman are diagrams of automobile engines turned on their heads, and they are paired below with an array of kitchen utensils, including a meat grinder and a pepper mill. All of these objects float on a background of scraps of sewing patterns, which Höch would have obtained through her job at Ullstein.

Most women would have responded immediately to the pattern tracings, for sewing was not merely an avocation at this time, it was a necessity in the midst of the postwar inflation. As frequent advertisements for clothes patterns in periodicals like *BIZ* and *Die Dame* noted, the "thrifty" woman of the early-1920s sewed her own clothes, the designs for which Höch herself was producing at Ullstein. Even more pertinent is the central figure in a bathing suit, with whom readers of the popular illustrated journals would also be very familiar. Since the end of the war, every summer the bourgeois press published photographs of famous people at the beach, including the one Höch snipped from a June 1921 issue of *Die Dame* and then used as the central image of this photocollage (fig. 5.6).[28] The original photograph shows the Russian ballerina Claudia Pavlova apparently taking time off from her rigorous tour of Germany to relax at water's edge. Pavlova's smiling face is typical of such photographs, which, without exception, portray only happy modern women. By replacing the smiling face of Pavlova with that of a melancholic woman who seems decidedly unhappy with the role her body plays, Höch called into question such popular representations. In her construct, Weimar's modern woman may indeed now have a career, be sporty and physically fit, and even display her legs, but ultimately she is still controlled by a male, technological world that disregards her achievements.

This was precisely how many German women felt. After the initial flush of optimism when women were granted the vote in 1919, disillusionment about the role women could play in postwar Germany rapidly set in. This was especially evident in leftist women's journals, where articles that once celebrated the impact women would have in the new, more humane society soon gave way to essays that questioned the ability of women to influence the body politic. Especially discouraging

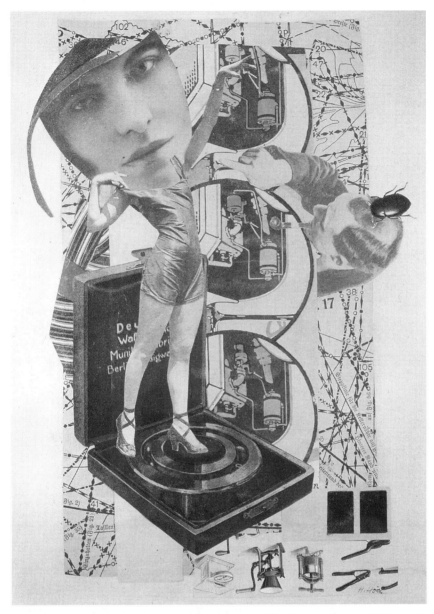

Figure 5.5. Hannah Höch, untitled photocollage (1921). Reprinted courtesy of Morton G. Neumann Family Collection.

Figure 5.6. "The first beautiful beach days: Dancer Claudia Pavlova of the St. Petersburg Ballet now on tour in Germany." *Die Dame* 48:18 (June 1921), 6. Reprinted courtesy of Staatliche Museen zu Berlin, Kunstbibliothek, Lipperheidesche Kostümbibliothek.

was Germany's demobilization policy, whereby working women were either re-tracked to lower-paying, unskilled jobs or fired to make room for returning soldiers. Not surprisingly, such treatment embittered women who had shouldered the double burden of housework and wage work during the long war and who had fully believed the promises of equality that had been made to them at the outset of the Weimar Republic.[29] Another cause for concern were the many husbands who returned from the war unwilling to accept the hard-won independence of their now very capable wives.[30] Discounted in their private lives, German women were similarly devalued in the public sphere. With the exception of the Communist party, the major political parties proved consistently reluctant to integrate women into their organizations, thereby making it difficult for the few elected women legislators to enact laws that would significantly help their constituency.[31] Though women now had the vote in theory, in fact it did them very little good. The New Woman of Weimar Germany was, finally, really not all that different from her counterpart in the Empire, and if the mainstream press like *BIZ* or *Die Dame* did not acknowledge this, leftist women's journals did.

So, too, did Hannah Höch, who was probably especially sensitive to the illusory emancipation of Weimar's New Woman because her own life proved disappointing on many levels. Although any biographical reading of the images discussed above is necessarily speculative, an account of Höch's professional situation in the immediate postwar period further contextualizes these works. While still in art school, Höch became involved with the dada group through her relationship with Raoul Hausmann, and was initially impressed and inspired by the progressive theories of the Communist-influenced dadaists as regards the role of women in society. Yet despite the lip service they all paid to women's emancipation, most of the male dadaists ultimately accorded Höch's professional achievements little if any genuine respect. George Grosz and John Heartfield opposed her participation in the First International Dada Fair of 1920,[32] and Hans Richter, the chronicler of the dada movement, condescendingly described Höch in *Dada: Art and Anti-Art* of 1965 as "a good girl" with a "tiny voice" whose main contribution to the dada movement was the "sandwiches, beer and coffee she managed somehow to conjure up despite the shortage of money.[33] But it was Hausmann, Höch's lover from 1915 to 1922 and the group's main proponent of women's emancipation, who proved Höch's most devastating critic, lecturing her like a child on aesthetics[34] and ridiculing her continued interest in easel painting.[35] Without perceiving his devastating slight, Hausmann even once asked Höch to help support him financially, because he, as an artist, should not have to waste time on such pecuniary affairs.[36]

Höch's public statements generally downplayed this lack of professional respect,[37] but her private correspondence suggests that she was deeply saddened and embittered by her exclusion from the dada group and its histories.[38] And on at least one occasion Höch even addressed her artwork to the hypocrisy of the male dadaists. *Da-Dandy* of 1919 (fig. 5.7) portrays five fragmented yet fashionable women dressed so similarly they appear as one. The two women who gaze outward wear frozen smiles

Figure 5.7. Hannah Höch, *Da-Dandy* (1919). Private Collection.

on their faces and, with the three other females pictured here, function not as active, independent subjects but as objects of titillation for the man in whose head they exist. His profile highlighted by a bit of red paper that circumscribes his silhouetted head and chest, this "da(daist)-dandy" may theoretically support women's emancipation but in fact objectifies women as much as any other contemporary male.

Höch's disillusionment with her professional status paralleled her disenchantment with her personal life, specifically, with her stormy relationship with Hausmann. The central points of contention between the two had their roots in Hausmann's belief that the Communist economic revolution could not be viable without a corresponding sexual revolution.[39] Arguing that the capitalist concept of ownership was rooted in the patriarchal organization of the family, he opposed legalized marriage, which he termed "the projection of rape into law." Instead, he advocated relationships in which women could experience a full range of sexuality outside the bonds of matrimony. This included the experience of motherhood, which Hausmann believed all women deeply desired. Hausmann thus repeatedly argued that Höch must bear a child with him to achieve total emancipation and to reach her full potential as a woman. Höch herself wanted children very much, but, ironically, Hausmann was already married and had a daughter and he was unwilling to separate legally or emotionally from his wife.[40] Höch's repeated demands that he break with her and Hausmann's tendency to respond by describing her emotional needs as "bourgeois" was the underlying cause of numerous confrontations, some of which were violent. Not only did Hausmann strike Höch and then justify his behavior by asserting that his brutality had been the only thing she could comprehend,[41] he even fantasized about killing her precisely so that Höch could no longer oppose him.[42] Not surprisingly, Höch chose not to bear the two children she conceived with Hausmann and underwent abortions in May 1916 and again in January 1918.

The profound contradictions between Hausmann's theory and practice illuminate Höch's gradual disenchantment with the role of the New Woman in the Weimar Republic, as visualized in the photocollages discussed above. They also shed light on Höch's own attitudes toward theory and, perhaps, on her critique of technology, especially as it had an impact on women. Ever anxious to expand her own intellectual horizons, Höch, like Hausmann, was initially a voracious reader of current philosophical and psychoanalytic thought. Faced with Hausmann's blatant hypocrisy, however, she soon lost patience with theoretical speculation. This is patently evident both in their correspondence and in a caustic short story Höch wrote around 1920.[43] "The Painter" chronicles the saga of Gotthold Heavenly-kingdom, an artist who is thrown into an intense spiritual crisis when his wife asks him to do the dishes. Knowing "enough about psychoanalysis to confront the woman with the truth that such demands always arise out of the desire to dominate, no matter what other reasons there might be," Gotthold goes on to theorize and then paint the "treacherous" female soul that "thwarted the boundless flight of his genius." As a spoof on Hausmann, "The Painter" not only attacks male chauvinism, it indicts the preeminently cerebral activity of (male) theoretical speculation that rationalizes human needs and emotions, or even discounts them entirely. Remarkably, just when Höch was becoming increasingly mistrustful of Hausmann and his ratiocinations, and when German society began both to renege on the promises made to women in the Weimar constitution and to rationalize women's lives and bodies, Höch's artwork became ever more critical of an in-humane, technological culture. Her initial enthusiasm about the role women and technology could play in a new postwar Germany, as visualized in *Cut with the Kitchen Knife*, was replaced by the disillusionment of *The Pretty Girl, Da-Dandy,* and the collage featuring Claudia Pavlova.

Two years before her death in 1978, Höch gave an interview in which she was asked about her Weimar photocollages of the New Woman. "My work did not at-tempt to glorify the modern woman," she replied. "On the contrary, I was con-cerned more with the suffering woman."[44] The implicit equation here of the "modern" and the "suffering" woman is explicit both in the 1920s left-wing women's press and in Höch's photocollages, especially in those works that portray technology as deleterious to women. Perhaps because Höch's own expectations about her personal and professional life had first been raised by Hausmann's tech-nical analyses of the male-female dynamic and then dashed by his inability to practice what he preached, Höch was unusually aware of the downside of an overly technological society. In any event, insofar as Höch intervened critically in debates about technology and the New Woman as early as 1919, her censure of modernity predated that of most of her male colleagues by nearly half a decade. Shaped by her uniquely female experience of Weimar Germany, Höch's vision was thus remarkably prescient indeed.

NOTES

This essay evolved out of a paper I delivered in a session on technology at the 1991 Ger-man Studies Association Conference, and I would like to express my gratitude to the coor-dinator, Peter Fritzsche, for his invitation to participate. For practical and intellectual help I am further indebted to the staff of the Berlinische Galerie, where the Hannah Höch Archive (subsequently referred to here as BG HHA) is located. Ralf Burmeister, Wolfgang Erler, Eckhard Fürlus, and Eva Züchner deserve special thanks for their many kindnesses and generosity. I would also like to acknowledge the Alexander von Humboldt Foundation and the National Endowment for the Humanities (NEH), which provided financial support that funded research for portions of this essay, and the participants of the 1992 NEH sum-mer seminar, "The City and Modernity: Film, Literature, and Urban Culture in the Weimar Republic." Their comments, especially those of Katharina von Ankum and of seminar director Anton Kaes, helped shape this essay. Above all, I would like to thank Neal Benezra, whose presence here is implicit.

1. Atina Grossmann, " 'Girlkultur' or Thoroughly Rationalized Female: A New Woman in Weimar Germany?" in *Women in Culture and Politics: A Century of Change,* ed. Judith Friedlander, Blanche Wiesen Cook, Alice Kessler-Harris, and Carroll Smith-Rosenberg (Bloomington: Indiana University Press, 1986), 62–80.

2. The exception here is Raoul Hausmann, who from the outset of the Weimar Re-public appears to have been more ambivalent about the machine than the other Berlin Dadaists. As Mathew Biro has pointed out in "The New Man as Cyborg: Figures of Tech-nology in Weimar Visual Culture," *New German Critique,* no. 62 (Spring-Summer 1994): 71–110, Hausmann's "cyborg" photomontages—those that figure the "new man" as a syn-

thesis of organic and technological elements—oscillate between a dystopian and a utopian view of modern technology, sometimes bringing both together in a single image.

3. Those studies on Höch that discuss her stance on technology include Jula Dech, *Schnitt mit dem Küchenmesser DADA durch die letzte Weimarer Bierbauchkulturepoche Deutschlands,* Form & Interesse, III, ed. Mg. Droste (Münster: Lit Verlag, 1981); Eberhard Roters, "Der mechanische Garten," *Hannah Höch, 1889–1978: Ihr Werk, Ihr Leben, Ihre Freunde,* ed. Berlinische Galerie (Berlin: Berlinische Galerie, 1989), 107–116; and Maud Lavin, *Cut with the Kitchen Knife: The Weimar Photomontages of Hannah Höch* (New Haven: Yale University Press, 1993). Ellen Maurer, "Symbolische Gemälde von Hannah Höch aus den Jahren 1920–1930," thesis, Ludwig-Maximilian-Universität, 1983, 17–23, analyzes the role technology plays in Höch's oil paintings. None of these studies suggests, as I do below, that Höch's attitudes toward technology changed over time.

4. For example, Lavin's *Cut with the Kitchen Knife* includes a great deal of biographical information, but only in the most general sense does it view Höch's work through a biographical lens. Courtney Federle's "Kuchenmesser: Hannah Höch's Cut through the Field of Vision," *Qui Parle* 5, no. 2 (Spring-Summer 1992): 120–134, does away with both biographical and contextual readings completely in favor of focusing on the tactics of Höch's montage practices.

5. On the experiences of Modersohn-Becker and Kollwitz at the school of the Verein der Künstlerinnen in Berlin, see J. Diane Radycki, "The Life of Lady Art Students: Changing Art Education at the Turn of the Century," *Art Journal* (Spring 1982): 9–13. On the Verein itself, see *Profession ohne Tradition: 125 Jahre Verein der Berliner Künstlerinnen* (Berlin: Berlinische Galerie, 1992). Renate Berger, *Malerinnen auf dem Weg ins 20. Jahrhundert: Kunstgeschichte als Sozialgeschichte* (Köln: DuMont, 1982), provides valuable information on the different career paths and educational opportunities open to German women artists.

6. In her unpublished autobiography "Für Huelsenbeck," BG HHA, as cited in Delia Güsselfeld, "Hannah Höch Freunde und Briefpartner 1915–1935," thesis, Freie Universität, 1984, 8, Höch intimated that she enrolled in the applied arts school so as not to upset her family.

7. The graphic collection of the Berlinische Galerie possesses numerous student works by Höch, from her painstaking exercises in lettering to accomplished designs for official documents of various sorts. Höch published embroidery designs in *Stickerei-und Spitzenrundschau* as early as February 1916, and throughout the 1910s and the first half of the 1920s her patterns continued to appear here and in Ullstein's women's magazines, cited below. I am grateful to Katharina Hoffmann of the graphic collection at the Berlinische Galerie for showing me Höch's calligraphy work, and to Heinrich and Eva-Maria Rössner for calling my attention to the *Stickerei-und Spitzenrundschau* magazines in the Höch Family Estate.

8. Lavin, *Cut with the Kitchen Knife,* 51–56, discusses the proliferation of Weimar's illustrated publications, especially the Ullstein publications. See also my essay in the 1996 Walker Art Center exhibition catalog on Hannah Höch's photocollages.

9. That Höch herself was an accomplished needleworker is evident from the scraps of lace- and crewelwork still extant in BG HHA. She probably executed these as models for the designs she then published in Ullstein journals. Höch commented on her work for Ullstein in an interview with Wolfgang Pehnt, "Jene zwanziger Jahre: Ein Gespräch mit Hannah Höch," Deutschlandfunk, 4 March 1973, a transcript of which is in BG HHA.

10. The designers of the fashions and handicrafts that appeared in Ullstein journals were usually not identified by name, but Höch, fortunately, removed and saved some of the

pages on which her designs appeared. Though now preserved in the BG HHA, these tear pages usually lack the pertinent issue and page numbers of the Ullstein journals from which they derive. I am indebted here to Michelle Cutler for the time and effort she took to locate the missing information for me. For an exact listing of these designs, see Kristin Makholm's chronology in the 1996 Walker Art Center exhibition catalog on Höch's photocollages.

11. Höch recounted these origins of photocollage in a lecture she delivered in Düsseldorf in 1966. The text of "Erinnerungen an DADA," now in BG HHA, was subsequently published in the exhibition catalog *Hannah Höch 1889–1978*, 201–213. See also the interviews she gave to Wolfgang Pehnt, "Jene zwanziger Jahre," and to Edouard Roditi, "Hannah Höch und die Berliner Dadaisten," *Der Monat* 12, no. 134 (November 1959): 61. Höch's short essay "Die Fotomontage," *Hannah Höch, 1889–1978*, 218–219, also addresses the beginnings of photocollage. Höch's account differs slightly from Hausmann's recollections, published in *Am Anfang war Dada*, 2d ed., Karl Riha and Günter Kämpf, with an afterword by Karl Riha (Giessen: Anabas Verlag, 1980), 45.

12. On the deconstructive nature of photomontage, see Maud Lavin, "Strategies of Pleasure and Deconstruction," in *The Divided Heritage: Themes and Problems in German Modernism*, ed. Irit Rogoff (Cambridge: Cambridge University Press, 1991), 101–102.

13. Heinz Ohff, *Hannah Höch* (Berlin: Gebrüder Mann, 1968), 17.

14. The literature is voluminous on the avant-garde's fascination with America. It includes Anton Kaes, "Brecht und der Amerikanismus im Theater der 20er Jahre: Unliterarische Tradition und Publikumsbezug," *Sprache im technischen Zeitalter* 56 (1975): 359–371; Karl Riha, "Amerika im Kopf der Dadaisten," *Sinn und Unsinn. Dada International*, Zwölftes Amherster Kolloquium zur deutschen Literatur, ed. Wolfgang Paulsen and Helmut G. Hermann (Bern: Francke Verlag, 1982), 249–264; Frank Costigliola, *Awkward Dominion: American Political, Economic, and Cultural Relations with Europe 1919–33* (Ithaca: Cornell University Press, 1984); Frank Trommler, "The Rise and Fall of Americanism in Germany," in *America and the Germans: An Assessment of a Three-Hundred-Year History*, ed. Frank Trommler and Joseph McVeigh (Philadelphia: University of Pennsylvania Press, 1985), 2:332–342; and especially the essays by John Czaplicka and Beeke Sell Tower in *Envisioning America: Prints, Drawings, and Photographs by George Grosz and his Contemporaries* (Cambridge: Busch-Reisinger Museum, 1990). Timothy Benson's "Mysticism, Materialism, and the Machine in Berlin Dada," *Art Journal* 46 (Spring 1987): 46–54, problematizes the dadaist fascination with technology by analyzing the interests of many dadaists in spirituality and mysticism. Benson's *Raoul Hausmann and Berlin Dada* (Ann Arbor: UMI Research Press, 1987) offers a more extended discussion of this and other issues. See also Biro, "The New Man as Cyborg."

15. For a more detailed analysis of this photocollage and its American sources and motifs, see Hanne Bergius, "Zur Wahrnehmung und Wahrnehmungskritik im Berliner Dadaismus," *Sprache im technischen Zeitalter* 53–56 (1975): 234–255, especially pp. 239 ff.; and Hanne Bergius, "Zur Wahrnehmung und Wahrnehmungskritik in der dadaistischen Phase von Grosz und Heartfield," in *Montage: John Heartfield*, ed. Eckhard Siepmann (Berlin: Elefanten Press Galerie, 1977), 43–47. "Universal City" is a pun on the Universal Filmgesellschaft, the German movie company for which Grosz and Heartfield worked in 1917 on a series of films, among them an anti-American propaganda film. It probably also refers to Universal Studios in Los Angeles.

16. On Taylorism, Fordism, and rationalization practices, see Charles S. Maier, "Between Taylorism and Technocracy: European Ideologies and the Vision of Industrial Productivity

in the 1920s," *Journal of Contemporary History* 5, no. 2 (1970): 27–61; Helmut Lethen, *Neue Sachlichkeit 1924–1932: Studien zur Literatur des "Weissen Sozialismus,"* Metzler Studienausgabe (Stuttgart: J. B. Metzlersche Verlagsbuchhandlung, 1970), 20–25; Detlev J. K. Peukert, *Die Weimarer Republik,* Neue Historische Bibliothek, Edition Suhrkamp, N.F. 282, ed. Hans-Ulrich Wehler (Frankfurt am Main: Suhrkamp, 1987), 111 ff.; and Mary Nolan, *Visions of Modernity: American Business and the Modernization of Germany* (New York: Oxford University Press, 1994).

17.   *Der Knüppel* no. 2 (February 1927): 5. The original photomontage to the reproduction still exists in the John-Heartfield-Archiv in the Akademie der Künste zu Berlin, Inventar Nr. 865.

18.   A small sampling of such celebratory articles might include "Das Taylor-System," *BIZ* 28, no. 21 (25 May 1919), 182–183; "Fords Europäische Pläne," *BIZ* 30, no. 1 (2 January 1921), 6; and "Bei Henry Ford: Wer ist der Mann? Und was ist sein Werk?" *BIZ* 33, no. 35 (31 August 1924), 1021–1024.

19.   *Hannah Höch: Collages, Peintures, Aquarelles, Gouaches, Dessins,* ed. Suzanne Pagé et al. (Paris and Berlin: Musée d'Art Moderne de la Ville de Paris and the Nationalgalerie Berlin Staatliche Museen Preussischer Kulturbesitz, 1976), 25.

20.   For an extended discussion of the work and its many meanings and sources, I refer the reader to Jula Dech, *Schnitt mit dem Küchenmesser DADA durch die letzte Weimarer Bierbauchkulturepoche Deutschlands,* which is the source of much of my discussion on *Cut with the Kitchen Knife.* Dech was among the first to identify the media sources of Höch's photomontages and thus deserves special note for pioneering a methodology that has proved so fruitful in Höch scholarship.

21.   These photos originally appeared as "Deutsche Kunstläufer beim Tanz auf der Eisbahn in Davos," *BIZ* 29, no. 9 (29 February 1920), 99; "Aus einer Ausstellung moderner Photographien: Die Tänzerin Sant M'hesa," *BIZ* 29, no. 2 (11 January 1920), title page; "Die volkstümlichen Filmschauspielerinnen in Deutschland: Pola Negri als Carmen," *BIZ* 28, no. 42 (19 October 1919), 428; "Pressephotograph, der zur Aufnahme einer Flottenparade im New Yorker Hafen auf die äusserste Spitze eines Schiffes klettert," *BIZ* 28, no. 50 (14 December 1919), 523; "Zwei deutsche Kunstspringerinnen Johanna und Charlotte Joseph (Schwimmclub Nixe Charlottenburg): Siegerinnen bei einem der letzten Wettkämpfe im Berliner Stadion," *BIZ* 28, no. 29 (20 July 1919), 270; "Mit 15 Jahren ein Tanzstern erster Grösse! Die Tänzerin Niddia Impekoven, die mit ausserordentlichem Erfolg in Berlin auftrat, als Pritzel-Puppe," *BIZ* 28, no. 45 (9 November 1919), 460; "Käthe Kollwitz, die Malerin und Radiererin, das erste weibliche Mitglied der Akademie der Künste," *BIZ* 28, no. 13 (30 March 1919), 101.

22.   These photos originally appeared as "Das Herz der Weltwirtschaft. Vor dem Börsengebäude in New York: Strassenbörse der Besucher, die im Saale keinen Platz haben," *BIZ* 29, no. 17 (25 April 1920), title page; "Bilder aus dem New York von heute: Der Sportenthusiasmus der Amerikaner. Die Menschenmenge vor dem Gebäude der Zeitung 'New York Times' in Erwartung des Berichts über den Verlauf eines Fussballspiels (während des Spiels)," *BIZ* 29, no. 18 (2 May 1920), 198; "Das neue Pennsylvania-Hotel mit 2200 Zimmern!" *BIZ* 29, no. 18 (2 May 1920), 199.

23.   See, for example, "New-York von Heute," *BIZ* 29, no. 18 (2 May 1920), 199; and "Das Heinzelmännchen-Hotel: Der modernste Gasthof-Typus," *BIZ* 30, no. 51 (18 December 1921), 825–827. Other articles in *BIZ* that celebrate American skyscrapers are "Sind deutsche Wolkenkratzer möglich?" *BIZ* 30, no. 7 (13 February 1921), 90–91; and "Fortschritt der Menschheit," *BIZ* 34, no. 46 (15 November 1925), 1492.

24. "Frauenwahlrecht—Kein Frauenwahlrecht," *BIZ* 28, no. 47 (23 November 1919), 482.

25. A small sampling of such articles would include "Frauen, lernt wählen," *Dies Blatt gehört der Hausfrau* 30, no. 14 (5 January 1919), 5; Luise von Brandt, "Arbeitsziele," *Neu-Deutschlands Frauen* (January 1919), 1–2; Lu Volbehr, "Frauenwahlpflicht," *Neu-Deutschlands Frauen* (January 1919), 2–6; "Neues Jahr—neue Pflichten!" *Fürs Haus* 37, no. 13 (29 December 1918), 1; "Politik und Mütterlichkeit," *Fürs Haus* 37, no. 19 (9 February 1919), 1.

26. "Ein aufblühender Sport," *BIZ* 29, no. 35 (29 August 1920), 399.

27. Raoul Hausmann, "Psychologie Dada," *Hannah Höch. Eine Lebenscollage* 1, 2 (Berlin: Berlinische Galerie, 1989) :743. On the sociopolitical significance of boxing for the Berlin avant-garde of the Weimar era, see David Bathrick, "Max Schmeling on the Canvas: Boxing as an Icon of Weimar Culture," *New German Critique*, no. 51 (Fall 1990): 113–136.

28. "Die ersten schönen Badetage an der See: Die Tänzerin Claudia Pawlowa vom Petersburger Ballet, die jetzt in Deutschland Gastspiele gibt," *Die Dame* 48, no. 18 (June 1921), 6. This collage is usually dated in the literature to 1920, but I have redated it here to 1921 on the basis of its media source.

29. For some characteristic reactions to demobilization, see the articles "Der Abbau der Frauenarbeit," *Neu-Deutschlands Frauen* (February 1919), 35–36; "Das Recht auf Arbeit," *Neu-Deutschlands Frauen* (March 1919), 35–36; "Die Frauen und der Personalabbau," *Neue Frauen-Zeit* 7, no. 1 (5 January 1924), 2. Other contemporaneous essays bemoan the unequal pay scale for men and women. See "Der volkswirtschaftliche Wert der Gehaltszählung nach Leistung!" *Neu-Deutschlands Frauen* (February 1920), 37–38; "Frauenlöhne nach Bedarf," *Neue Frauen-Zeit* 6, no. 24 (15 June 1923), 1; and Anna Blos, "Die Bewertung der Frau im Staat," *Neue Frauen-Zeit* 6, no. 37 (22 September 1923), 1.

30. Hanns Martin Elfster, "Mit den Augen des Heimgekehrten . . . ," *Neu-Deutschlands Frauen* (May 1919), 7–12; and Trude Bez-Mennicke, "Die Not, Mütter," *Neu-Deutschlands Frauen* (April 1920), 5–8.

31. The disappointment that leftist women felt in this regard is evident even in generally upbeat articles like Elfe Frobenius, "Parlamentarische Frauenberufe," *Neu-Deutschlands Frauen* (February 1920), 11–13; and Ilse Hamel, "Politische Arbeitsgemeinschaften," *Neu-Deutschlands Frauen* (May 1920), 39–40. For a lengthier treatment of the subject, see Renate Bridenthal and Claudia Koonz, "Beyond *Kinder, Küche, Kirche:* Weimar Women in Politics and Work," in *When Biology Became Destiny,* ed. Renate Bridenthal, Atina Grossmann, and Marion Kaplan (New York: Monthly Review Press, 1984), 33–65.

32. Hanne Bergius, *Das Lachen Dadas: Die Berliner Dadisten und ihre Aktionen,* Werkbund-Archiv Reihe, no. 19 (Giessen: Anabas-Verlag, 1989), 130.

33. Hans Richter, *Dada: Art and Anti-Art* (New York: McGraw-Hill, 1965), 132.

34. Hausmann to Höch, 5 June 1918, *Eine Lebenscollage* 1,1:393–395.

35. Höch's longtime friend and biographer, Heinz Ohff, recounted that in the final years of their relationship Höch would only paint in secret, behind Hausmann's back. Heinz Ohff, "Was fürs Erste nicht erscheinen kann," unpublished manuscript, Heinz-Ohff-Archiv, Berlinische Galerie.

36. Hausmann to Höch, 21 August 1915, *Eine Lebenscollage* 1,1:128–129. Ohff says that Höch used her salary from Ullstein to support both her and Hausmann for the entire time they were together. Heinz Ohff, "Was fürs Erste nicht erscheinen kann."

37. See, for example, Suzanne Pagé, "Interview mit Hannah Höch," in *Hannah Höch: Collages, Peintures, Aquarelles, Gouaches, Dessins,* 26. In response to a question from Page about why Höch had been discovered much later than other Dadaists who also worked with pho-

tomontage, Höch replied, "Naturally I suffered from being a woman, but this was more the exception than the rule. My works were accepted—and that was enough for me."

38. Höch's letters to Richard Huelsenbeck, 3 April 1958 and 18 February 1964, BG HHA, express irritation at having been excluded from the exhibitions Huelsenbeck organized and omitted from the books he wrote. Höch was particularly indignant about Hans Richter's description of her as a "good girl" in *Dada: Art and Anti-Art,* writing him after its publication that they could no longer remain friends after he had so misrepresented her. Höch to Richter, 13 December 1965, BG HHA. They later appeared to have reconciled, for their subsequent correspondence is again cordial.

39. On Hausmann's complex theories, see Benson, *Raoul Hausmann and Berlin Dada;* and *Eine Lebenscollage* 1,1 and 1,2, passim.

40. Since 1905 Hausmann had lived with Elfriede Schaeffer, with whom he had a daughter, Vera, in 1907. Hausmann and Schaeffer married in 1908.

41. "Understand one thing: I hit you only because that was the last means [I had available] to reach you." Hausmann to Höch, 27 March 1918, BG HHA. This unpublished letter is merely described in *Eine Lebenscollage* 1,1:352. The incident, which made Höch so fearful that she fled her own apartment and hid at her brother's, was preceded by another in which Hausmann smashed a teacup in anger. Höch interpreted his action as an attempt on her life. See Hausmann to Höch, 23 March 1918, BG HHA. This unpublished letter is merely described in *Eine Lebenscollage* 1:351–352. Other occasions on which Hausmann struck Höch were in July 1917 and June 1918. See Hausmann to Höch, 11 July 1917 and 4 June 1918, *Eine Lebenscollage* 1,1:288–289, 389–393. Particularly on the latter occasion, Hausmann demonstrated his incapacity to live up to his theories about women's emancipation and marriage. After Höch again fled Hausmann, he wrote her ordering her to return. "I demand that you behave as such, which you would unquestionably do if we were married." Hausmann to Höch, 3 June 1918, BG HHA. This unpublished letter is merely described in *Eine Lebenscollage* 1:389.

42. See, for example, Hausmann to Höch, 28 September 1917 and 5 February 1918, *Eine Lebenscollage* 1,1:299–301, 341–342. Höch took such fantasies seriously, writing her sister during one of many altercations with Hausmann that it was "a horrible time for me. I can't escape this Todesangst." Höch to Grete Höch, 8 April 1918, *Eine Lebenscollage* 1,1:356.

43. The German text to this story is published in *Eine Lebenscollage* 1:746–749. Lavin, *Cut with the Kitchen Knife,* published a translated version, pp. 216–218. For other evidence of Höch's impatience with Hausmann's theorizing, see Höch to Hausmann, 17 June 1918, and Hausmann to Höch, September/October 1916, 26 April 1918, 12 June 1918, and 13 July 1918, *Eine Lebenscollage* 1,1:400–402, 220–224, 371, 395–396, 422–423.

44. Pagé, "Interview mit Hannah Höch," 27.

SIX

Metropolis and the Technosexual Woman of German Modernity

Janet Lungstrum

As the robot-woman in Fritz Lang's science fiction film *Metropolis* (premiered in 1927) so entertainingly suggests, the "woman question" of this century corresponds—at least in her cinematic, literary, and political representations—not only to the perennial "German question"[1] but also to the Heideggerian "question concerning technology."[2] In the industrial era of Western modernity as well as in our own cybernetically postmodern times, the effect of technology has been to cast woman in a provocative pose, a position not unlike that of woman in the male imagination: she is the sex-machine locus of her creators' fear and fascination. As addictive projections of male desire, woman and technology are represented as fusing cathectically into one great (or monstrous) body housing (or engulfing) mankind. Is the re-creation of this feminine machine inherently self-violating not only for woman but for human society? Is it "always already" exploitative—or, alternatively, can it ever be deemed an act of new creative possibilities? The possible prosthetic benefits for feminist criticism of what may be termed woman's twentieth-century technosexuality need to be explored. In considering the machine-discourses of German modernity, this essay will present a simulacrum that aims to help resituate woman in response to the Frankensteinian transmutation already enacted upon her.

"Our age," wrote Heidegger, "is not a technological age because it is the age of the machine; it is an age of the machine because it is the technological age."[3] A Foucauldian addendum to this comment would be that having opened up our civic, living, and work spaces to rationalized measurement, we must tolerate being counted by the same capillary system of society, architecture, or machine we thought we had invented. Technological man, who has successfully patented his inventions in much the same way as the male literary writer, fashion designer, advertiser, or filmmaker, has produced woman (for example, the apparently liberated New Woman of the 1920s, or the technologically efficient new housewife of the same decade), pays a price for his technological dominance over nature and the ensuing automatization of sexuality. Reflecting back from the items he had created to delineate his strength comes a disturbing image of the modern Western male's crisis in subjectivity and sexuality. At the peak of the process of urban modernization—and hence, in theory, of male power—arose a new state of anxiety or "intensity of nervousness," as Georg Simmel first noticed about city life's increased tempo in 1903.[4] This crisis of extremes, in which the modern male oscillates between his own technological empowerment and his own automatization/feminization, is especially prevalent in the interwar Weimar German period. The Weimar Republic offers a prime locus of how technology and woman intersect; reasons for this are found in its multiple industrial, political, and economic transformations and ensuing social crises. Weimar was when the sense of German nationhood was in an insecure, emasculated limbo between the demobilization of one world war and the remobilization for the next; when disabled former front soldiers embarrassed the public gaze with their physical deformities; when the Republic's democratic chaos and economic fiascos became increasingly analogized by the right wing with the social, sexual, and professional emancipation of woman; when New Objectivity in architecture and design rejected ornamental artistic traditions in favor of engineering-as-art; when German film production reached an early apex and sought to emulate its archrival, Hollywood; and when Germany, particularly Berlin, underwent a radically swift technologization process. The all-too-human results of German modernization were hence those of discontinuity and shock, not only in the perceptual sense that Walter Benjamin iterated for the urban flaneur or film spectator, but also as regards gender relations.

The overuse of woman as a symbolic projection of the desires of an essentially male mass psyche did not of course happen for the first time with the onset of industrial modernity, but it was certainly accentuated by it. Creating woman as technosexual Other is, in its impetus at least, the ultimate Pygmalionesque fantasy of control for the male inventor, such as in the robot-woman introduced to America by the character of Thomas Edison in Villiers de l'Isle Adam's novel, *L'Eve future* (1886). Olympia, Spalanzani's invention in E. T. A. Hoffmann's romantic tale "Der Sandmann" (1816), is a perfect pre-city precursor of subsequent configurations in that she is the responsive mirror-image doll of her impotent lover's desires. What is interesting in the case of Germany is to note the swift "descent" (in moral terms) undergone by the figure of woman from the pure protectress figure of the nineteenth century, namely, Germania or Berolina, to the figure of Weimar Berlin as mechanized whore and Babylonian dominatrix, as depicted in Alfred Döblin's novel of 1929, *Berlin, Alexanderplatz*.[5] For Berlin had indeed sold herself to America(nism), just as Germany had become the mistress of the U.S.A.'s Dawes Plan of 1924 to survive reparation payments and the 1923 inflation crisis; it was the metropolis that served as the site of Weimar Germany's belated, hence overly rushed and wholesale adoption of the productivity ethics of psychotechnical Fordism.[6] The population of Berlin exploded from a prewar figure of two million to more than four and a half million by 1925—masses whose fantasies regarding these all-too-abrupt social and economic changes were best realized on the silent silver screen.[7] Weimar German cities gave birth, in caesarean manner, to Karl Marx's vision of the factory as "mechanical monster," as well as to Oswald Spengler's heralding of the (female) machine as the "real ruler (*Herrin*) of the century."[8] Again, for Siegfried Kracauer in his 1927 essay "The Mass Ornament," it is the "monstrous figure" of the capitalist "organization," engendered feminine, that is the invisible, panoptic overseer of the industrialized masses.[9] All along the political spectrum of these coagulations of woman, city, and technology, we find Walter Benjamin's notion of "dream-/desire(d)-images" (*Wunschbilder*) at work: that is, images of the new material means of technological production that are projected forth by the collective consciousness but yet remain ineluctably linked to a mythological, preindustrial past.[10] This genderized regressive tendency was all the more striking (and hence also needed) in the Weimar age of Weberian, postreligious "disenchantment" and of the interwar masculinist *kalte persona*.[11] The significance of technologized woman as myth, as the "desire(d)" and feared image of modern Germany's access to the capitalist production line of commodity fetishism, was made concomitantly more primal and more demoniac by this nation's relatively retarded entry into the world market and by the serious instability of the Weimar Republic.

The literary and filmic imagination of the industrial age failed to contain its image of woman and machine as programmable mistress (an instrumental view), or as iconic, maternal reproductive organ for the benefit of society (a view that is repressively essentializing).[12] This wishfully safe compartmentalization is what breaks out of its containment in the course of Lang's film, *Metropolis*, when the body of Maria is cloned onto that of the robot (both played by the previously unknown actress Brigitte Helm) and sexual and mechanical chaos ensues. No matter how much programming goes on, woman and machine refuse to be man's perfect creations. Indeed, one could say that, in late nineteenth- and particularly early twentieth-century Europe, the more the worker and capitalist alike felt alienated through the mechanization and bureaucratization of their city lives, the greater the need to depict and avenge this frustration in the body of woman (think of Zola's Nana, Wilde's Salomé, or Wedekind's/Pabst's Lulu, the vamps). The unconscious sublime produces images of ecstasy and terror via the Freudian degenerate "dark continent" of female sexuality and via out-of-control workings of machinery. This excessive representation of the femme fatale is certainly misogynistic (for the plot always dictates that all demon machines must die).[13] Nonetheless, the Medusa remains an important mise-en-scène of the perennial automation-autonomy dilemma[14] in technological relations.

According to Freud in his two-page fragment called "Medusa's Head" of 1922,[15] the terror of witnessing the decapitated head of the mythic Medusa figure is that of the little boy seeing the castrated naked genitalia of woman, namely, his mother. It can (and perhaps most definitely should) be argued against Freud, how-

ever, that man's turning to stone occurs more at the sight of a woman in possession of the phallus than at the sight of its horrifying lack. The Medusa's plural
phallus (her gaze, her snakelike hair, her devouring teeth) is a sign to men of her
potential power in her own sexual and cerebral jouissance, not of her resentment-
laden castration. For the turning-to-stone to become its opposite reflex, namely, an
erection (as detailed by Freud), it has been necessary for the male to re-create the
woman-machine. In Lang's *Metropolis*, Rotwang, the futuristic yet medieval inventor, has built the robot-woman so that he can fully possess his own re-created version of the late Hel, the woman he once lost to Joh Fredersen and who gave birth
to Freder.[16] But just as uncanny Olympia signaled only mechanized, frenzied
death for her lover, so Rotwang lost a hand in the process (a sign of castration).[17]
Freder's father, Joh Fredersen—as the capitalist controller of Metropolis and the
one behind the idea to send the robot-woman to cause trouble among the workers
in their labyrinthine, neo-Christian revolutionary prayer meetings, by cloning the
robot into the likeness of Maria, their spiritual leader—serves to remind us that
woman in her capacity as tyrant's plaything is still a male invention, as in Hitler's
programming and feminizing of the German state by turning it into a war machine.[18] Medusa's automation is thus a useful front for these men to hide behind.

In the futuristic scheme of things to come for German modernity (according to
the scriptwriter/filmbook author Thea von Harbou, Lang's wife and future Nazi
supporter), it is apparent that the underground workers who operate the machinery providing comfort for the inhabitants of Metropolis aboveground are no more
than alienated drones, emasculated puppets of this Medusa-machine; their movements of ten-hour shifts are totally governed by her operational demands. The ultimate scene of workers' castration by the *vagina dentata* occurs when the machine
at the power plant explodes and workers are killed, and Freder has a vision of the
machine turning into a Moloch's mouth demanding human sacrifice.[19] There is
not much difference between the strict choreography demanded by the exploitative Metropolis-machine and the compulsory mass calisthenics enacted by factory
workers in Nazi Germany: these overly trained men are not the castrating machine but her castrated tools. This is a role imposed on the dial-face workers (and
by Freder, who substitutes for one of them out of pity); they must enact a series of
slavish movements to connect the pressure points of the breastlike dial. Freder's
second hallucination of woman as sex machine, this time of the "false" Robot-
Maria as she dances nearly nude before the transfixed gaze of the city's upper-
class males, is ended by the figure of the Grim Reaper swinging his scythe: as if to
say that no social caste can avoid seduction by the Medusa. This scene includes a
peculiar collection of hanging globes, like superimposed iris-centered eyeballs, located behind the dancing robot (fig. 6.1), as well as a montage shot consisting
purely of male voyeuristic eyes in extreme close-up, fixed on following the enticing
movements of Robot-Maria. Thus, even though this woman is a performer for the
visual pleasure of men, she is more than just the Mulveyesque receiving object of
the male gaze from the profilmic and actual audiences: the reproduction of the

Figure 6.1. Robot-Maria's Dance in *Metropolis*. Reprinted courtesy of Stiftung Deutsche Kinemathek, Berlin.

eyeball is shown not only as a male activity looking at her but as part of her own dance act on stage, staring back at and dominating the men.

The question one should consider here is whether these two scenes of mass male castration both below ground and above, both machinic and sexual, are serving the pleasure principle of the Medusa-machine (be this understood as the engulfing body of the power plant or of Robot-Maria) or still serving the will to power of her male creators. Either way, one could maintain that woman-as-technology just continues to take the blame. Indeed, this subservient position of woman despite her omnivorous technosexual representation is reflected in the relative silence regarding the film's representation of woman in the immediate press reception of *Metropolis:* German reviewers concentrated, both negatively and positively, on the self-monumentalizing aspects of the film as shown in the technology of special effects, class and labor warfare, modern urban architecture, and, above all, in the immense marketing for the film devised by the production company Ufa (Universal Film Aktiengesellschaft), which practically bankrupted itself during the two years Lang required to make the film. Brigitte Helm was certainly launched into ten years of vamp-stardom, but the ramifications of the specifically *female* gender and sexuality of her *Maschinenmensch* were curiously played down.[20]

I wish to take a detour at this point, to illustrate how an alternative configuration of female technosexuality can be found via the writings of Franz Kafka. In Kafka's troubled textual body, the nightmare vision of woman as sex machine of modernity is actually internalized (rather than projected) by the male protagonist, in a series of sadomasochistic, self-inscribing, homoerotic moves.[21] As Gilles Deleuze and Félix Guattari have suggested, there is no shoring up of the male defenses going on in Kafka, no *re*territorialization, but instead an open confession of the radical *de*territorialization of modern man by collective and social machines.[22] While Deleuze and Guattari are accurate in their description of the Kafka-machine as an ongoing process of desire, it is possible to go one step further and say that the psychic mechanism in Kafka, in addition to its "bachelor-machine" attributes, is also female, that is, that it can be interpreted for feminist purposes.[23] In "The Metamorphosis" (1912), for example, Gregor's becoming an insect in bed one morning is a Medusan process, his multiple legs and orifices resembling her snakes and mouth; he actually becomes a terrifying symbol of the societal machine governing and castrating his life. As a bug among humans, he is powerless and doomed; but as an inverted affect, as a bodily transformation into and literal realization of the male fear of the technological/sexual feminine, he is most monstrous; indeed the story relates with relish his discoveries of his new grotesque physical deformity and his (albeit short-lived) Medusan effects on his family and environment. In Kafka, the repeated scenario of Medusan castration amounts to the writer's becoming one with the machine in a self-sodomizing motion. This is at its most extreme in the story "In the Penal Colony" (1919), in which we are presented with a torture apparatus designed by the late commander of the colony and maintained with slavish devotion by the officer. That this machine and her officer form a peculiar remnant of a former fascist past now without their Führer goes without saying. The officer's suicide pact with his mistress-machine provides the male explorer and the reader with a cinematically voyeuristic scene of sex unto death.

> His hand had only to approach the Harrow for it to rise and sink several times till it was adjusted to the right position for receiving him; he touched only the edge of the Bed and already it was vibrating: the felt gag came to meet his mouth, one could see that the officer was really reluctant to take it but he shrank from it only a moment, soon he submitted and received it.[24]

And so the choreography of the Medusan dance begins; male becomes female as the harrow of the (type-)writing machine inscribes the judgment onto the naked body of her own custodian, but this union of man and machine is too fast, too absolute, too out of control. As the explorer notes, "exquisite torture" becomes "plain murder" when the machine goes to pieces. As with the explosion of the Metropolis machine and Robot-Maria's subsequent instigation of the workers to destroy the machinery and flood their own homes, the unleashed power of female orgasm literally floods her own mechanism and short-circuits.[25] Robot-Maria goes laughing to the stake. The contribution to male technological society of woman as the desiring-machine is, in Deleuzian terms, one of *anti*production,[26] a wrench in the works.

While the more obvious feminist response here would be an extratechnological one, following the woman-as-*physis* line which exorcises both man and machine, there is another possibility, namely, the reappropriation, or re-creation, by woman of her own technosexuality in German modernity and beyond. The unusual aspect to this approach lies in the fact that one is not seeking to attack, sublimate, or avoid the unavoidable social formation of (post)modern woman into an image of Medusan, machinic Otherness; rather, one adopts, adapts, and empowers a phallocentric discourse into a hybrid feminist re-production.

To do this one can refer first to what the later Heidegger calls the "essence" of technology (technology is his name for the Being of today in his 1953 essay, "The Question Concerning Technology"). His name for this essence is *Gestell*—that is, that which he terms the linked assemblage of what is "posited" or "enframed" by technology and not the actual separate objects, events, and mechanisms of technology itself.

> Modern technology as an ordering revealing is . . . no merely human doing. Therefore we must take that challenging that sets upon man to order the real as standing-reserve in accordance with the way in which it shows itself. That challenging gathers man into ordering. This gathering concentrates man upon ordering the real as standing-reserve.
>
> That which primordially unfolds the mountains into mountain ranges and courses through them in their unfolded togetherness is the gathering that we call "*Ge*birg" (mountain chain).
>
> That original gathering from which unfold the ways in which we have feelings of one kind or another we name "*Ge*müt" (disposition).
>
> We now name that challenging claim which gathers man thither to order the self-revealing as standing-reserve: "*Ge-stell*" (Enframing).[27]

Heidegger states that the best reflection on technology occurs not in an instrumental way (whether for or against), but rather in taking on the challenge posed by technology, namely, its claim toward the totalizing ordering, or "Enframing," of society. He believes that the mysterious Gestell of technology threatens man as a "way of revealing which is a destining," and that man can respond to this challenge by re-producing art as *technē*, as ontological disclosure that gives rise to a new "saving power" for humans despite the "frenziedness of [technological] ordering."[28]

The term "Gestell" can be adopted for the purposes of this study in a sense that goes beyond (or can be deconstructed within) Heidegger's own, namely, by seeing the modern representation of woman's technosexuality as a parallel sphinxlike challenge of Enframing, whereby the (male-perceived) ordering of engulfment is that projected by the Medusan sexual Other.[29] Heidegger, even if unconsciously, situates technological Gestell well within the realm of the threatening feminine; Enframing (like the feminine) "threatens revealing" in truth.[30] In the same way that Heidegger never explicitly acknowledges Auschwitz as the "caesura of our times," to quote Philippe Lacoue-Labarthe,[31] so too does Heidegger consistently omit to address sexual difference—at least in his main text, as Derrida has pointed out.[32] Heidegger's warnings about Gestell as the "frenziedness of technology" reproducing itself for its own sake, as the "ambiguous essence of technology" offering both good and bad prospects, are an apparent condemnation of Nazism after the deed, but his remarks can also be read to suggest the question concerning the fearful woman-machine.[33] In the interview he gave in 1966 to *Der Spiegel*, Heidegger recommends an attitude of *Gelassenheit*, or "releasement," toward the Gestell, to stop the flow of all this dangerous "functioning" he sees going on around him in technology.[34] One should ask at this point: what is it in technology's power that scares the postwar Heidegger so, for he had surely favored her unquestioning use when appropriately saddled into service for the fascist rebuilding of the German empire, as was made clear by his 1935 statement about the "inner truth and greatness" of the National Socialist movement having to do with the "encounter between global technology and modern man."[35] It is, in fact, the self-regenerative aspect of (especially postmodern) technology, her desiring of herself, that most disturbs and activates his reactionary stance. Thus his ostensible critique of the "Will to Will" in technology betrays a more originary will on his part to harness the feminine *Gestell* from getting out of his (man's) control.[36]

Heidegger's implicit or unconscious conflation of woman as technological *Gestell* is played out in *Metropolis* with some surprising profeminist results, particularly in the key transmutation scene, where the "soul" of Maria is cloned by the know-how of Rotwang onto the robot-woman, producing thereby the "false" Robot-Maria. Now, the postwar Kracauer criticized the skilled technical effects of this scene for not being intrinsic to the plot, for being ornamental and surface-driven.[37] Not only does he fail to see in this any indication of the film escaping its Harbou entrapment—specifically, how woman may escape moral reification by turning the tables on her machinic-filmic spectacle[38]—but he simply cannot bring himself to engage the sexual circuitry at work here.[39] Initially in this scene, Rotwang appears as the master of ceremonies, having kidnapped Maria and installed her, naked and unconscious, in a metallic pod that is, one might say, wired for cloning. But what in fact happens in this scene makes Rotwang fade into a non-controlling, peripheral appendage to his own invention.[40] Shots of the Frankensteinian cloning laboratory are intercut and superimposed with close-up images of seemingly alive, bubbling fluids, which indicate to the viewer the power of the feminine about to be released and transferred from natural organism to artificial machine. Life itself is donated from Maria via (so we are to believe) the bright streams of electrical discharge from her "hooked-up" body: first to the ascending and descending circular tubes of light encircling the seated robot and then to the attached robot herself, giving her a cyborg's hybrid equivalent of heart and arteries. In this new figure, the "body-without-organs" (to use Deleuze and Guattari's term for the feminine, flooding desire of the unconscious, which in fact originally set the design pattern for all our societal and sexual machinery), that is, the engine-city Metropolis, reflects herself to herself.[41]

Through this superimposition of Maria's exterior characteristics, Robot-Maria's face and body emerge as the ultimate challenge of Gestell. As an uncontrollable figure of technological jouissance, she is nobody's tool. Unlike the man-serving combination of the real Alicia with the artificial Hadaly in Villiers's *Eve future*—and unlike the reactionary sexual emplotment in Thea von Harbou's script-cum-best-seller novel[42]—the filmic image of Robot-Maria serves nobody but herself. A subversive sex machine is being nonborn; this is woman-to-woman parthenogenesis. Here one can take up Donna Haraway's feminist discourse as a response to Heidegger's depiction of Gestell. As Haraway states of the theory of the cyborg-woman, she is a reassembling and disassembling "design," not an essence, with many advantages emerging for her in this radical loss of "distinctions between organism and machine."[43] According to Haraway, recrafted woman can reclaim and make very good use of her identity as the cyborg-Other of modernity. The desiring, pulsating body of technology, like the cavernous world of Kafka's "The Burrow," is only as threatening as the burrower wants to make it. It is not insignificant in this respect that Heidegger explicitly withdrew from "cybernetics," the self-referential side of modern technology, since he was unable to deal with this independently "functioning" aspect and the loss of the human-versus-machine distinction.[44] Deleuze and Guattari would maintain here, against the Heideggerian hesitation before the same, that the schizoid body-without-organs is a welcome "functioning" aspect of technology, constantly making and dissolving connections, and infinitely preferable to any ego-machine of reterritorialized stasis. Likewise, Haraway's cyborg replicates, she is not forced to breed.[45] And, as Hélène Cixous has stated of the Medusa, it is fine to meet her gaze: "She's not deadly. She's beautiful and she's laughing."[46]

A good macrocosmic representation of this female desiring-machine is the image of the city itself as presented in Walter Ruttmann's film of 1927, *Berlin, die Sinfonie der Grossstadt* (Berlin, Symphony of the City), one of the first "day-in-the-life-of" documentaries. The body of mechanized Berlin, created in the style of New Objectivity, is the main protagonist. The city's inhabitants are ironically depicted, in a series of parallel editing, on equal footing with the mechanized dummies in the shop windows or the milk bottles on the unceasing production line; however, the mechanized workings of the factories, communications, and vehicles are shown not as exploiting their human users but rather as creating a new urban interfacing of constant information and motion. In Ruttmann's *Berlin*, everything moves constantly in a sexually interactive circuitry, with the camera crosscutting to and fro between close-ups of the pistons of the factory machinery, the legs of the commuters, the dancers' Charlestoning legs, the soldiers' marching legs, and the legs of the cattle. Life's human functions (e.g., sleep, work, love, eating, entertainment) are depicted as an incessant, independent, technological functioning. *Berlin's* provocative, machinic body of urban display provides the viewer with a visual pleasure not totally unlike that of the implied male gaze's voyeuristic fetishism of woman's body image in narrative cinema,[47] but it is a pleasure that avoids identificatory reification of woman, because this film is consistent in its anti-identificatory decentering and dissociating techniques. Its logic is not narrative but a visual montage of the musical-machinic-organic. It thus provides a cinematic mise-en-abyme of the body of Robot-Maria herself.

In this way, Ruttmann's symphonic symmetry of independently functioning urban technology signifies a celebration of the Kracauerian self-sufficient mass ornament, as typified by the celebrated American dancing troupe, the Tiller Girls. Robot-Maria, Ruttmann's film of Berlin, and the movements of the Tiller Girls all partake of the amoral ethos of the new (feminine) technologized, self-renewing, and self-repeating capitalist (re-)production of display and excess for its own sake. Even though, as Kracauer notes, the "mass ornament is the aesthetic reflex of the rationality striven for by the dominant economic system," there is in this capitalist "end in itself" (*Selbstzweck*) no inherent rationale behind its infinitely self-perpetuating form—no matter how "rationally" it was conceived.[48] The ultimate by-product of the production-line process is a new grace of movement that responds only to itself. Thus the liberated new technosexuality of the Weimar woman (as mechanized robot, city symphony, or dance troupe) is a twentieth-century version of the preindustrial, suprahuman, dancing puppets who were free of gravity and fallible self-consciousness in Heinrich von Kleist's essay, "Über das Marionettentheater."

At this point of welcoming the pluralized becoming-machine in female subjectivity, a historical caveat must be mentioned—one that is heralded by the Harbou plot ending of *Metropolis* itself, in its final scenes of reordering and re-Enframing of the technological threat into renewed submission under the rule of Freder as the new Mediator. This end effect is not the ontological disclosure that the postwar Heidegger had in mind; nor does it allow for the continuation of the feminist cyborg's disruptions. The ultimate becoming-machine or reification of modern technology surely occurred in the machinery of the death camps and the gas chambers, used to get rid of all those who did not fit into the Nazi religion of the *Volkskörper* as the machine-in-itself. Fascism has amply demonstrated its skill at taking technology to adapt her according to its own specifications. Her operator must accordingly be the Jünger-inspired or Freikorps type of armored male, as Klaus Theweleit has elaborated.[49] An article from the Nazi export *Signal* magazine of 1944 on gender-specific differences between male and female crane operators makes it clear that the controlled-yet-controlling robot-man's work is preferred over the woman's, who, if allowed to operate the machinery of the German state, is portrayed as inefficient, weighing the workers down (she has too much flow).

> In the transport work that a man operator does with his crane, he is animated by satisfaction in his method of organization, and by its quick and precise functioning: perhaps he is pleased, too, in the play of cable, chains and his own manly strength. . . . But the woman for her part is filled with pleasure in helping, in looking after loads, in passing them on to others who need what she is helping to transport.[50]

It is perhaps not too surprising that in contrast to the magazine's image of the male crane operator, the female worker is depicted operating literally without a

Figure 6.2. Nazi description of female crane-operator: "But the woman for her part is filled with pleasure in helping, in looking after loads, in passing them on to others who need what she is helping to transport." Reproduced from *Signal: Years of Retreat 1943–1944. Hitler's Wartime Pictures Magazine,* ed. S. L. Mayer (Greenwich: Bison/Brompton Books, 1979). Reprinted by permission of the publisher.

crane (fig. 6.2). In the Nazi *Gesamtkunstwerk*, woman as desiring-machine is displaced: her place now is in the breeding process for which she must be conditioned and paraded.[51] And yet the mechanics of her desire are still being pressed into service.

As Benjamin had feared, the fascist "violation of the masses" is best effected by mass ritual, using the "violation of an apparatus."[52] Hitler's apparatus was first and foremost the medium of film, which had the power to transvalue the effect of all other technological weapons.[53] Thanks to Nazi propaganda, woman's new technosexuality was made over into film itself, and used to seduce the masses into specular overidentification. The ever-present potential hypostatization of the political power of film occurred first with Leni Riefenstahl's filming of the 1934

Nürnberg party rally. Images of the femme fatale as body sensual are substituted via the film apparatus with a machinic body politic in the fascist state, and the male gaze becomes unhesitatingly a captive audience of his own creations. All the more complicitous, then, is Riefenstahl's willingness to shape and edit this vision in *Triumph des Willens* (1935) (the film credits state "gestaltet von"). She is allowed to operate the medium of film in the name of what she called beauty and power, but only in obedient service to the Nazi vision. The aim is an *absolute* becoming-machine, a coming-in-machine, where every group movement and every individual gaze is choreographed in a communal, responsive lust for Hitler, the machine's controller who is staging himself as both masculine Führer and feminine body of desire.[54] Recall the mirroring words of Hess: "The Party is Hitler—but Hitler is Germany—as Germany is Hitler!" The viewer of the spectacle *Triumph des Willens*, whether in the cinema hall or at the rally, is meant to come ecstatically, but only on the "Heil" command as a mechanized collective being.[55] Hitler himself, in *Mein Kampf* (1925–1926), indicated his will for nothing less than a total "intoxication" of the spectator from individual to mass entity, whether via the implied immediacy of the filmic medium or, ideally, via the certain immediacy of mass meetings.[56] The orgy was to prove as illusory as the promised redemption for Kafka's officer in the body of the penal machine.

By way of conclusion, it is useful to iterate the three guiding principles behind this essay. First, the rejection of technology per se is a *dystopian* approach conflating technology with the fascist abuse of the same; this is as simplistic, and as irresponsible, as the *utopian* acceptance of machine progress. Second, the desire to rape, and especially to be raped, by the power of technology is not "out there," not just a former dictator's sin, or an Other's will to power, but a part of our continuing inherent wish to gain passive arousal before the power of the social/filmic machine—that which Deleuze and Guattari have called desire desiring its own repression;[57] hence it is something we always have to counteract in our bionic creations. Third, it is apparent by now that it has been the primary intention of this essay to show how one path of self-empowerment for woman lies not in avoiding but in truly "becoming what she is," which amounts to more than her fate as technologized carrier of modernity, that is, what she has been forced to become by the hegemonic male discourse. The challenge now is to take this "Ms.-representation" as and when it occurs, and to make it a non-abused and nonabusive desire (and there are surely more imaginative ways than borrowing, like Madonna, Robot-Maria's metallic breastplates in a mere simulacrum of a cyborg manifesto).[58] This essay, precisely in *not* denoting woman's new technosexuality as a cause for separatist feminist politics, has sought instead to demonstrate the benefits of accepting this image in order to transform the automated product into autonomous productivity. Being a shocking artwork in the age of technological reproducibility is not necessarily a bad thing.

NOTES

All translations are the author's unless otherwise indicated.

1. For related views on the "German question," see Ralf Dahrendorf's *Society and Democracy in Germany* (New York: Norton, 1965), and Detlev Peukert's *Die Weimarer Republik: Krisenjahre der klassischen Moderne* (Frankfurt am Main: Suhrkamp, 1987). A main contention of Dahrendorf's is that post-1871 Germany's rush into industrialization should not be confused with the process of true democratization, which was sorely lacking in this still feudalistic-militaristic society; and Peukert insists that the descent into National Socialism has most to do with Germany's crisis of modernization.

2. Martin Heidegger, "The Question Concerning Technology," in *Basic Writings* (New York: Harper and Row, 1977).

3. Martin Heidegger, *What Is Called Thinking?* trans. Fred D. Wieck and J. Glenn Gray (New York: Harper and Row, 1972), 24.

4. Georg Simmel's "Die Grosstädte und das Geistesleben," in *Die Grosstadt*, ed. Karl Bücher et al. (Dresden: Zahn and Jaensch, 1903), 188.

5. For a discussion of the sociosexual symbolism of castrated males and castrating females during the Weimar Republic, see Richard W. McCormick, "From *Caligari* to Dietrich: Sexual, Social, and Cinematic Discourses in Weimar Film," *Signs* 18, no. 3 (1993):644–648. See also George L. Mosse's sociohistorical discussion of Germania as nineteenth-century symbol, in *Nationalism and Sexuality* (New York: Howard Fertig, 1985), 94–96. For a philosophical discussion of Western man's castrating female complex, see Alice Jardine, *Gynesis: Configurations of Woman and Modernity* (Ithaca: Cornell University Press, 1985), 76.

6. For the absorption of American Fordism by Germany (and by *Metropolis*), see Peter Wollen's "Cinema/Americanism/The Robot," *New Formations* 5 (1989): 7–35. Peter Gendolla, in *Zeit: Zur Geschichte der Zeiterfahrung* (Cologne: Dumont, 1992), comments on Germany's unsuccessful attempt to make current the German word *Befleissigung* for industrialization (after its Latin origin, *industria*); but Gendolla does not address why this sociolinguistic nonevent occurred.

7. See Anton Kaes's chapter "Film in der Weimarer Republik" in *Geschichte des deutschen Films*, ed. Wolfgang Jacobsen, Anton Kaes, and Hans Helmut Prinzler (Stuttgart: Metzler, 1993), 62.

8. Oswald Spengler, *Der Untergang des Abendlandes: Umrisse einer Morphologie der Weltgeschichte* (Munich: C. H. Beck'sche Verlagsbuchhandlung, 1923), 628. For Marx, see Marc Le Bot et al., *The Bachelor Machines* (New York: Rizzoli, 1975), 61.

9. Siegfried Kracauer, *Das Ornament der Masse* (Frankfurt am Main: Suhrkamp, 1963), 54.

10. Walter Benjamin, "Paris: Die Hauptstadt des XIX Jahrhunderts" (1935), in *Gesammelte Schriften*, vol. 1, ed. Rolf Tiedemann and Hermann Schweppenhäuser (Frankfurt am Main: Suhrkamp, 1972), 408.

11. See Helmut Lethen, *Verhaltenslehren der Kälte: Lebensversuche zwischen den Kriegen* (Frankfurt am Main: Suhrkamp, 1994). See also Wilfried Wang, "Geometrie und Raster: Der mechanisierte Mensch," in *Expressionismus und Neue Sachlichkeit: Moderne Architektur in Deutschland 1900 bis 1945*, ed. Vittorio Lampugnani and Romana Scheider (Stuttgart: Hatje, 1994), 32–49.

12. Bertolt Brecht, in his Weimar poem "700 Intellektuelle beten einen Öltank an," made fun of the search for deliverance via the new carriers of the technological sublime,

such as oil tankers (*Gesammelte Werke*, vol. 8 [Frankfurt am Main: Suhrkamp, 1967], 316). See also Klaus Theweleit's discussion of how the deindividualization process of modernity, with its tendency toward the mass ornamentalization of the female body, is linked to the much older need to build figures of ordered "universal harmony" (*Buch der Könige: Orpheus und Eurydike* [Frankfurt am Main: Stroemfeld/Roter Stern, 1986], 928).

13. Mary Ann Doane criticizes the ambivalence of cinema as modernity's "technology of representation," for giving a home to the femme fatale as a "carrier" of power, not as a subject. See her *Femmes Fatales: Feminism, Film Theory, Psychoanalysis* (New York: Routledge, 1991), 2.

14. See William Leiss on the root metaphor for the machine being master and servant: "Technology and Degeneration: The Sublime Machine," in *Degeneration: The Dark Side of Progress*, ed. J. Edward Chamberlin and Sander L. Gilman (New York: Columbia University Press, 1985), 149.

15. Sigmund Freud, "Medusa's Head," in *Sexuality and the Psychology of Love* (New York: Macmillan, 1963), 212–213.

16. Writing before Giorgio Moroder's 1984 reedited version of the film, Andreas Huyssen, in his groundbreaking article on Lang's film, does not refer to the Hel motivation behind Rotwang's re-creation of woman. In finding a "simple and deeply problematic [male-projected] homology" between woman and machine in *Metropolis* (p. 27), Huyssen adroitly links the expressionist fear of technology to castration anxiety, and situates the film's other stylistic half within New Objectivity machine worship. See Huyssen's "The Vamp and the Machine: Technology and Sexuality in Fritz Lang's *Metropolis*," *New German Critique*, no. 24–25 (1981–1982), 221–237.

17. Anton Kaes points out the association of Rotwang and his robot with the psychic threat for the Weimar mass public represented by the film director and the created technological product, namely, film (Jacobsen, Kaes, and Prinzler, *Geschichte des deutschen Films*, 64).

18. Adolf Hitler stresses that the German masses are "feminine" and therefore fit only to be propagandized, so as to transform them into a self-sacrificing, singularized body. See *Mein Kampf* (Munich: Verlag Franz Eher Nachfolger, 1934), 201.

19. See Huyssen, "The Vamp and the Machine," 234–235.

20. See, for example, the review articles by Axel Eggebrecht in *Welt am Abend* (11 January 1927) and by Rudolf Arnheim in 1927 (*Kritiken und Aufsätze zum Film*, ed. Helmut H. Diederichs [Munich: Carl Hanser, 1977], 184–186), and the review in *Die Form* 2, no. 2 (1927): 63–64. The prevailing tendency was to accept unquestionably Harbou's moral division between the "right" and the "wrong" or "artificial" Maria, even if the review in question was simultaneously critical of the film's ending, which oversimplistically "mediated" between capitalist ("brain") and workers ("hand").

21. Richard Jayne discusses the Benjaminian concept of mechanical reproduction in Kafka but does not link it to sexual identity. See "The Work of Art as a Serial Reproduction: Kafka and Benjamin," *Journal of the Kafka Society of America* 1–2 (1988):27–41.

22. Gilles Deleuze and Félix Guattari, *Kafka: Toward a Minor Literature*, trans. Dana Polan (Minneapolis: University of Minnesota Press, 1986), 58.

23. The term "bachelor machine" has its origins in Marcel Duchamp's artwork, *The Large Glass: The Bride Stripped Bare by Her Bachelors, Even*, and has been further theorized by Michel Carrouges's *Les machines célibataires* (Paris: Le Chêne, 1954), and by the exhibition catalog, Marc Le Bot et al., ed., *The Bachelor Machines* (New York: Rizzoli, 1975). See also Constance Penley's demand for a feminist transformation of the "bachelor machine" within ap-

paratus theory in film studies, to deconstruct the male masturbatory narcissism within and to open it up instead to sexual difference via fantasy: *The Future of an Illusion: Film, Feminism, and Psychoanalysis* (Minneapolis: University of Minnesota Press, 1989), 57–80. Penley takes issue with Michel de Certeau's assertion that the Kafkaesque "bachelor machine does not agree to write the woman as well" ("Arts of Dying: Anti-Mystical Writing," in Le Bot et al., *The Bachelor Machines*, 95).

24. Franz Kafka, "In the Penal Colony," in *The Metamorphosis, The Penal Colony, and Other Stories*, trans. Willa Muir and Edwin Muir (New York: Schocken, 1975), 221–222.

25. See Klaus Theweleit, who studies the male fascist fear of the (menstrual) flow of female sexuality, understood along Deleuzian lines as a desiring-machine of the unconscious, in *Male Fantasies*, vol. 1, trans. Stephen Conway (Minneapolis: University of Minnesota Press, 1987), 225.

26. Gilles Deleuze and Félix Guattari, *Anti-Oedipus* (Minneapolis: University of Minnesota Press, 1983), 32.

27. Heidegger, "The Question Concerning Technology," 300–301.

28. Ibid., 311, 314.

29. See Avital Ronell's discussion of Heideggerian Gestell in *The Telephone Book* (Lincoln: University of Nebraska Press, 1991), 40, 196. See also Michael Heim's reference to Heidegger's speculations on Gestell as a "sphinx" with a "puzzling lack of specificity": "The Computer Age as Component: Heidegger and McCluhan," *Philosophy and Literature* 16 (1992):306.

30. Heidegger, "The Question Concerning Technology," 315.

31. Philippe Lacoue-Labarthe, *Heidegger, Art and Politics*, trans. Chris Turner (Cambridge: Basil Blackwell, 1990), 46.

32. Jacques Derrida, "Sexual Difference, Ontological Difference" (1983), in *A Derrida Reader: Between the Blinds*, ed. Peggy Kamuf (New York: Columbia University Press, 1991), 380–381. See also Patrice Petro's discussion of Heidegger's effective neutralization (via *das Dasein*) of gender, sexuality, and woman's cultural and historical role, in *The Joyless Streets: Women and Melodramatic Representation in Weimar Germany* (Princeton: Princeton University Press, 1989), 56.

33. Heidegger, "The Question Concerning Technology," 316, 315.

34. Heidegger, " 'Only a God Can Save Us': The *Spiegel* Interview," trans. William T. Richardson, in *Heidegger: The Man and the Thinker*, ed. Thomas Sheehan (Chicago: Precedent, 1981), 277.

35. Heidegger, *An Introduction to Metaphysics*, trans. Ralph Manheim (New Haven: Yale University Press, 1987), 199.

36. Heidegger, "The Word of Nietzsche," in *The Question Concerning Technology*, trans. William Lovitt (New York: Harper and Row, 1977), 78. As Michael E. Zimmerman comments, "The self-organizing, self-perpetuating character of modern technology was profoundly disturbing for Heidegger" *(Heidegger's Confrontations with Modernity, Technology, Politics, Art* [Bloomington: Indiana University Press, 1990], 201).

37. Kracauer, *From Caligari to Hitler: A Psychological History of the German Film* (Princeton: Princeton University Press, 1947), 149.

38. See Wollen, "Cinema/Americanism/The Robot," 19.

39. Cf. Huyssen, "The Vamp and the Machine," 222.

40. Patricia Mellencamp, in contrast, reads the film more as an exclusively male narrative and hence attributes less power to the clone and more power to Rotwang, her creator ("Oedipus and the Robot in *Metropolis*," *Enclitic* 5, no. 1 [1981]:39).

41. See Michael Töteberg's "Der Turmbau zu Babelsberg: Fritz Lang's *Metropolis*," in *Das Ufa-Buch*, ed. Hans-Michael Bock and Michael Töteberg (Frankfurt am Main: Zweitausendeins, 1992), 182.

42. In 1927, Luis Buñuel was among the first to complain about the film's sentimental plot line contradicting the "picture-book." Buñuel's review was originally published in *Gaceta Literaria* (Madrid, 1927) and is republished in *Metropolis. Un film de Fritz Lang. Images d'un tournage* (Paris: Centre National de la Photographie et de la Cinémathèque française, 1985). See also Paul Coates's cross-reading of von Harbou's novel-script with the film, in *The Gorgon's Gaze: German Cinema, Expressionism, and the Image of Horror* (New York: Cambridge University Press, 1991), 41–52. R. L. Rutsky further develops the Harbou novel's potentially protofascistic advocacy of mass subservience and control in his article, "The Mediation of Technology and Gender: *Metropolis*, Nazism, Modernism," *New German Critique*, no. 60 (1993):3–32.

43. Donna Haraway, "A Manifesto for Cyborgs: Science, Technology, and Socialist Feminism in the 1980s" (1985), in *Feminism/Postmodernism*, ed. Linda J. Nicholson (New York: Routledge, 1990), 204, 216. See also Stacy Alaimo's consideration of the pros and cons of feminist cyborgism in "Cyborg and Ecofeminist Interventions: Challenges for an Environmental Feminism," *Feminist Studies* 20, no. 1 (1994), 133–152.

44. Heidegger, "Only a God Can Save Us," 279.

45. Haraway, "Manifesto for Cyborgs," 203.

46. Hélène Cixous, "The Laugh of the Medusa" (1975), in *New French Feminism*, ed. Elaine Marks and Isabelle de Courtivon (New York: Schocken Books, 1981), 255.

47. Sabine Hake links this film's self-referential, specular representation of the city to theories of visual pleasure in her essay, "Ruttmann's *Berlin, Symphony of the Big City*," in *Dancing on the Volcano: Essays on the Culture of the Weimar Republic*, ed. Thomas W. Kniesche and Stephen Brockmann (Columbia: Camden House, 1994). Cf. Laura Mulvey, "Visual Pleasure and Narrative Cinema," in *Woman and Film: Both Sides of the Camera*, ed. E. Ann Kaplan (New York: Methuen, 1983). See also Mary Ann Doane, who critiques the antitechnological (and ultimately antifeminist) assumption behind Jean-Louis Baudry's apparatus theory, in which the spectator is always already duped by the camera into Platonic idealism (or reification of the female body on screen): Doane's point is to caution against assuming that the (male) gaze inevitably possesses the camera and repeats this representational error ("Remembering Women: Psychical and Historical Constructions in Film Theory," in *Psychoanalysis and Cinema*, ed. E. Ann Kaplan [New York: Routledge, 1990], 51).

48. Kracauer, *Das Ornament der Masse*, 54, 53.

49. Cf. Theweleit, *Male Fantasies*, 2:162.

50. "Woman: Autonomous in her Sphere," *Signal: Years of Retreat 1943–1944*, ed. S. L. Mayer (Englewood Cliffs, N.J.: Prentice Hall, 1979).

51. See the photo-booklet by Friedrich Mau and Bernhard Woischnit, *Freude am Kind* (Berlin: Deutscher Verlag für Politik und Wirtschaft, 1945), 43. Here, for example, it is stated that "sport increases [women's] joy in their work."

52. Walter Benjamin, "The Work of Art in the Age of Mechanical Reproduction," in *Illuminations*, trans. Harry Zohn (New York: Schocken Books, 1969), 241. See also Anton Kaes's chapter 1 in *From Hitler to Heimat: The Return of History as Film* (Cambridge, Mass.: Harvard University Press, 1989), 3–35.

53. Cf. Gilles Deleuze: "machines can take hold so fully on man that it awakens the most ancient powers, and the moving machine [cinema as psychomechanics] becomes one

with the psychological automaton pure and simple, at the service of a frightening new order." *Cinema 2: The Time-Image*, trans. Hugh Tomlinson and Robert Galeta (Minneapolis: University of Minnesota Press, 1989), 263.

54. Cf. Steve Neale, "*Triumph of the Will:* Notes on Documentary and Spectacle," *Screen* 20, no. 1 (1979):69.

55. Cf. Susan Sontag's 1972 essay, "Fascinating Fascism," on the theatrical, sado-masochistic setting of Hitler making the crowd come, in *Under the Sign of Saturn* (New York: Farrar, Straus, Giroux, 1972), 102–105. See also Deleuze and Guattari regarding Hitler's "coercive machine" that "got the fascists sexually aroused" (*Anti-Oedipus*, 293).

56. Hitler, *Mein Kampf,* 536.

57. Deleuze and Guattari, *Anti-Oedipus*, 346.

58. In addition to general personal mimicry of Robot-Maria, Madonna invested a lot from *Metropolis* in her music video *Express Yourself* (1989). Melanie Morton believes that the video improves on (rather than weakly repeats) the "dialectics of domination" in Lang's film: "Don't Go for Second Sex, Baby!" in *The Madonna Connection*, ed. Cathy Schwichtenberg (Boulder, Colo.: Westview Press, 1993), 216.

SEVEN

Femininity, the Primitive, and Modern Urban Space: Josephine Baker in Berlin

Nancy Nenno

"The Ladies with the Lip have arrived!" proclaimed an article in the Berlin daily *Tempo* in April of 1931, announcing the newest sensational *Völkerschau* (ethnographic exhibition) at the Berlin Zoological Gardens.[1] The accompanying photo showed several African women who, with the lower half of their faces covered by scarves and with heads slightly bent, resembled camera-shy film stars as they hurried through a crowd of curious onlookers. They looked different from their audience, for they were dark-skinned while the gapers were light, even in newsprint. But what was really different lay behind the scarves: their mouths. These mouths not only spoke a foreign tongue, they also looked foreign. In a city where fashionable women self-consciously attempted to draw attention to themselves, these African women made news. For it was not only their clothes that were different, but their bodies as well. Set in downtown Berlin, next to the fashionable shopping district of the Kurfürstendamm, the exhibition promised to display "primitive" cultural tradition in the form of lip-stretching. In the midst of the jungle of the big city, the primitive was commodified as spectacle.

Merely blocks away, at Rudolf Nelson's exclusive Theater am Kurfürstendamm, Josephine Baker had made news six years before by stylizing herself according to current expectations of the primitive. Following its overwhelming success at the Théâtre des Champs-Elysées in Paris, Carolyn Dudley Reagan's all-black revue, *La Révue Nègre*, traveled to Berlin and held a guest performance on 31 December 1925. "In her the wildness of her forefathers, who were transplanted from the Congo Basin to the Mississippi, is preserved most authentically; she breathes life, the power of nature, a wantonness that can hardly be contained," praised a reviewer for the *Berliner Tageblatt*.[2] Like the African women in the 1931 Völkerschau, Josephine Baker was heralded in Berlin as the incarnation of the primitive.

Between these two spectacular exhibitions of female bodies emerges a discourse about the place and function of the primitive in modern urban space.

Situated within the wealthiest, most consumer-oriented entertainment district of Berlin in the Weimar Republic, such spectacles spoke much more about European modernity than they did about the bodies they claimed to exhibit. They tell us about the function of the primitive in modernity as Other and mirror. They expose the commodification of difference through the medium of the female body. And they mark those liminal spaces in the modern city that provided a stage for the meeting of the modern and the primitive.

It was this rhetoric that enabled the teenaged Josephine Baker to conquer Berlin. Throughout the Weimar Republic, Berlin conducted a love affair with things American, attempting to model itself as Europe's most modern city. At the same time, it created an image of itself as the wildest, most sexually excessive city in the European landscape. Although consistently associated with Paris in the Twenties, Josephine Baker was also a major star in Berlin during this time. During the so-called Golden Twenties, she toured with *La Révue Nègre*, returning in 1928 as the conservative tendencies of Weimar began to reassert their power, with *Bitte Einsteigen*. She even considered a permanent move to Berlin. Berlin not only loved her, but she in turn was fascinated by this city of lights and promiscuity. In her performances, Baker negotiated discourses about the relationship of the primitive and modernity. As an icon of jazz, her Charleston echoed the sounds of the city. As an American, she represented ultra-up-to-dateness. The color of her skin signaled her status as the primitive Other, a symbol of Europe's rejuvenation following the First World War; but her identity as an African-American marked her as (partially) assimilated and assimilable. And as a woman, she successfully mitigated the German popular fear of primitive sexuality associated with the "Black Horror." In this manner, she not only engaged German fears and desires associated with the introduction of the primitive into the modern cityscape but also effectively came to embody all those contradictions of Berlin's own modernity.

The European reception of Baker differed markedly from the way that Americans perceived her performances. When she was discovered by Carolyn Dudley Reagan, Josephine Baker had just completed a tour of the United States with Noble Sissle and Eubie Blake's *The Chocolate Dandies* in which she had been praised for her comic genius. Smeared in blackface—long a tradition among black performers—and dressed in pickaninny outfits, Baker played on the dominant, non-threatening images of the American black favored by white America.[3] As the critic Homi Bhabha has suggested, the racial, and more often racist, stereotype offers the dominant culture a pleasurable experience of that which could be threatening.[4] All-black revues in the United States, like *Darktown Follies*, *The Chocolate Dandies*, and *Shuffle Along*, engaged white anxieties about black Americans by enhancing their blackness and mitigated these same fears through humor and sentimentality. In this manner, Josephine Baker's performances actively replicated the stereotype of the American black as humorous entertainer. Her performances allowed her white audiences to identify with her and not feel threatened by her.[5] Indeed, in another revue, *Shuffle Along*, she was even billed as "That Comedy Chorus Girl."[6]

But stereotypes depend on a particular cultural and temporal context, a specific cultural experience of that which is being stereotyped. Blacks were an integral part of the socioeconomic structure of American society, but in Europe they were still perceived as completely foreign, and as such a novelty. European colonialism in Africa had created a repository of popular myths that linked the black body to Africa and further to the concept of the primitive.[7] In this way, European response to Baker was predicated on an essentialization of the black body as African. The black body thus became a screen on which European desires for authenticity were projected.

Although purportedly giving "a cross section of Negro life in America," *La Révue Nègre* literally presented a review or survey of representations of the *Nègre*, or Negro, in accordance with European expectations.[8] This is illustrated by the seven sketches that comprised *La Révue Nègre:* Mississippi Steam Boat Race, New York Skyscraper, Louisiana Camp-Meeting, Les Strutting Babies, Darky Impressions, Les pieds qui parlent, and Charleston Cabaret. While all these numbers carried overt associations with modern America—the city, technology and transportation, urban entertainment—it was the latent ascription of primitivity to the black body that linked the sketches. In contrast to America, where lighter skin tone was prized, European audiences set a premium on black performers with darker skin, believing that the authenticity of the primitive was legible on the surface of the body. As a result, Baker and several of the other female performers had to be prevented from powdering their skin to make it appear lighter. The German terms *Neger, Nigger, Schwarze*, which were used to address all blacks—whether African natives, colonial subjects, or black American—without regard to racial, national, or cultural identity, underscore the essentialist conception of the black body.[9] Within this discourse, the terms proved multivalent and all-inclusive. The black body came to represent the entire continuum from untamed to civilized while maintaining traces of its African heritage. The notion of the black body as the primitive incarnate is epitomized by one review of *The Chocolate Kiddies.* After praising this revue's celebration of the black performers' natural talents, the reviewer criticized their attempts to acculturate to the norms of the revue and varieté: "It completely contradicts the entire meaning, spirit and style of this undertaking which seeks to play up the naturalness and elementariness of these black [*schwärzlichen*] hopping-geniuses."[10] (See fig. 7.1.)

La Révue Nègre presented a range of contexts for the performance of "blackness." Beginning in the modern American context, the narrative "regressed" back to the African jungle. Baker began with "Yes sir, that's my baby" in blackface, performing grotesque gestures and crossing her eyes. Singing "I Want to Yodel," she played the urban American, and Charlestoned in front of a backdrop of a skyscraper. While one critic referred to her performance in "Darky Impressions" as her big number,[11] it was the final sequence, the infamous "Danse sauvage," that made her name in Berlin. In the revue's final sketch, she portrayed the dead prey of a hunter played by an African native, Joe Alex. Both appeared on stage naked

Charleston-Darstellung
Ende der zwanziger Jahre

Figure 7.1. A portrayal of the Charleston from the late 1920s. In the public domain.

except for strategically placed beads and feathers, Baker draped across his shoulders. As the tempo of the drumbeats increased, the prey came to life, sliding down and around the hunter's naked body.

It was not simply the color of her body but also her gender that linked Baker to the concept of the primitive in the German mind. In Sigmund Freud's *Civilization and Its Discontents,* woman, like primitive man, is relegated to the realm prior to civilization. She is both physically and emotionally incapable of participating in the system of social exchanges that constitute civilization. For this reason she appears as a potentially disruptive element within the fabric of civilization. "Forced into the background by the claims of civilization," wrote Freud in 1930, woman "adopts a hostile attitude towards it."[12] Numerous texts in the 1920s addressed this mystery of woman from medical, psychological, anthropological, and cultural standpoints. Her mystery, which falls outside the parameters of civilization, thus became an object of exchange and the currency of the homosocial bond.[13]

The dynamic of exchange reached an apex in the institution of the modern urban revue. Like the city itself, which was in constant motion, the review embodied the aspects of urban space that signified its modernity. Staged in theaters with large seating capacities, the revue offered constant movement and change to the blasé urban audience of the metropolis. Each short scene or sketch boasted unending visual stimulation in the form of opulent costumes and backdrops, exotic locations and performers. Although nominally linked by a narrative or thematic core, the various revue sketches worked more on the principle of montage, thus affirming the fragmented, stepped-up pace of urban life. This dynamic of modernity was overtly disclosed and negotiated through the fetishization of the female body for a paying audience. "The whole point of a revue . . . is its sensuality. . . . Whoever goes to a revue, wants to see pretty, tantalizingly clothed and unclothed girls."[14] James Klein, one of the primary revue impresarios in Berlin, was notorious for staging nude displays in the name of popular entertainment. Like the performers in the Celly de Rheidt ballets of the early 1920s, who danced in veils that revealed more than they concealed, the revue Girls cavorted about the stage, more naked than clothed. These bodies were perceived to be "mediators of heightened desires."[15] And in this manner, the revue exploited the desires of decadent, middle- and upper-class audiences seeking (expensive) thrills.[16]

At the same time, the sensuality of the revue also mediated fears associated with modernity. For many, including Siegfried Kracauer, the world-famous revue favorites, the British Tiller Girls and their imitations—the Empire Girls, the Hoffmann Girls, the Jackson Girls—came to represent the precision and mechanization of the modern city: "What is it that they, like an image become flesh, embody? The *functioning* of a flourishing economy."[17] The synchronized movements of the Girl troupes molded them together into a single machinelike mass, in which the overt display of sensuality appeared controlled. By deemphasizing the individual sexuality of each Girl, they presented female sexuality as a product and fringe benefit of modernity. As a fetish of modernization, the desexualized female body no longer threatened to produce anxiety, but instead desire and pleasure. In this way, the female body became a screen on which fears regarding modernization and modernity could be projected and subsequently fetishized into a pleasurable experience.

While modernity was the overt theme of the revue, it was also the tacit subtext of the urban Völkerschau.[18] The display of "primitive" native bodies in the Völkerschau served to confirm the modernity of German urban culture; their primitiveness merely underscored the rewards of civilization. In this manner, both institutions affirmed the goals of modernity. Like the revue, the Völkerschau operated according to principles of voyeurism, the desire to see more, and the spectacle of difference. And the exotic costumes and narrative motifs of many revues echoed the primitivist discourse of the Völkerschau, which exhibited virtually naked natives—both male and female—in their "natural state." The exoticized and naked female body in the Weimar revue thus seemed to confirm Freud's 1930 dictum that woman represented the primitive within civilization, for the female body became the site where the primitive and the modern met. And where Baker's performances in the revue format resonated with the all-white revues in Weimar Berlin, it also evoked the displays of the primitive body in the *Völkerschauen*. As a black American woman, Josephine Baker's body represented the confluence of both the black body and the feminine, the primitive and the modern.

Following her performance with *La Révue Nègre*, Baker became a household word in the capital of the Weimar Republic. Welcomed to the city with open arms, she was showered with gifts and offers of contracts—including one from Max Reinhardt. Her influence was already being felt in Paris, where fashionable women now sported arms covered in bracelets and wore turbans, and she continued to inspire new trends in Germany as well.[19] As a result of her fame, black models were even permitted on German fashion show runways.[20] The German popular press, which had Germanified her name to "Josefine," regularly reported on her current projects and the scandals surrounding her. "Die Bakerin" even inspired parodies of her performances—a true sign of her name and face recognition.[21]

"Exactly what is it about Josephine Baker?"[22] is a question we ourselves might pose about her reception in Berlin. What was so attractive, so seductive about her persona? To what desires did she respond, and which questions did she seem to answer? Was she merely a passive victim of discourses about the primitive, or was she also an active participant in this stylization? And why was she so beloved in the modern city of Berlin? (See fig. 7.2.)

It was her performance of the primitive that earned her kudos in Weimar Berlin. Numerous articles attest to the popular perception of Baker as a representative of all that was the opposite of European urban modernity. As the embodiment of "life, nature, wantonness," the primitive took the guise of the repressed Other of civilization. However, as Marianna Torgovnick has suggested, the primitive does not constitute a singular, monolithic identity, but is rather the creation of the modern, according to the needs and desires of the latter.[23] As we shall see, in the cultural context of the Weimar Republic, the primitive possessed several faces, from threatening to fascinating to amusing. The evaluation of each depended on the degree to which it could be assimilated into modern culture, as well its potential threat to that order.

To some extent, this balance between assimilation and threat posed by the primitive depended on how "foreign" the particular representative of the primitive appeared to be. In the case of the 1931 Völkerschau, the twelve African women seemed very foreign indeed. But any threat posed by their difference was mitigated by the ethnographic context of their exhibition, which circumscribed their presence and their meaning. Few in number and always separated from their audiences, they posed a limited threat to the order of modernity. And similar to the objects displayed in ethnographic museums, such as the Berliner Museum für Völkerkunde, they were contained within a scientific, positivist discourse that contextualized their differences from the Germans in cultural terms. The Völkerschauen created a stage for the performance of the primitive that was always contained and controlled within modern urban topographical space.

The generally positive response to the Völkerschauen contrasts sharply with the German reception of the deployment of French African colonial troops to the Rhineland following the Treaty of Versailles. Whereas in the former, the primitive inhabited a proscribed space within the modern landscape, the so-called Schwarze

Figure 7.2. *Josephine Baker. Neueste Aufnahme* (Latest Portrait), photographed by Walery. *Das Magazin* 38:4 (October 1927), 1477. Reprinted courtesy of Bildarchiv Preussischer Kulturbesitz.

Schmach am Rhein (Black Horror on the Rhine) represented an undesirable, uncontrolled, and anxiety-provoking invasion of the primitive Other into German urban space.

German popular discussions interpreted the French employment of African troops in the postwar occupation of the Rhineland as the ultimate proof of Germany's humiliating defeat. Stripped of its colonies by the Treaty of Versailles, the former imperialist nation now experienced an overturning of the colonialist paradigm as the "savages" they had once dominated now occupied their territory.[24] The German translation of this term "Black Horror," as *die schwarze Schmach* (the black humiliation), *die schwarze Not* (the black peril), and *die schwarze Schande* (the black disgrace) all suggest how the presence of colonial soldiers from Africa was perceived as a threat to civilization itself, upsetting the hierarchical balance between the civilized and the primitive.

On 9 April 1920, the liberal British newspaper the *Daily Herald* ran the following headline: "FRANKFURT RUNS WITH BLOOD. FRENCH TROOPS USE MACHINE GUNS ON CIVILIANS."[25] On 6 April, French troops, including three divisions of soldiers from the African colonies, had marched into the cities of Darmstadt, Hanau, Homburg, and Frankfurt am Main. During the general mayhem in Frankfurt, Moroccan soldiers reportedly had fired into the populace, an act that infuriated not only the Germans but numerous other Western nations as well.[26] Outrageous stories circulated about how African troops were being quartered in Goethe's house, desecrating this temple to civilization. And France, the country that some credited with having invented civilization,[27] was attacked for initiating the downfall of Western civilization by bringing the primitives into "one of the most civilized areas of Europe."[28]

The arguments surrounding the Black Horror were based on a binary opposition between modern, civilized urban space and the primitive savagery of the African jungle, and the necessity of their separation and differentiation.[29] The popular press, both in Germany and internationally, represented the African soldiers as dirty, uncivilized, and even incapable of civilization. Popularly represented as weapon-toting gorillas in French uniforms, for many Germans they came to represent the imminent demise of civilization. Further, the "horror" or danger of this presence became inflected with an erotic element once stories of the sexual misuse of girls, women, and young boys began to emanate from the Rhineland. "The occupied Germans no longer find sanctity in their houses. And if necessary, the blond prey can be hunted down in its own home."[30] Rhetoric such as this consistently constructed the African soldiers as animals who, possessed by an excessive and perverse sexual drive, threatened modern Europe with their jungle mentality.[31]

The discourse about the danger posed by this uncontrolled, primitive, African, male sexuality in turn fueled discussions about the demise of white civilization. Cast as the (castrated) passive feminine and essentialized into a homogeneous unit, white civilization was perceived as being put at risk by the "animalistic bestiality of the Blacks."[32] In this scenario, civilized Germany became infantilized and feminized by its forcible disarmament in the Treaty of Versailles, placed at the mercy of uncivilized or only semicivilized men. It was feared that the uncontrolled sexuality of the African troops would infect and overwhelm white civilization. Reports that all the African troops carried syphilis, which they then communicated to their victims, further supported the discourse about the infectiousness of primitivity.[33]

The Black Horror on the Rhine formed a nodal point for the aggregation of discourses about Africans and Europeans, the primitive and civilization, and the breakdown of clear-cut geographic borders in the early Weimar Republic. For the defeated Germans, their presence as conquerors upset the traditional colonialist hierarchies, representing the ultimate in defeat. In contrast to the zoological gardens, the physical and imaginary confines of which guaranteed a protected experience of the primitive within the city, the Black Horror fed upon and contributed to anxieties revolving around the primitive.

African colonial troops had not been the only black soldiers to invade the borders of predominantly white Europe in the First World War. During its short and decisive engagement, the United States had also deployed black American troops, still segregated into their own divisions, into the European field of battle. With them, they paved the way for the jazz wave of the mid-1920s.[34] "Jazz is the rhythm of our time," declared one critic after seeing a performance of Sam Wooding's all-black revue, *The Chocolate Kiddies*, at Hermann Haller's Theater im Admiralpalast in May 1925.[35] And the jazz he praised was that of black Americans. In contrast to white appropriations of jazz, which were characterized by technical virtuosity, black jazz was seen as being spontaneous and improvisational, full of life, emotion, and the "African wild."

"The Negroes are conquering Europe!" declared Yvan Goll. "The Negroes are conquering Paris. They are conquering Berlin. They have already filled the whole continent with their howls, with their laughter. And we are not shocked, we are not amazed: on the contrary, the old world calls on its failing strength to applaud them."[36] Consciously parodying the rhetoric of the Black Horror, Goll inverted the anxieties about the presence of the primitive within German urban modernity. Contrasted with the defensive responses to the African colonial troops, the reception of this all-black revue in the German capital was overwhelmingly positive. In Goll's text, the Neger, who in the discourse about the Black Horror would overwhelm and destroy white civilization, became a source of renewal.

"Negroes dance with their senses. (While Europeans can only dance with their minds)," continued Goll.

> They dance with their legs, breasts, and bellies. This was the dance of the Egyptians, the whole of antiquity, the Orient. This is the dance of the Negroes. One can only envy them, for this is life, sun, primeval forests, the singing of birds and the roar of a leopard, earth. They never dance naked: and yet, how naked is the dance! They have put on clothes only to show that clothes do not exist for them.[37]

In Goll's text, the Neger are portrayed as natural beings, whose bodies dictate their actions. In this way, he participates in the rhetoric that casts all blacks as natural beings. At the same time that he reveals the absurdity of the rhetoric of the Black Horror, Goll created a new role for the black body to play within modern (white) civilization: the agent of rejuvenation. "These Negroes come out of the darkest parts of New York. . . . They do not come from the primeval forests at all. . . . But they are a new unspoiled race. They dance with their blood, with their life, with all the memories of their short history."[38]

As the star of *La Révue Nègre,* Josephine Baker was celebrated as Europe's rejuvenation. Erich Maria Remarque called her "a breath from the jungle," Oscar Bie saw in her performance "the remains of genuine paganism, of idol worship, of grotesque orgies," and Fernand Devoire, author of the introduction to Baker's autobiography, *Voyages et aventures,* translated into German in 1932, praised her as a representation of renewal: "Josephine Baker, our lives on the banks of the Seine were weary and depressing before you came along. In the eyes of Paris, you are the virgin forest. You bring us a savage rejuvenation."[39] But what was the nature of this rejuvenation? Was it purely an infusion of the primitive into war-weary Europe, as these quotes suggest? Or was there another element that ameliorated fear of the primitive which made it palatable, assimilable, and nonthreatening to German urban audiences?

As the rejuvenating quality of the primitive, jazz offered a way to forget the past and to focus purely on the present. The sensual terms in which German critics described jazz reflected the way in which it came to be figured as the absolute opposite to European intellectualism and its obsession with the past. Writers of popular colonialist novels such as Frieda von Bülow had used the term *Urwaldmusik* (jungle music) in a pejorative sense—a meaning preserved in the racist rhetoric of the extreme Right in the Weimar Republic.[40] But in the patoise of the 1920s, "Urwaldmusik" also came to signify the life-affirming quality of jazz. Constructed as a genetic characteristic of an "unspoiled race," jazz was channeled through the modern bodies of African-Americans. Characterized by its infectious rhythm, syncopation, and improvisation, jazz captured both the performers and the audience, breaking down the invisible wall between them.[41] Kracauer praised jazz for providing access to "untrammeled physicality," teaching war-weary bodies how to function once again.[42] And in its capacity as healing tonic, it joined the ranks of such "liberating" drugs as alcohol, cocaine, morphine, and opium as a narcotic that promoted the erasure of the recent past from current memory.[43] In contrast to the African troops on the Rhine, the "African" origins of American black jazz seemed to promise a renewal of, rather than a threat to, modern civilization.

Baker's success in Berlin was intimately linked to her being seen as the personification of the African-inspired jazz spirit that had introduced the wildly popular Charleston to Germany. But the quality of the primitive that inflected her reception was mediated by its origin in America, that most modern of nations. On 17 February 1926, after seeing the *Negerrevue* at Nelson's, Count Harry Kessler noted in his diary, "They are products of both the jungle and the skyscraper; the same with their music, jazz, in tone and rhythm. Ultramodern and ultraprimitive."[44] In a similar manner, another paper called her the "representative of ultra-up-to-date modernity."[45] Read as both African and American, Josephine Baker seemed to embody what jazz had come to represent to the German urbanite: the constellation of the "ultramodern and the ultraprimitive" in one body.

For the German public, Josephine Baker was not merely the primitive but also the elegant, well-dressed, modern American woman who conquered its capital. Josephine Baker's persona and her performances coincided with Berlin's own image as both highly elegant and exceedingly decadent, as combining both American and European elements. During the 1920s, Berlin was fascinated with America and actively sought to model itself as the most "American" of European cities.[46] In part as a result of its identification with America—whose financial support had helped put Germany back on its economic feet after the inflation during the early years of the Weimar Republic—Berlin had become a city marked by its tempo and the mechanization and precision of its movements.

"The movement and rhythm of dance today differ from those of Strauss's blissful times. They are born out of the new turbulence of life, its whipped-up and driving tempo!"[47] Like the urban revue, Baker's dances and the rhythm of the jazz music replicated the tact and tempo of the city's streets, echoing and thematizing the constant movement of the traffic. A quarter century earlier, Georg Simmel had asserted that one of the primary characteristics of the modern metropolis was its stepped-up pace, and Baker's Charleston was renowned for its frenetic tempo. But more than that, her performances as the wild primitive woman whose sexuality knows no bounds also resonated with the sexual labyrinths of Berlin; the image of the city as a modern Sodom and Gomorrah.[48]

It is no wonder that Josephine Baker conquered Berlin, for she offered a point of identification for the various aspects of the city, both primitive and modern. In this manner, her body became the site of competing aspects of the primitive, from decadent to naive to threatening to life-giving. But her self-stylization also posed a question about the relationship of this constructed primitive to modernity, whereby her body became a stage on which different interpretations of the primitive—as both African and feminine—were enacted and negotiated. The provocative nudity of her performances resonated with the profusion of naked female bodies on the Berlin stages. Offstage, her numerous love affairs served as a notorious advertisement for the unbridled, voracious sexuality attributed to, and expected of, the black woman since the Hottentot Venus.[49] Numerous eyewitnesses claimed to have been greeted by a totally naked Josephine at all hours of the day and night in her home.[50] And yet the sexual element of her nudity was tempered by her image as the representative of the primitive-as-childlike. "She dances so primitively and so genderless, that one doesn't know if one is watching a girl or a lovely boy," wrote Theodor Lessing.[51] The potentially disruptive element of her feminine sexuality could be ameliorated by her identification with the natural, wild, and primitive. And this primitiveness was considered to be assimilable by European modernity. Indeed, it revealed itself as an integral constituent of modernity as evidenced by the fascination that Baker held for both intellectual and artistic circles.

Since the turn of the century artists had appropriated "primitive motifs" into literary and visual modernism. One of the most influential figures in the "redis-covery" of African art was Carl Einstein, who first published his *Negerplastik* in 1915, portions of which were republished in *Die Freie Welt* in protest against the German discourse of the Black Horror ("Kunst und Dichtung," 4–5). Juxtaposing African art with the nineteenth-century European traditions of realism and the rationality of scientific thought, Einstein insisted on its stature as the only true art. And in his translations of African legends (*Afrikanische Legenden*, 1925), he empha-sizes their similarity to European legends, thus articulating a particular modernist obsession with the primitive as a source of a unifying mythology. Although Ein-stein was not the first to praise African art, particularly sculpture, he was the first to reach a wide audience.[52]

While the European avant-garde was fascinated with African art, they also in-sisted that their contact with primitive sculpture and masks was an *influence* and not an appropriation.[53] Members of *Der blaue Reiter* asserted their own "interiorization and expansion" of primitive art without direct borrowing.[54] But the attraction of non-European, primitive art for these artists lay not merely in its distance from post-Renaissance European aesthetic traditions of realism but also in its perceived oppo-sition to modernity.[55] The art historian Jill Lloyd has offered a critique of modernist primitivism that captures both the reactionary and the modern qualities of this fas-cination, whereby "primitivism could be used as a critical tool to question the dom-inant values of Western bourgeois society—or as a panacea, a cure for all ills."[56]

As a panacea, primitive art seemed to bear affinities to simpler, more pleasur-able states, prior to modern civilization. Max Deri wrote, "Children's drawings, folk paintings, Negro art: all bring joy in 'primitiveness,' for which the overripe culture of decadence longed. They allow the hurried inhabitants of large cities to glimpse the recovery of an hour and so to counterfeit a psychological 'gathering together.' "[57] However, as Deri's words illustrate, the fascination with the primitive was less about the primitive than about modernity. An antidote to the fragmenta-tion and mechanization of modern urban life, the primitive provided a medium for connection and community. Through the bodies and artworks of marginalized and nonthreatening agents, such as children, the *Volk*, and the insane, primitive art was now unearthed as an integral part of European art.

In a similar manner, Josephine Baker also offered a link to the primitive African jungle, mediated through her American body, uncovering the primitive within the midst of the modern. This is what the cultural pessimist Theodor Lessing sug-gested when he wrote that Baker's performances held a mirror up to Europe, reflecting it in all its primitivity. But, he continued, in contrast to the complicated and complex-ridden civilized man, the "unspoiled, natural, naked monkey-child" gyrates wildly, spurning civilization with a clear conscience. "And this, esteemed contemporaries, is the meaning of our phenomenon: Josephine Baker."[58]

But Baker's enactment of the primitive was anything but uncomplicated. For Josephine Baker was no native, freshly imported from the jungles of the Dark Continent, but rather a young woman from St. Louis, Missouri. She constructed her image to coincide with the desires of her European audience, negotiating anxieties about the African primitive with humorous renditions of established stereotypes as well as alluding to American modernity. She actively intervened in the discourse of the primitive in creating her personae, using the modern media to further promote herself. Capitalizing on the image of herself as a child of the jungle, she imported a leopard, Chiquita, from Hamburg and roamed the streets of Paris—in effect, continuing her performance outside of the theater. Beginning in 1927, she embarked on a series of autobiographies with the French journalist Marcel Sauvage: *Mémoires* (1927; German translation, 1927), *Voyages et aventures avec Joséphine Baker* (1931; German translation, 1931–1932), *Une vie dans toutes les couleurs* (1935). Even her beauty secrets, revealed to German women's magazines, actively replicated stereotypes of the primitive: "The *Arkanum* [private secret] of Josefine Baker consists of rubbing herself with the juice of bananas that have been soaked in alcohol; she sleeps in the nude."[59] Like the natives on display in the Völkerschau, Baker became a commodity, but she also participated in this very act of commodification; for Christmas 1926, a Joséphine Baker doll appeared in the stores. And she formed her own company with her longtime companion, Pepito Abatino, and marketed a popular hair pomade called *le Baker fix*, which brought in almost as much money as her performances.[60]

Baker returned to Berlin once more in 1928 as part of her two-year, twenty-five-country tour. This was when she performed the infamous dance with the skirt of artificial bananas at the Theater des Westens which continues to serve as the dominant icon of her identity. Considering a permanent move from Paris to Berlin, she bought a house in the Grunewald and was photographed in a little skiff on the lake. Bringing a little bit of Paris to the German capital, she opened a new "Chez Joséphine" at 53 Behrensstrasse, where she sang and danced nightly both for and with her audiences. In addition, she performed in a new revue entitled *Bitte Einsteigen (Joséphine)*. Only after reviews rejected the piece as unadulterated kitsch did she flee the city.

Times had changed. By the end of the 1920s, the image of the primitive had shifted and transformed itself again, this time into a more palatable version of the modern primitive. Amid economic distress, the "decadence" of her performances no longer stood in her favor, and the conservative voices that had long denounced her performances in the German-speaking countries as degenerate and immoral gained in popularity. And in the increasingly conservative atmosphere of the late Weimar Republic, Baker's body came to iconize the double function of the primitive as both life-giving and as threatening. Bruno Frank's *Politische Novelle* (1928) explicitly links the political threat posed by the primitive,[61] the foreign, and the feminine in the body of the black dancer Becky Floyd, who was modeled on Josephine Baker.[62]

As a result of the change in political climate, Baker began to downplay her role as the sexually uninhibited primitive and began to perform as the representative of a partially domesticated and integrated, colonized nation. Although her performances in Germany had long been the focus of protests by National Socialists and other ultraconservative forces, after the stock market crash in 1929, the situation intensified. Conservative rhetoric, like that of Hitler's *Mein Kampf,* which denounced the frivolousness of a society that lauded "half-apes," found more resonance in a population weary of economic uncertainty. As a result, Baker's 1928–1930 European tour was often overshadowed by attempts on the part of the Right to prevent her from performing. In Vienna, right-wing students, supported by the Roman Catholic hierarchy, protested her performance as "pornographic." And in 1929, the Munich police categorically refused to issue her a performance permit because they considered her a potentially corrupting influence.

However, Baker's influence as a cultural icon still remained in place. Four years after the National Socialists came to power, the Metropol theater, well known for its opulent revue-operettas during the Weimar Republic, staged a new piece entitled *Maske in Blau.*[63] Set in San Remo, the throw-away plot revolves around the identity of a woman, the "masked woman in blue." "You are a mystery to me, wonderful woman!" sings the male protagonist, Armando Cellini. When finally the dénouement comes, and the identity of the masked woman is revealed, the stage is filled with Argentinean "natives." And in the midst of this revuelike chorus line steps a woman in blackface, entirely naked but for a banana skirt. She has no name, but she dominates center stage. In a sense, Josephine Baker never left Berlin, for she had always been an imaginary construction of the city's urban modernity.

NOTES

All translations are the author's unless otherwise indicated.

1. "Die Damen mit der Lippe sind da!" *Tempo,* 21 April 1931, 4.

2. Quoted in Peter Jelavitch, *Berlin Cabaret* (Cambridge, Mass.: Harvard University Press, 1993), 171.

3. See Bryan Hammond and Patrick O'Connor, *Josephine Baker* (Boston: Little, Brown, 1988), 7.

4. Homi K. Bhabha, "The Other Question: Difference, Discrimination and the Discourse of Colonialism," in *Out There: Marginalization and Contemporary Cultures,* ed. Russell Ferguson et al. (New York: New Museum of Contemporary Art, 1990), 71–87.

5. This is not to say that parodic representations of stereotypes cannot be subversive, even if that subversive quality is not recognized by those at whom it is aimed. Indeed, Baker's performances could be read as consistently and openly mocking precisely those who most praised her.

6. Hammond and O'Brien, *Josephine Baker,* 9.

7. For more on blacks in German culture, see Sander L. Gilman, *On Blackness without Blacks: Essays on the Image of the Black in Germany* (Boston: Hall, 1982), and Reinhold Grimm and Jost Hermand, *Blacks and German Culture* (Madison: University of Wisconsin Press, 1986).

8. Ottomar Starke, "Révue Nègre," *Querschnitt* 2 (1926): 118.

9. The question of address is always a difficult one, especially since the terms from the mid-1920s bear such pejorative overtones for us. The term "African-American" would be eminently fitting in such a discussion of the reception of Josephine Baker in Berlin as both African *and* American. However, because the question is one of translation and an attempt to fidelity to the historical contextualization of terms, I have elected to use an anachronistic term, "black," to mark the emphasis on skin color and race in German cultural constructions of Africans and African-Americans.

10. Alfred Polgar, "Chocolate Kiddies," *Weltbühne* 6 (1926): 224.

11. Starke, "Révue Nègre," 119.

12. Sigmund Freud, *Civilization and Its Discontents*, trans. James Strachey (New York: W. W. Norton, 1961), 50.

13. Numerous classical feminist texts have addressed this functional objectification of women, from Luce Irigaray to Gayle Rubin and most recently Eve Kosofsky Sedgwick. See Luce Irigaray, *The Sex Which Is Not One*, trans. Catherine Porter with Carolyn Burke (Ithaca: Cornell University Press, 1985); Gayle Rubin, "The Traffic in Women," in *Toward an Anthropology of Women*, ed. Rayna R. Reiter (New York: Monthly Review Press, 1975); Eve Kosofsky Sedgwick, *Between Men: English Literature and Male Homosocial Desire* (New York: Columbia University Press, 1985).

14. Wolfgang Petzet, "Kitsch und Kunst im Tonfilm," *Der Kunstwart* 3 (1930): 209.

15. Theodor Lücke, "Gedanken der Revue," *Die Scene* 4 (1926): 114.

16. For more on the discourse of thrill-seeking in the modern city, see Siegfried Kracauer, "Kult der Zerstreuung" and "Langeweile," in *Das Ornament der Masse* (Frankfurt am Main: Suhrkamp, 1963); and "Rollercoaster," in "Loitering: Four Encounters in Berlin," trans. Courtney Federle and Thomas Y. Levin, *Qui Parle* 5, no. 2 (1991): 51–60.

17. Siegfried Kracauer, "Girls and Crisis," in *The Weimar Republic Sourcebook*, ed. Anton Kaes, Martin Jay, and Edward Dimendberg, *Weimar and Now: German Cultural Criticism* 3 (Berkeley and Los Angeles: University of California Press, 1994), 565.

18. For more on the institution of the Völkerschau, see Cornelia Essner, "Berlins Völkerkunde-Museum in der Kolonialära: Betrachtungen zum Verhältnis von Ethnologie und Kolonialismus in Deutschland," in *Berlin in Geschichte und Gegenwart: Jahrbuch des Landesarchivs Berlin*, ed. Hans J. Reichardt (Berlin: Siedler Verlag, 1986), 65–94; and Jill Lloyd, *German Expressionism: Primitivism and Modernity* (New Haven: Yale University Press, 1991).

19. Valerie Steele, *Paris Fashion: A Cultural History* (New York: Oxford University Press, 1988).

20. "Es begann die Zeit der Maskierung," in *Wir erlebten das Ende der Weimarer Republic: Zeitgenossen berichten*, ed. Rolf Italiaander (Düsseldorf: Droste, 1982), 98.

21. For example, "Die Tänzerin Jenny Steiner in einer witzigen Josephine Baker-Parodie" (Nelsons Künstlerspiele in Berlin)," *Berliner Illustrirte Zeitung*, 24 January 1929, 159.

22. Phyllis Rose, "Exactly What Is It About Josephine Baker?" *New York Times*, 10 March 1991, 31, 35.

23. Marianna Torgovnick, *Gone Primitive: Savage Intellects, Modern Lives* (Chicago: University of Chicago Press, 1990), 34.

24. Some of the troops fighting with the French army did indeed come from former German colonies, which only served to further enrage the Germans. See Reiner Pommerin, *Sterilisierung der Rheinlandbastarde: Das Schicksal einer farbigen deutschen Minderheit, 1918–1937* (Düsseldorf: Droste, 1979), 19.

25. Robert C. Reinders, "Racialism on the Left: E. D. Morel and the 'Black Horror on the Rhine,' " *International Review of Social History* 13 (1968): 1.

26. Pommerin, *Sterilisierung der Rheinlandbastarde*, 12.

27. Martin Hobohm, "Die französische Schande im Rheinland," *Deutsche Politik*, 20 August 1920, 242–243.

28. France Evelyn, Countess of Warwick, "Schwarze Truppen und weisse Frauen: Ein Appell an die Engländerinnen," *Neue Freie Presse*, 23 July 1992, 3; Francesco Nitti, *Der Niedergang Europas: Die Wege zum Wiederaufbau*, trans. C. Dericksweiler (Frankfurt am Main: Frankfurter Societäts-Druckerei, 1922).

29. Naturally this distinction was not made by all segments of society. Numerous authors of the New Objectivity adopted the motif of the jungle as a metaphor for the modern city: Bertolt Brecht (*Im Dickicht der Städte*), Alfred Döblin (*Berlin Alexanderplatz*), and Robert Müller (*Tropen*). See Gerhard Riecke, "Vom Dschungel zum Fahnenwald," in *Die Metropole: Industriekultur deutscher Städte und Regionen; Berlin 2* (Munich: Beck, 1986), 230–237; Wolfgang Reif, *Zivilisationsflucht und literarische Wunschräume: Der exotische Roman im ersten Viertel des 20. Jahrhunderts* (Stuttgart: Metzler, 1975).

30. Hobohm, "Die französische Schande in Rheinland," 244.

31. Ibid., 243; "Die schwarze Schmach," *Hamburger Nachrichten*, 30 December 1921, 1; Count Max Montgelas, "Die schwarze Schande," *Deutsche Politik*, 4 June 1920, 681–685.

32. "Die 'schwarze Pest' am Rhein: Eine Amerikanerin über die Verbrechen der schwarzen Franzosen," *Leipziger Neueste Nachrichten*, 26 February 1921, 2.

33. Pommerin, *Sterilisierung der Rheinlandbastarde*, 24; "Die 'schwarze Pest' am Rhein," 2. Pommerin also addresses the racial hygiene protest against miscegenation; pp. 22–41.

34. For summaries on the history of jazz in Germany, see Wolfgang Jansen, *Glanzrevuen der Zwanziger Jahre*. Stätten der Geschichte Berlins 25 (Berlin: Edition Hentrich, 1987), 132–135; Michael H. Kater, "Forbidden Fruit? Jazz in the Third Reich," *American Historical Review* 94, no. 1 (1989): 11–43; and Marc A. Weiner, "Urwaldmusik and the Borders of German Identity: Jazz in Literature of the Weimar Republic," *German Quarterly* 64, no. 4 (1991): 475–487. The influence of African-Americans who lived in Europe during this time is also charted in Paul Gilroy's study, *The Black Atlantic: Modernity and Double Consciousness* (Cambridge, Mass.: Harvard University Press, 1993).

35. Klaus Pringsheim, "Jazz," *Die Weltbühne* 46 (1926): 793.

36. Yvan Goll, "The Negroes are conquering Europe," in Kaes, Jay, and Dimendberg, *Weimar Republic Sourcebook*, 559.

37. Kaes, Jay, and Dimendberg, *Weimar Republic Sourcebook*, 559.

38. Ibid., 560.

39. Quoted in Lynn Hadley, *Naked at the Feast: A Biography of Josephine Baker* (New York: Dodd, Mead, 1988), 83, 99, 131; Jelavitch, *Berlin Cabaret*, 171.

40. Amadou Booker Sadji, *Das Bild des Negro-Afrikaners in der deutschen Kolonialliteratur, 1884–1945: Ein Beitrag zur literarischen Imagologie Schwarzafrikas*, Beiträge zur Kulturanthropologie (Berlin: Dietrich Reimer, 1985), 263.

41. The possession of the body by jazz is illustrated by one observer's memory of Josephine dancing to jazz music at a private party: "that is, she swept her hips over the rug, and beat the drum with her wild pelvis so that her feet could scarcely keep up, so much was her lower body possessed by running to jazz music." Fred Hildenbrand, "Josephine Baker," *Die Scene* 1 (1926): 16.

42. Siegfried Kracauer, "Renovierter Jazz," *Schriften* 5, no. 2, *Aufsätze 1927–32*, ed. Inka Mülder-Bach (Frankfurt am Main: Suhrkamp, 1990), 391.

43. Hans Siemsen, "Jazz-band," *Die Weltbühne* 10 (1926): 287.

44. Harry Graf Kessler, *Tagebücher 1918–1937*, ed. Wolfgang Pfeiffer (Frankfurt am Main: Insel, 1961), 458.

45. "Die Kunst der Primitiven," *Der Filmspiegel*, 6 June 1928, 16.

46. Michael Bienert, *Die eingebildete Metropole: Berlin im Feuilleton der Weimarer Republik* (Stuttgart: J. B. Metzler'sche Verlagsbuchhandlung, 1992).

47. Katharine Rathaus, "Charleston," *Uhu* 3 (1926): 120.

48. During the Weimar Republic, Berlin was often figured as the modern equivalent of Sodom and Gomorrah, as in the title of Yvan Goll's *Sodom und Berlin*. See also Hanne Bergius, "Berlin als Hure Babylon," in *Die Metropole*, 102–119; John J. White, "Sexual Mecca, Nazi Metropolis, City of Doom," in *Berlin: Literary Images of a City, Eine Grosstadt im Spiegel der Literatur*, ed. Derck Glass, Dietmar Rösler, and John J. White (Berlin: Erich Schmidt Verlag, 1989), 124–145.

49. The Hottentot Venus, an African native who was exhibited during the nineteenth century in France and Britain, and whose genitals and buttocks remain on display at the Musée de l'Homme, represents one example of the black woman as the figure of concupiscence. For an extended discussion, see Sander L. Gilman, "Black Bodies, White Bodies: Towards an Iconography of Female Sexuality in Late Nineteenth-Century Art, Medicine, and Literature," *Critical Inquiry* 12, no. 1 (1985): 204–242.

50. Hadley, *Naked at the Feast*, 131.

51. Theodor Lessing, "Josephine," *Das Stachelschwein* 1 (1928): 29.

52. Christoph Braun, *Carl Einstein. Zwischen Ästhetik und Anarchismus. Zu Leben und Werk eines expressionistischen Schriftstellers* (Munich: Iudicium, 1987), 207.

53. Recent publications on representations of black in modern art include Jill Lloyd, *German Expressionsm: The Image of the Black in Western Art*, vol. 1, ed. Hugh Honour (Fribourg: Office du livre; Cambridge, Mass.: Harvard University Press, 1976); *Primitivism in Twentieth Century Art: Affinity of the Tribal and the Modern*, ed. William Stanley Rubin (New York: Museum of Modern Art, 1984).

54. See Robert Goldwater, *Primitivism in Modern Art* (Cambridge, Mass.: Bellknap Press of Harvard University Press, [1938] 1986), 126.

55. Herbert Kühn, *Die Kunst der Primitiven* (Munich: Delphin, 1923), 31.

56. Jill Lloyd, *German Expressionism: Primitivism and Modernity* (New Haven: Yale University Press, 1991), vii.

57. Max Deri, "Die Neue Malerei: Sechs Vorträge" (1921), quoted in Goldwater, *Primitivism in Modern Art*, xx.

58. Lessing, "Josephine," 31.

59. Johannes Kunde, "Von Pappaa zu Josefina," *Die schöne Frau* 7 (1928–1929), 25.

60. Jean-Claude Baker and Chris Chase, *Josephine: The Hungry Heart* (New York: Random House, 1993), 144, 171.

61. Bruno Frank, *Politische Novelle* (Berlin: Rowohlt, 1928).

62. Marc Weiner and Bernd Widdig have both named Baker as the source for Frank's character. Widdig explores the relationship of sexual politics and political culture of Frank's novel in *Männerbünde und Massen: Zur Krise männlicher Identität in der Literatur der Moderne* (Opladen: Westdeutscher Verlag, 1992).

63. *Maske in Blau*, by Fred Raymond, lyrics by G. Schwenn, directed by Heinz Hentschke, Metropol Theater, Berlin, 27 September 1937.

EIGHT

Gendered Urban Spaces in Irmgard Keun's
Das kunstseidene Mädchen

Katharina von Ankum

And yesterday I was with a man who came on to me and took me for something that I am not—that I am not, even now. But there are whores standing around everywhere in the evening—so many around the Alex, so many, along the Kurfürstendamm and Joachimsthaler Strasse and at the Friedrichsstrasse Station and everywhere. And they don't always look at all the part, they walk in such a hesitant way. It's not always the face that makes a whore—I am looking into my mirror—; it's the way a person walks when her heart has gone to sleep.[1]

In this diary entry, Irmgard Keun's "artificial silk girl" Doris reflects a specifically female perspective on the modern metropolis that is unusual for the literature of the New Objectivity. Allowing her protagonist to stroll through the streets of Berlin as a *flaneuse,* the female counterpart to the flaneur, Keun dis/uncovers the patriarchal foundation of modernity in which the commodity character of the female body is brought to light undisguised. In her essay "Women on the Market," Luce Irigaray postulates the commodity character of woman as constitutive for modern society that is "hommo-sexual," that is, a society in which men relate to other men and constitute relationships through exchanges with other men.[2] In addition to her natural use value, which is determined by reproductive labor, a symbolic exchange or surplus value is attributed to woman which is, as it were, a desire value (*Begehrwert*) allotted to her only in comparison to other women's bodies. With the theft of the fur coat, with which she positions herself outside bourgeois society and from which she is unable to separate herself throughout the entire course of her adventure in Berlin, Keun situates her heroine in this discourse that postulates the exchangeability of the female body as prominent marker of modernity. Doris creates for herself a "second skin," a costly but impenetrable shell that heightens her exchange value and also makes her outwardly recognizable as a commodity. The fur coat is the material embodiment of Doris's identity as the mirror image of male desire. As Irigaray expounds,

For the commodity, there is no mirror that copies itself so that it may be at once it-self and its "own" reflection. One commodity cannot be mirrored in another, as man is mirrored in his fellow man. For when we are dealing with commodities the self-same, mirrored, is not "its" own likeness, contains nothing of its properties, its qual-ities, its "skin and hair." The likeness here is only a measure expressing the *fabricated* character of the commodity, its trans-formation by man's (social, symbolic) labor. . . . Commodities, women, are a mirror of value of and for man.[3]

Returning to the quote with which I began: at that moment at which the man, by accosting her, makes Doris aware of her sexual availability, her own self-perception, her image of herself, is adapted to the man's image of her. The metropolis threatens her female identity in that it gives her to understand that the institutionalized mod-els for woman—either mother/madonna or whore—are stronger than her own claim to emancipation. The following discussion is an attempt to read Irmgard Keun's *Das kunstseidene Mädchen* (The Artificial Silk Girl) as the story of female urban experience of modernity. A montage of citations will be used to reconstruct the con-temporary discourse on female sexuality and modernity through which Keun's text not only negates the possibility of female *flanerie* but also reflects on the limitations placed on the struggle for woman's emancipation in the Weimar period.

I

In the male-determined discourse of modernity, the metropolis is engendered as woman.[4] In contrast to the female bourgeois city dweller of the nineteenth cen-tury, who rarely appeared in the image of the city, the modern woman conquered a clearly visible place for herself in the public sphere of the first two decades of the twentieth century. The forerunners of this conquest of the city—motivated pri-marily by economic need but simultaneously creating new, personal free spaces for women—were the servant girls whose numbers more than doubled between 1880 and 1905.[5] As a result of the impoverishment of private households after World War I and fostered by the rationalization and restructuring of businesses and offices, the likewise gender-specialized profession of office worker/employee re-placed that of servant girl as a typically female employment option in the 1920s. While the percentage of servant girls and domestic employees sank from 16.1 per-cent in 1907 to 11.4 percent in 1925, the number of female office employees rose from 6.5 percent to 12.6 percent during the same period,[6] from 55,100 in 1907 to 1,433,700 in 1925. Women were everywhere: behind desks in offices and in public buildings, behind the sales counters at department stores, on the street on their way to and from work. It is thus not surprising that the female office employee was perceived as the typical working woman of the masses.

Anyone who walks through the business district of a big city just before 8:00 A.M. or in the evening just after the shops and offices have closed will typically encounter an army of girls and women who are either hurrying to get to work in the big office buildings or coming home tired from work. These are the crowds of working women. They provide the dominant image of the city street, they give the characteristic stamp to the department store and to the company stenographic office.[7]

Even more than the presumed displacement of a more highly paid male workforce by less expensive women and machines, the intermixing of a gender-specific assignment of space defined male experience of modernity.[8] While the public sphere of public life had been assigned to men alone in bourgeois nineteenth-century society, women's activities, at least of those better positioned socially, remained restricted to private and public interior arenas.[9]

Prostitutes were the only women who ostentatiously practiced their trade in public space. The red-light district appeared as the blank spot on the city map of the male flaneur, for whom flanerie functioned as a surrogate orgasm. Siegfried Kracauer's "Recollection of a Paris Street" reflects the attraction of urban activity as well as the anxiety felt by the male individual who has lost his way in the hustle and bustle of the streets.

> Even the occasional encounters with women seemed to me like a dereliction of duty, like a foolish diversion of the streets that laid claim to me with a far greater degree of intensity than any individual girl. I took pleasure in them blindly and let myself be exhausted by them, and although I consistently returned home depleted from the orgies, there was nothing that could prevent me from succumbing to my passion again another day.[10]

The streets become demanding, jealous lovers from whose magic spell the man is unable to break away. Having gone astray through the street district he describes, the narrator drifts compulsively in the course of investigating the labyrinth into the tentacles of a monster, from which he is able to escape only with difficulty.

> Suddenly I wanted to traverse the narrow distance that separated me from the main thoroughfare. But then it happened. Hardly had I freed myself from the white, excessively high wall of the theater, when it suddenly became difficult for me to continue, and I felt the invisible net holding me back. The street in which I found myself wouldn't let me go.[11]

What captivates the narrator, what both ensnares and fascinates him, is more properly the suggestive gaze of the "sloppily dressed females" whom he identifies as prostitutes. The threat represented by the chaos of the seedy street district is his fear of unbridled female sexuality, from which a man can save himself only with difficulty and that he henceforth will try to avoid: "Like a swimmer who struggles against the current, I strove with a desperate effort in the direction of the street's opening. . . . Although I have been in Paris often since then, I have never again risked setting foot near this street."[12] The experience of voyeurism exhausts and threatens the sexual potency of the flaneur. Alienation, chaos, and the orientation toward consumption explain the fascination, but also the threatening quality of the modern metropolis that is infused with female sexuality.

Walter Benjamin's characterization of urban prostitution reflects the definition of the masses as feminine, typical of his time, in contrast to which the male individual had to differentiate himself.[13]

> One of its most powerful appeals fell to prostitution for the first time in the metropolis. It is its effect within the masses and through them. It is the masses that first allows prostitution to be dispersed over a broad section of the city.[14]

Caught in its fascination with modern commodification, the comment ignores the actual social situation of the women in question, who have been forced into prostitution. The majority of prostitutes were recruited from the ranks of women who worked as servant girls, waitresses, sales clerks, and seasonal workers, the majority of whom had migrated to the city from rural areas to find work. The spread of prostitution was thus a concrete result of forced industrialization and urbanization.[15] The distanced, voyeuristic gaze of the flaneur strolling across the modern metropolis, a gaze that consciously denied social reality, was thus clearly determined and limited by his gender.[16]

The transformation of the city of Berlin into a "city of women" was one of the clearest indications of the ongoing process of social transformation, the push toward modernization, that characterized the postwar society of the Weimar Republic. Certainly, the new women's professions such as postal and telegraph employee, office worker, and sales clerk allowed great numbers of even bourgeois girls and women—at least until they married—a relatively self-determined lifestyle for which earning money outside the household was a prerequisite. This, however, did not mean that male prejudices about unaccompanied, unmarried women in public had disappeared. Sexual advances were considered an occupational hazard for women, and the sex appeal exuded by a stenographer or sales clerk was considered at least as important as her professional qualifications.[17] In G. W. Pabst's film *Die freudlose Gasse* (The Joyless Street), Greta's boss feels encouraged by her new, only seemingly unlawfully acquired coat to offer his office employee a lucrative love affair, which she declines with horror. In contrast to Greta, who innocently and unsuspectingly becomes the victim of her situation, Doris in Irmgard Keun's *Das kunstseidene Mädchen* attempts to put her feminine art of seduction to use in order to mask her inability to properly place commas.

> And he looks over my letters and inserts commas with ink—I think, what have you got to lose! and inadvertently brush up against him slightly. And he keeps adding in commas and crossing things out and making corrections, and with one letter starts to say that it must be done over again. But at the "over again" I press my breasts against his shoulder, and because he stares at them, I make my nostrils flare out for all they are worth, because I want to leave and don't want to write another word about Blasewitz's molars or about Frau Gumpel's installments for her stinking creamery. And so I had to avert my expression of disgust and twitch my nostrils like a giant Belgian rabbit eating cabbage.[18]

Her sovereignty is merely illusory, however. Doris ultimately loses in her attempt to maintain this balancing act, and must quit her job because she is not willing to secure her position by means of an undesired love affair.

The unmarried working woman or the woman who appeared alone in public was immediately labeled with a reputation for being sexually available. The greater freedom of movement enjoyed by the bourgeois woman, on the one hand, and the increase in the numbers of prostitutes among women from the lower classes, on the other, collided in the modern metropolis in a way that made it increasingly difficult to maintain the polarization of women into either whores or wives and mothers that had been established by bourgeois morality. The decisive argument in favor of the regulation of prostitution discussed in the late nineteenth century had therefore been the threat posed to the virtuous reputations of upstanding bourgeois women and girls: "Frightened half to death, our wives and daughters come home in a state of incessant concern at having been mistaken for prostitutes. It is the simplest and plainest of truths to state that licentiousness and vice dominate the streets."[19] Newspapers repeatedly reported unpleasant incidents in which women unaccompanied by men were accosted, especially in the areas of the city that were known to be the favorite haunts of prostitutes, such as the theater and entertainment quarter near Friedrichstrasse (fig. 8.1).

To curtail the number of such misunderstandings, policemen received extremely detailed instructions as to how to treat a woman they suspected of prostitution without offending her as a lady, which she was considered to be until taken into custody. In only apparent contradiction to this, prostitutes were obliged by a police ordinance to pursue their trade in such a way that it would be concealed from the eyes of passersby.

> The Berlin police intended to permit prostitutes to walk the streets who comported themselves with the same good manners as respectable women. Thus under no circumstances were the notorious women of Friedrichstrasse allowed to return a gaze or pass in front of a store window, or to stand in one place with a gentleman or even speak to one.[20]

On the outside, the decency and the morality of the society were to be protected. Streetwalkers were supposed to renounce their commodity character in that they were to avoid the very behaviors that could bring them a client. To maintain the double standard of bourgeois morality, prostitutes were expected to jeopardize the basis of their own existence.

Because of the increasing unrecognizability of girls who sold themselves, police in Berlin, where prostitution had never been regulated to a particular quarter, saw themselves forced to protect the reputations of "respectable" bourgeois women.[21] In 1903, a criminal police force was established for their protection.

> The Criminal Patrol to protect respectable women from being accosted on the street, which was founded in September of 1903, had 158 opportunities to intervene last year. The initial reluctance on the part of women to accept the protection thus

Figure 8.1. Prostitutes on Friedrichstrasse (1930). Reproduced from WEKA, "Stätten der Berliner Prostitution" (Berlin: Auffenberg Verlag, 1930). Courtesy of Landesarchiv, Berlin.

offered quickly disappeared. In 58 cases, the accosters were brought to trial and sentenced to terms of up to six weeks and a fine for gross misdemeanors, and to prison terms of up to six months for slander. The service of the patrol is constantly in demand. In addition, it is the duty of all police personnel who are on duty on the streets, whether in uniform or in plain clothes, to respond to any request expressed by women or girls for protection against being accosted. It is to be hoped that the serious consequences of improper behavior toward women on the streets will provide an impressive warning.[22]

A woman could not move within urban space without entrusting herself to male protection, and thus submitting one way or the other to male social surveillance. While a man could experience flanerie as an extension of his private sphere, the flaneuse was limited to the role of the prostitute. A flaneur could stroll through the streets unmolested and without purpose. A woman doing the same thing was perceived as a streetwalker, as illustrated by Doris's experience in Berlin.[23]

> If I go with my fur coat and my smoked fish, two of them with caviar in their bellies, someone will most certainly accost me. "You are making an enormous mistake in talking to me," I say. Not another word. With a regal movement of the hand, I cut off any further conversation. By the way, I will definitely have to get his black shoes fixed tomorrow.[24]

The satisfaction with which Doris narrates this story of misrecognition—emphasizing her albeit temporarily secured role as housewife and legitimating her presence on the street through the necessity of having to run errands—betrays the desperate effort with which she tries to maintain the supposed difference between her own situation and the fate of prostitutes. Her resort to the presumed safety of the bourgeois moral code after she has found refuge as homemaker for a lonely man abandoned by his wife indicates that Doris had to quickly and completely subordinate her initial claim to emancipation to the reality of the modern metropolis.

II

Popular women's novels in the early twentieth century urgently reflected the moral threat that the city represented for innocent, naive young women from the countryside. In Clara Viebig's *Das tägliche Brot* (Our Daily Bread) of 1901, Mine is indebted to the extraordinary strength of her character, not to mention her farm-girl looks, for the fact that she does not slip into prostitution.[25] In the fictitious diary of M. I. Breme, *Vom Leben getötet* (A Casualty of Life, 1927), the young woman's mother attempts to prove her daughter's innocence and moral stability, which have been brought into question by her fellow townspeople after a brief adventure in Berlin.[26] Neither Mine nor Margarethe remain unpunished for having chosen to step outside the social boundaries of the family and lead an unsupervised independent existence in the big city. Both protagonists are not allowed to return to their hometowns once they have set foot in the metropolis. Margarethe pays for her adventure with her life. On her return home she is taken into custody on suspicion of having worked as a prostitute in Berlin and dies as the result of a compulsory routine treatment for syphilis.[27]

In contrast to Viebig and Breme, whose novels can be understood as urgent warnings to their female readers not to succumb to the attraction of the metropolis, Anita Loos's novel *Gentlemen Prefer Blondes* (1925) describes female urban experience as an inconsequential adventure, in the course of which the woman protagonist even succeeds in arranging a lucrative marriage.

Paris is devine. I mean Dorothy and I got to Paris yesterday, and it really is devine. Because the French are devine. . . . So then we went to dinner and then we went to Monmart and it really was devine because we saw them all over again. . . . So the French veecount is going to call up in the morning but I am not going to see him again. Because French gentlemen are really quite deceeving. I mean they take you to quite cute places and they make you feel quite good about yourself and you really seem to have a delightful time but when you get home and come to think it all over, all you have got is a fan that only cost 20 francs and a doll that they gave you away for nothing in a restaurant. I mean a girl has to look out in Paris, or she would have such a good time in Paris that she would not get anywheres. So I really think that American gentlemen are the best after all, because kissing your hand may make you feel very very good but a diamond and safire bracelet lasts forever.[28]

Loos's novel, which had first been published in the American magazine *Harper's Bazaar*, appeared in German translation as a serialized novel in the fashion magazine *Die Dame* in 1925.[29] Unlike the heroines portrayed by Viebig and Breme, Loos's protagonist is a woman who manages to make her way in modern metropolitan society self-confidently and with deliberation to her own advantage. Tactically clever, she employs beauty and feminine naïveté to gain material advantages through male patronage and rise in society.

Irmgard Keun undoubtedly used Loos's society novel as the pattern for the style and plot sequencing of *Das kunstseidene Mädchen*.[30] At the same time, however, she links the model she takes from Hollywood with the moral and didactic tradition of the German bourgeois women's novel. While Loos's best-seller deludes its women readers into thinking that they could also succeed by way of cold calculation in defeating men with their own means, Keun shows the illusory nature of such a strategy, which fails to appreciate the powerful conventions of bourgeois morality and the magnitude of the price that must be paid for callousness. Unlike Loos's protagonist, who can observe Paris from her safe tourist perspective, Keun throws her juvenile delinquent Doris into the fray of the metropolitan throng. Her experience of the city is that of the New Woman of the 1920s—doomed to failure in the metropolis in spite of her newly won professional and sexual freedoms—because the patriarchal economic structures have remained intact.

I am in Berlin. Since a couple of days ago. With a return ticket and ninety marks left over. I will have to live on this until other sources of money present themselves. I have experienced a great deal. Berlin has dropped down onto me like a comforter covered with sparkling flowers. The "West" is elegant with a great deal of light—quite expensive like fabulous stones and with such an ornate setting. Here we have illuminated advertisements that are quite excessive. There was a glittering light all around me. And I with my fur coat. And chic men like white slave traders, without exactly trafficking in women, those no longer exist—but they look as if they would do this if there was any profit to be made by it. A lot of shining black hair and deep-set night eyes. Exciting. There are many women on the Kurfürstendamm. They simply walk. They have the same faces and a lot of moleskin furs—not exactly first-class, in other words—but still chic—with arrogant legs and a great waft of perfume about them.

> There is a subway, it is like an illuminated coffin on skis—under the ground and
> musty, and one is squashed. That is what I ride on. It is interesting and travels fast.[31]

Like Loos, Keun uses the female-identified genre of the diary. Despite her use
of this genre, Doris wants explicitly to break out of this private form of writing
and know her life as understood by public interest: "I am not thinking about the
diary—that is ridiculous for a girl of eighteen who's on top of things. But I do
want to write something like a film, for that is what my life is like and what it will
increasingly be like. . . . And if I read later on, it will all be like the movies—I will
see myself in images."[32] In contrast to Loos's novel, which was used as the basis for
the successful 1953 film with Marilyn Monroe, *Gentlemen Prefer Blondes*, Keun's ambivalent, problem-oriented presentation of the fate of her protagonist contradicts
the conventional Hollywood presentation.[33] But there can be no doubt that Doris
has "movies on her mind." The telegram style of her diary entries reflects the unceasing tempo of the metropolis.[34] She records image material like a camera, material that she then projects before the eyes of the reader. Keun's visual narrative
style is most apparent in the scenes in which Doris "collects sight" for her landlady's
blind husband.[35] As if she were looking into a kaleidoscope, Doris constructs constantly shifting vignettes for the blind man, and captures what is characteristic and
important to the atmosphere of the situation with her pithy language. Film and advertising are the cultural spheres that are familiar terrain for Doris. Publicly limited in terms of her ability to express herself linguistically, she uses popular culture
as her means of communication. In evoking a situation in a movie or referring to
a well-known film personality, she is trying to make certain that the right image appears before the eyes of the contemporary reader. Determined by her own marginal metropolitan existence, Doris's critical-documentary gaze captures the contrasts that characterized the metropolis of the early 1930s.

> I have seen—a man with a sign around his neck, "I will accept any work"—with the
> "any" underlined three times in red—and a spiteful mouth, the corners of which
> were drawn increasingly down—and when a woman gave him ten pfennings, they
> were yellow, and he rolled them on the pavement in which they were reflected be-
> cause of the cinemas and nightclubs.[36]

Doris's perception is indeed marked by the accelerated pace of life in the city and
by the film medium, but it consciously differentiates between make-believe illusion
and reality: "Well, I could still go to the movies. Then I can sit in the film café from
morning till night, all year round. Some day they will discover me as a starved
corpse to use as an extra. Filthy swine."[37]

Doris is not blond like Lillian Harvey, nor would she stand a chance as a revue
girl, given her unevenly proportioned legs. From personal experience she knows
full well that a correspondingly handsome character usually isn't hiding behind
every Conrad Veidt–like face.

> Movies on their minds: damsels in distress are rescued in exclusive nightclubs by
> refined gentlemen while drinking refined drinks—waiter, two more glasses of

wine!—and the small-town girl marries the senior executive from Berlin. Have you seen the movie? Renate Müller as a private secretary. Unbelievable nonsense! But the artificial silk girls believe in it. They have to believe in something . . . although they really know better. Really, they know so much! They have seen so much! No one will easily get away with anything with them! 8.80 support a week, 2 marks for a furnished room, with 5 pfennings extra for a basin of hot water, and then someone comes along and buys them silk shoes from Pinet for 40 marks! Simply because they are pretty![38]

With her portrait of Doris, Irmgard Keun counters Kracauer's condescending description of the "little shop girls" with a female film spectator whose perspective is both active and critical.[39] The fantasy of marrying the boss is a welcome escape from the difficulty of everyday life for the unemployed, but it in no way reflects their grasp on reality. What links the film plot with their personal experience, however, is that they are condemned to passivity: whether in the movies, in the office, or in the shoe store, a woman must wait to be discovered by a man.

With the assumption that she is ultimately disclosing her personal life to a public audience, Doris's diary entries are like letters home, and some are even addressed directly to her mother or girlfriend. Doris wants to stand out from the anonymity of the metropolis. From the onset, she identifies herself as someone who is seen: "A glittering light around me. And I with my fur coat." Although she questions the existence of white slave traders—"And chic men like white slave traders, without actually trafficking in women, those no longer exist"—she is intuitively conscious of her potential commodity character. Doris has completely internalized her object character. The juxtaposition of these two statements also implies that she is at least subconsciously aware of the possibility of social descent and perceives herself as endangered as a woman in the urban environment.

Within the parameters of prostitution, the traffick in girls and women had developed into a blossoming business. Go-betweens as well as bar businesses functioned as agencies handling the organized trade in girls and women.

According to the *Schöneberger Tageblatt* of 8 September 1899, an agent received between 30 and 50 marks for a waitress from the Berlin restaurants, and from 60 to 75 from restaurants in the elegant resort locations. As proof, the agent presented the postal receipts that he had received in one week. There were 38 of them, and thus it is to be assumed that they can make around 30 transactions in just a week. "The business is really very simple," the agent continued, "there is never any time-consuming correspondence, the transactions are usually finalized by telegram. There we simply say, 'One, two or three boxes are requested.' . . . 'Boxes' are what we in the business call waitresses."[40]

The trade in young women was understood as an unavoidable side effect of modernity, resulting from "the general market quality of the modern man of culture," embodied in its most extreme form by woman. Here it is not economic need or lack of enlightenment of the girls that is problematized, but rather the "women's lack of power to assert themselves," which is said to result in the fact that women "in increasing numbers knowingly [lower] their economic value to the level of mere commodities."[41]

Doris's first diary entry in Berlin documents a combination of her desire for adventure and enthusiasm for the metropolis that promises independence and new possibilities, on the one hand, and an undercurrent of fear that she will have to "pay the price" by selling herself, on the other. Her first impression of the metropolis reflects the image of Berlin as a city of the underworld, in which willing provincials could experience a minor adventure whenever they please. In publications such as Kurt Moreck's *Führer durch das lasterhafte Berlin* (Guide to Depraved Berlin, 1930) or Hans Ostwald's *Sittengeschichte der Inflation* (History of Moral Customs During the Inflation, 1931), the male visitor who was unfamiliar with the place found detailed instructions as to how and where he could best study and enjoy the licentiousness of the metropolis. From her perspective as a woman, Doris is unable to share in this sort of unrestricted fascination with the city. The sight of a fellow woman walking aimlessly down the Kurfürstendamm brings into question Doris's struggle for individual happiness, and from the onset mirrors the possibility that she, too, will fail in the metropolis.[42]

Doris is visibly impressed by the electric lighting that puts her and her fur coat in the right light. The invention of electric gas lanterns, through which a natural sense of time was transcended and a "third time of day" developed, was among the most significant and most visible changes of city life.[43]

> It would be difficult to separate the phenomenon of the street as interior, in which the phantasmagoria of the flaneur is concentrated, from that of gas lighting. . . . Under Napoleon III, the number of gas street lanterns in Paris increased in rapid succession. This increased the sense of security in the city; it made the crowds out in the street feel at home there even at night.[44]

In contrast to the male flaneur, for whom the illuminated street could become a home, for his female counterpart, the streetwalker, it became a place to work. Walter Benjamin illustrates this in his essay on Baudelaire, quoting from the poem "Le crépuscule du soir," the first lines of which read "A travers les luers que tormente le vent / La prostitution s'allume dans les rues" (55). While nighttime street lighting made it possible for prostitutes to practice their trade unhindered, it simultaneously subjected them to increased control. What looks like security from a male perspective is, from a female perspective, another example of homosocial surveillance.

A respectable lady distinguished herself not only through her moral behavior but also through her controlled consumption. The home journal *Die praktische Berlinerin* admonished its readers in 1925,

> It certainly can be fun for a woman to take a look at the splendors of the store displays, without making any purchases herself. However, it is irresponsible for women to linger for long periods of time in shops without intending to buy anything, and have goods shown to them, none of which fit, of course, since there is no intention of making a purchase in the first place.[45]

In the opening scene of Joe May's *Asphalt* (1928), the camera slowly zooms in on a single woman within a crowd of people populating a street. Her long, intense observation of the window display in a jewelry store suggests to the viewer that this woman has no intention of making an honest purchase.

While men could engage in criminal activities without completely losing their moral integrity, women who were found guilty of vagrancy or of petty larceny were labeled "fallen women" and thus placed on the same level as prostitutes. The term "fallen" was applied to all girls and women who violated the standards of morality and decency that were linked to the image of the proper and virtuous housewife and mother. A gender-specific evaluation of offenses led to the same behavior being criminalized differently for men and women.[46]

In contrast to Franz Biberkopf in Alfred Döblin's *Berlin, Alexanderplatz*, who swears to remain "decent," that is, to not do anything that will land him in jail again after his release from Tegel prison, Doris questions the purpose of moral irreproachability from the beginning. Her image of herself as a modern, emancipated woman prompts her to lay claim to the same sexual freedoms that have always been granted men. In this she identifies herself as an adherent of the call for free love for both men and women that was represented by the progressive wing of the bourgeois women's movement. In contrast to the advocates of the conservative position who wanted to approach the problem of ever-increasing numbers of prostitutes with the moral call for abstinence, the activists around Helene Stöcker contended that women as well as men should fully enjoy their sexuality, even before marriage.[47] As a result, the institution of marriage itself was brought into question.

> If a young woman with money marries an old man because of money and for no other reason and makes love to him for hours and has a pious look on her face, then she is a German mother of children and a decent woman. If a young woman with no money sleeps with a man with no money because he has smooth skin and she likes him, then she is a whore and a pig.[48]

This is Doris's on-target synopsis of the hypocrisy of the double standard of bourgeois morality. While she can still react with rage and contempt to the advice of her former lover Hubert to remain a decent girl and "give herself to no man until she is married" while in her average town, her experience as an unattached woman in the metropolis brings her to the realization that the distance she initially self-assuredly presumes separates her from her neighbor, Hulla the whore, can shrink to nothing in no time. Without the moral protection and financial security of a family or husband, she is forced to realize that, from the perspective of the bourgeois man, there is very little that distinguishes her from the woman who puts her body up for sale.

> I walked slowly past the Memorial church, down the Tauentzien, walking farther and with an attitude of indifference in the backs of my knees, and thus my walking was a sort of staying in place between wanting to walk on farther and a desire to walk

back again, in that I really didn't want to do either. And then my body came to a stop at the corner, for corners create in one's back such a longing for contact with the sharp edge that is called a corner, and you just want to lean up once against them and feel them intensely. . . . I kept on going, the whores were standing on the corners and plying their trade, and there was a sort of mechanism in me that duplicated precisely their walking and standing still. And then a man spoke to me, someone who thought himself my better, and I said, "I am not 'my child' to you, I am a lady."[49]

Just as on her first day in Berlin, when Doris noticed with amazement the women who "are just walking," it is once again her gait that distinguishes the decent woman from the prospective streetwalker. While Doris initially differentiates herself critically from the women "walking" along the Kurfürstendamm, she now identifies herself, albeit at first only capriciously, with her fellow women through the way she walks (fig. 8.2). As soon as Doris realizes that a woman's sexual freedom can only be the illusion of freedom as long as economic power continues to be concentrated in the hands of men, she also understands her own social descent as a gain in power. In accepting gainful employment, a woman only resigns herself to another form of dependency on men, a dependency that will continue as long as men remain exclusively in positions of seniority and women are exclusively employees with no chance of promotion. A woman can be a self-sufficient entrepreneuse only by putting her body up for sale: "In this a whore has more stress, but at least she's running her own business."[50] Since Doris cannot attain an adequate standard of living through "honest" work, prostitution becomes the only viable professional alternative.

> You have 120 [marks] with deductions to turn in at home or live on it. You're hardly worth more, but are hardly satisfied in spite of it all. And you want a few nice clothes, but at least then you are no longer a complete nobody. And also you want a coffee once in a while with music and an elegant peach melba in very elegant goblets—and that is not at all something you can muster alone, again you need the big industrialists for that, and you might as well just start turning tricks. Without an eight-hour day.[51]

Doris refuses to be enlisted in the alienating labor process of modern society that does not even offer her the economic independence necessary to indemnify herself for the monotony of everyday life through participation in the culture of distraction.

In that Keun directly links economic discrimination against woman with her decision to become a prostitute, her fictive life story of a "fallen women" can be distinguished from the majority of pseudoscientific attempts prevalent at the time which try to link a necessary critique of patriarchal society to a weakness in female character, describing prostitutes as individuals with a natural aversion to work and an exaggerated fondness for fancy clothes.[52] The report by a Dr. Hager published in *Der Abolitionist* of 1 July 1931, on the homeless girls who fall under his care, reads not only like a model for Doris's life. Beyond that it demonstrates the wide

Figure 8.2. *Quo vadis?* Sketch by Paul Simmel from *Lustige Blätter*, Berlin. Reproduced in Leo Schidrowitz, *Sittengeschichte des Intimsten*. Reprinted courtesy of Archiv des Instituts für Sexualforschung Dr. Magnus Hirschfeld.

dissemination and acceptance, even in progressive and liberal circles, of such attempts to explain prostitution and demoralization in exclusively psychological and moral terms.

> I first take quite simple, quite childlike young girls with no particular psychological condition, because they are very small sized, for the most part a little weak-willed, very helpless, very spineless. They are usually very anxious, seeking protection and if their speech is arrogant and insolent, this is to be understood only as overcompensation, that is, a way of balancing their sense of their own insufficiency and their fear. On their own under average conditions, they would be able to remain completely sociable in simple life situations; something external must happen to drive them to prostitution. Minor household conflicts, external disadvantages of their circumstances, sometimes even a lack of experience are what tip the scale here. Frequently they come in from outside (such children should never be left alone in the big city, a regulation that strictly forbids it is urgently needed!)—some also come out of impoverished urban situations that they often have entered into for quite childish reasons. In the man who accosts them they often see the prince from the fairy tale, in the café, cinema, and hotel the wonder that is Berlin, the wonder of life. Often enough the man is indeed their salvation from the emergency situation they have created for themselves (hunger, homelessness).

Not only psychic instability but also the social milieu—the absence or alcoholism of the father, the promiscuity of the mother—and the family background of the girls were held responsible for their choice of an "immoral" way of life. Keun, in contrast, does not use Doris's illegitimate birth to a mother who had to sell her body because she needed money to provide a genetic or Darwinistic precondition for the fate of her protagonist. Instead, she uses it as a point of departure for developing a concept of female solidarity.

> Dear mother, you had a beautiful face, you have eyes that look like you desire something, you were poor, like I am poor, you slept with men because you liked them or because you needed money—I do that, too. Whenever anyone calls me names, they call you names as well—I hate everyone, I hate everyone—to hell with the world, mother, to hell with the world.[53]

Doris also expresses solidarity with her friend Margarethe—"what is happening to you can also happen to me" (p. 48)—and ultimately with the prostitute Hulla as well, after she has recognized the prostitute's fate as the embodiment of the pattern of her own female existence. The wrath of the socially powerless against patriarchal society and the bourgeois moral double standard that is expressed in the passage cited above remains an isolated instance, however. Aware of her powerlessness, Doris does not become violent, but instead attempts to defeat her enemies with their own means—callousness and calculation. But in her attempt to exploit the market value of her femininity, she in turn overlooks the boundaries that bourgeois morality erects to prevent her from rising in society. Disillusioned by the possibility of getting ahead economically through her own labor, and in the realization that social betterment can only be achieved through connection to a man, Doris allows herself to be kept by different men. She becomes a consumer par excellence in that she indiscriminately accumulates material possessions and makes a point of demanding payment for the traditionally feminine quality of listening: "Things are progressing. I have five blouses made of Bemberg silk with hand-sewn seams, a handbag made of cowhide with some crocodile appliqué, a small grey felt hat and a pair of shoes with lizard toes."[54]

Doris at first falsely considers her frenzied collecting of material possessions the first step on the road to social recognition and economic security: "I've made it. I am—O, God!—Mother, I've gone on a shopping spree. A little fur jacket and hat and the finest saveloy—is it a dream? I am powerful. I am bursting with excitement."[55] The luxury items and articles of clothing that Doris bags on her raids through the male world for plunder lend her at least the outward appearance of the desired "glamour" that she has been seeking in the city, but they concurrently lower her social status. She is now the lover, the mistress, who is showered by the man who keeps her with transitory fashionable objects such as hats and furs. In contrast to the wife, who is surrounded by furniture as the status symbol and possession of her husband—as the surrogate wife of Ernst, Doris buys a carpet to make the living quarters they share seem more "homey"—the presents that the girlfriend receives from her more often than not married lover usually are of less permanent value.

The purchasing of clothing by a wealthy man for a pretty stranger has been a standard scene in Hollywood cinema from *Palm Beach Story* (1942) to *Pretty Woman* (1990). When the woman exhibits on her body the things obtained through his buying power, she is reflected in his eyes and herself becomes a purchasable object. As one who is looked at (*Gesehene*), who draws the gazes of passersby on the street, Doris has no unmediated experience of the city, a fact that prevents her from controlling her own existence. Even in her romantic relationship with Brenner, the blind husband of her landlady, in which Doris is no longer subjected to the objectification of the male gaze, she does not develop her own but rather a surrogate perspective on Berlin—she needs a "middleman to the world."[56] Her relationship to her own body betrays the extent to which Doris is alienated from herself and has internalized the male gaze: "Doris is now an enormous, clever man, and looks at Doris and says, like a medical doctor would, 'Well, my dear child, you have a very pretty figure, but it is a little skinny, but that's very fashionable right now.' "[57] The perspective from which Doris attempts to describe herself is not only a male one but also the "desexualized" and "objective" perspective of a medical doctor. Although Doris appears as narrator and author of her own story, she can ultimately represent herself only as the projection of the male gaze. Her understanding of herself as a woman remains "derive[d] from elsewhere."[58]

The dichotomy between the sexualized woman outside, that is, the woman who tries to survive on her own in the city without the protection and supervision of a man, and the desexualized woman inside, who possesses material security and moral acceptance, is especially apparent in Doris's relationship with Ernst.

It is always such a strange feeling, to stand in front of a door when someone else opens it and in a strange apartment house. The marble smells so cold and doesn't like me. . . . And then one has respect toward a person who has a ring of keys, that makes a clinking sound and is such a mystery of many keys, only one person knows it. And there you stand, powerless. . . . There he has an apartment with cork flooring, three rooms and a bath, a rubber tree plant and a divan, so wide, with a silk cover and fine steel dentist office lamps—he has everything, and yet he howls and moans about some woman who's taken off. But there are so many. He has a lacquer bed, so smooth, and little night tables like Japanese hay boxes and rings around his eyes because of a woman. And there are hordes of us walking from Alexanderplatz to the Memorial Church and from the Tauentzien to Friedrichstrasse.[59]

Possession of the apartment strengthens the man's position of power vis-à-vis the woman in the streets. In her description, Doris perceives the woman whom she imagines as a piece of furniture in the midst of the fashionably decorated apartment as an exchangeable object. The man can choose a girl from the masses of homeless girls of the street, take her into his apartment, and thus give her a home that she cannot attain for herself in the city.

The possession of a place to live, hardly thought about before the war, was now something of such value that women looking for husbands offered themselves in the marriage ads with "a beautiful home" or a "completely furnished apartment." Many of those who listed themselves on the marriage market in this way wanted only an escape from agonizing loneliness. For the majority of them were undoubtedly complying with the womanly goal of paying for it honestly with body and soul.[60]

Hans Ostwald's comment elucidates the commodity character of woman in that he draws a parallel between the apartment market and the marriage market. The assurance that the honor of the German woman would be saved in that she wanted to "pay honestly with body and soul" does not succeed in clarifying the morally irreproachable female motivation for wanting to marry but rather indicates, albeit unintentionally, the essential formal similarity of the wife and the prostitute.

Despite the increasing number of single working women, the prospect of living alone as a woman seemed a difficult, unnatural condition that had to be overcome as soon as possible. However, in giving up the role of housewife, the modern woman had relinquished her claim to a place to call home. Her only domain became the street.[61] Homelessness is an inevitable part of woman's experience of the city and modernity. Like Margarethe Breme, who notes in her diary, "we walk around like pursued wild animals and are for the moment homeless,"[62] Doris never overcomes the feeling of being lost in Berlin: "And Berlin is very splendid, but it doesn't offer any sense of being at home, because it is closed off."[63] To find a home in the metropolis, Doris must relinquish her claim to unlimited mobility and the free experience of her sexuality and withdraw into the limited experiential sphere of the housewife. While she is living with Ernst, her excursions into metropolitan space are restricted to going shopping and taking walks in the evening with her "husband." She continues to enjoy the public sphere only as a contrast to the feeling of well-being she senses at being able to soon go home.

> And then I sit here alone and always feel only one thing: I'll be going right home. I have to look at all the people who fill up the place here and . . . are they going home? Thank you, I have only a little time, I'm meeting someone to go home, I am something quite secure, and every word I speak is love for the man of my life.[64]

The failure of Doris's attempt to slip into the role of the bourgeois housewife and to make Ernst's apartment a home betrays the impossibility of returning to the world of the nineteenth century—split into interior and exterior—in which the interior, characterized as feminine, still represented a place of refuge, at least for the male.

> The inhabitant of the interior during the Gründerzeit sought a fixed point within the circulation of money and commodities. Thus he created for himself the fiction of static "property" in the form of furniture, medieval in its immobility, that helped him bear the tension between the necessary mobility of capital and the desire for personal duration: the interior as the repression of permanent exchange.[65]

The hypermodern interior of Ernst's apartment, in which not only the furniture is no longer a "fixed point," but woman as the "guardian of the hearth" has become exchangeable, can obviously not offer any sense of home, "for it is written in the signature of this shifting time period that the final bell has tolled for living in the old sense, wherein security was a first priority."[66]

Having found no satisfaction in the unstable existence of the New Woman, whom she initially embodied externally as well as in her lifestyle, Doris sees her last chance to win back her lost sense of home in becoming the companion of Karl, who lives in a garden colony on the outskirts of Berlin. Her experience of the metropolis has prompted her to give up the struggle for emancipation and undertake the futile attempt to fit into a traditional, male-defined woman's life pattern. Like so many of her real-life contemporaries, Doris longs to exchange the emancipatory myth of the metropolis with the security of the traditional female role.

> The emancipated woman, having emerged from the muddy pond (or, if you will, the clear lake) of her previous state, found herself on a bleak shore, surrounded here and there by skyscrapers that blocked her view. She simply noted: I have less time than my mother had. I have less money, less joy, less hope, less consolation. And thus she too, with a quiet disillusion, defiantly returns to the ranks of the backward-looking.[67]

Forced rationalization of female existence, as well as the unchanged discrimination against the female workforce, prompted increasing numbers of women to recognize the flip side of the role of the New Woman. Irmgard Keun's *Das kunstseidene Mädchen* reflects this process of disillusionment that was building up in the early 1930s, but at the same time it illustrates the problems inherent in a solution oriented toward traditional models of femininity. One indication of the dubiousness of the lifestyle idealized by the novel's protagonist is the fact that Doris's source of self-expression, her diary, threatens to run out at the moment when her existence is secure and she defines herself exclusively in relation to a man.[68] The choice with which Doris is faced at the end of her Berlin adventure in the Bahnhof Zoo waiting room—an idyllic life with Karl in a garden colony outside the actual city limits or a life of prostitution in the Tauentzien district—is obviously not a satisfying choice and points to the limitations of the parameters for emancipation actually allowed for the New Woman.[69] "My life is Berlin, and I am Berlin,"[70] writes Doris, reflecting the identification of woman with the city and modernity, and defining her pursuit of happiness as entirely within the context of metropolitan existence. Her failure in Berlin brings into question the possibility of female self-realization in the rationally and functionally determined society of modernity, but it also insists on the search for an alternative that will not play into the hands of the forces of reactionary antifeminism.

Translated by Jamie Owen Daniel

NOTES

1. Irmgard Keun, *Das kunstseidene Mädchen* (Munich: dtv, 1989), 92. The first edition was published by Universitas in Berlin in 1932.

2. Luce Irigaray, *This Sex Which Is Not One*, trans. Catherine Porter with Carolyn Burke (Ithaca: Cornell University Press, 1985), 170–191.

3. Ibid., 176–177.

4. Patrice Petro, *Joyless Streets: Women and Melodramatic Representation in Weimar Germany* (Princeton: Princeton University Press, 1988), 39–78.

5. On the role of the servant girl in the process of urbanization at the turn of the century, see Karin Walser, "Der Zug in die Stadt: Berliner Dienstmädchen um 1900," in *Triumph und Scheitern in der Metropole: Zur Rolle der Weiblichkeit in der Geschichte Berlins*, ed. Sigrun Anselm and Barbara Beck (Berlin: Dietrich Reimer, 1987), 75–90.

6. Dieter Peukert, *Die Weimarer Republik* (Frankfurt am Main: Suhrkamp, 1987), 101.

7. Susanne Suhr, "Die weiblichen Angestellten" (1930), in *Frauenarbeit und Beruf*, ed. Gisela Brinker-Gabler (Frankfurt am Main: Fischer, 1979), 329–330.

8. The rapidly increasing rate of unemployment was frequently discussed in the context of the increasing rate of women's employment. In fact, however, the majority of women continued to be employed in family businesses as unpaid assistants or were occupied with the production of consumer goods that had previously been produced at home. This misinterpretation of clear statistical information, on the one hand, surely occurred in the interests of intensified capitalist competition, and, on the other, expressed the repressed sexual anxieties of the male population. See Suhr, "Die weiblichen Angestellten," 300, and Hilde Walter, "Frauendämmerung?" *Weltbühne* 27 (7 July 1931): 24–26.

9. In Walter Benjamin's description of his childhood experience of Berlin, Gabriele Geiger deduces the restriction of woman's experience of the city and contrasts it to the diffuse male conquest of metropolitan space: "And also when walking at mother's side, the

talk is of 'errands' that must be run, but that will doubtless be limited to the district in which we live because they are within walking distance. The space of the city, to the extent that bourgeois women perceive it, is traversed . . . by them. What counted for them were the places: places for social encounters. . . . In addition, there were the places of choice for personal purchases. . . . The paths to these places are escape and dream, however. . . . The perspective of the women on the world remained that of an observer. . . . In public, the bourgeois women is separated from the 'masses' by a ramp." Gabriele Geiger, *Frauen-Körper-Bauten* (Munich: Profil, 1986), 137.

10. Siegfried Kracauer, *Strassen in Berlin und anderswo* (Berlin: Arsenal, 1987), 7.

11. Ibid., 8.

12. Ibid., 11. A similarly subconsciously sexualized description of the city can be found in Walter Benjamin, as well as in Sigmund Freud and Adolf Hitler. See Elizabeth Wilson, *The Sphinx in the City: Urban Life, the Control of Disorder, and Women* (Berkeley and Los Angeles: University of California Press, 1991); and Susan Buck-Morss, "The Flaneur, the Sandwichman and the Whore," *New German Critique*, no. 39(1986): 128–129.

13. See Andreas Huyssen, "Mass Culture as Woman: Modernism's Other," in Huyssen, *After the Great Divide: Modernism, Mass Culture, Postmodernism* (Bloomington: Indiana University Press, 1986), 44–62.

14. Walter Benjamin, *Das Passagenwerk* (Frankfurt am Main: Suhrkamp, 1982), 427.

15. Regina Schulte, *Sperrbezirke: Tugendhaftigkeit und Prostitution in der bürgerlichen Welt* (Frankfurt am Main: Syndikat, 1984).

16. Buck-Morss ("The Flaneur, the Sandwichman and the Whore") explains Benjamin's critical mass consciousness, which ignores class and gender differences in reference to the figure of the sandwichman, as the expression of a consumption orientation that also encompasses literature: "The flaneur-as-writer was thus the prototype of the author-as-producer of mass culture. Rather than reflecting the true conditions of urban life, he diverted readers from its tedium. Observed by his public while he 'works' at loitering, the flaneur-as-writer may have social prominence, but not dominance. His protests against the social order are never more than gestures because . . . he needs money" (pp. 111–112). Gender-based differences, as Buck-Morss goes on to note, cannot be explained away as the outgrowth of capitalism as can class differences in an examination of the phenomenon of flanerie, for "sexual difference complicates the politics of loitering. . . . Prostitution was indeed the female version of flanerie. Yet sexual difference makes visible the privileged position of males within public space. I mean this: the flaneur was simply the name of a man who loitered, but all women who loitered risked being seen as whores, as the term 'streetwalker' or 'tramp' applied to women makes clear" (pp. 118–119).

17. In her study of the situation in which women white-collar workers found themselves, Susanne Suhr explains the difference in age between office employees and sales girls by the fact that "the fresh, youthful appearance of the sales girl was an advertisement for the store" ("Die weiblichen Angestellten," 334). In other words, not only was the product being sold, but indirectly so was the body of the woman; that is, the female workforce in general was sexualized. Sexual services that are coerced from office personnel play a central role in Christa Anita Brück's novel, *Schicksale hinter Schreibmaschinen* (Destinies behind the Typewriter) (Berlin: Sieben Stäbe, 1930).

18. Keun, *Das kunstseidene Mädchen*, 16.

19. From the records of a Dr. Zahn on the relegalization of prostitution in Nuremberg, 1872, cited in Geiger, *Frauen-Körper-Bauten*, 136.

20. Robert Hessen, *Die Prostitution in Deutschland* (Munich: Albert Langen, 1910), 1977.

21. A stricter dress code in the nineteenth century served to make it possible to differentiate between bourgeois women and women of the street. Even Doris, herself an "artificial silk girl," pays close attention to the clothing worn by her fellow women and notes its "second-class" characteristics critically: "There are many women on the Kurfürstendamm. . . . They have the same faces and a lot of moleskin furs—not exactly first-class, in other words—but still chic—with arrogant legs and a great waft of perfume about them" (p. 43). See also Richard Sennett, *The Fall of Public Man* (New York: Knopf, 1974), 67–68.

22. *Der Abolitionist*, 1 July 1905.

23. Janet Wolff, "The Invisible Flaneuse: Women and the Literature of Modernity," *Theory, Culture and Society* 2, no. 3 (1982): 45. See also Buck-Morss, "The Flaneur, the Sandwichman and the Whore," 118–119.

24. Keun, *Der kunstseidene Mädchen*, 111–12.

25. Clara Viebig, *Das tägliche Brot* (Berlin: Fontane, 1901).

26. M. I. Breme, *Vom Leben getötet: Bekenntnisse eines Kindes* (Freiburg: Herder, 1927).

27. On the reception of this factually based novel, see Elisabeth Meyer-Renschhausen, "The Bremen Morality Scandal," in *When Biology Became Destiny*, ed. Renate Bridenthal, Atina Grossmann, and Marion Kaplan (New York: Monthly Review Press, 1984), 87–108.

28. Anita Loos, *Gentlemen Prefer Blondes, But Gentlemen Marry Brunettes* (1925, 1928) (London: Penguin, 1989), 93, 99–100.

29. *Die Dame* 53, beginning with the November 2 edition.

30. It was impossible for contemporary criticism to overlook the parallels between the two novels. See Friedrich Weissinger, "Das kunstseidene Mädchen," *Die literarische Welt* (29 July 1932). See also a letter to Irmgard Keun from Kurt Tucholsky, dated 16 July 1932, in which he accuses the author of plagiarizing from Robert Neumann's novel, *Karriere*. Reprinted in Gabriele Kreis, *Was man glaubt, gibt es: Das Leben der Irmgard Keun* (Zurich: Arche, 1991), 105–106. A comparative discussion of the two novels can be found in Livia Z. Wittman, "Erfolgschancen eines Gaukelspiels: Vergleichende Beobachtungen zu 'Gentlemen Prefer Blondes' (Anita Loos) und 'Das kunstseidene Mädchen' (Irmgard Keun)," *Carleton Germanic Papers* 11 (1983): 35–49. For a more detailed discussion of this point, see my article "Material Girls: Consumer Culture and the 'New Woman' in Anita Loos' *Gentlemen Prefer Blondes* and Irmgard Keun's *Das kunstseidene Mädchen*," *Colloquia Germanica* 27, no. 2 (1994): 159–172.

31. Keun, *Das kunstseidene Mädchen*, 43.

32. Ibid., 6.

33. Leo Lensing, "Cinema, Society, and Literature in Irmgard Keun's *Das kunstseidene Mädchen*," *Germanic Review* 9, no. 4 (Fall 1985): 129–134. Loos's novel was filmed first in 1928. In the 1958 version with Marilyn Monroe in the central role, the plot sequence is changed in an interesting way. The heroine in the book enjoys herself in Europe at the expense of her rich lover and ultimately returns to good things in New York. In the film, by contrast, the rich lover comes to Paris, having been upset by Lorelei's skill in seduction, to cut off her credit. Left without resources in a matter of seconds, Lorelei takes a job as a dancer in a variety theater, again a situation from which she can be freed only by a rich man willing to compromise. The end of the film version is thus similar to the plot patterns of melodramas such as *Blonde Venus* or *Joyless Streets*. While Lorelei in Loos's novel succeeds in pulling the wool over men's eyes and in maintaining her self-sufficiency in spite of financial support, the heroine in the film must sell her body and finally be rescued by a man. Obviously, the

recipe for success of the "American matriarch" in the 1950s was too risqué to be propagated before a mass audience.

34. Anton Kaes, *Kino-Debatte: Literatur und Film 1909–29* (Tübingen: Niemeyer, 1978), 4–9.

35. Lensing, "Cinema, Society, and Literature," 131. See also Ursula Krechel, "Irmgard Keun: Die Zerstörung der kalten Ordnung: Auch ein Versuch über das Vergessen weiblicher Kulturleistungen," *Literaturmagazin* 10 (1979): 112.

36. Keun, *Das kunstseidene Mädchen*, 65.

37. Ibid., 85.

38. Irmgard Keun in conversation with Johannes Tralow. Cited in Kreis, *Was man glaubt, gibt es*, 90.

39. Siegfried Kracauer, "Die kleinen Ladenmädchen gehen ins Kino" (1927), in *Das Ornament der Masse* (Frankfurt am Main: Suhrkamp, 1977), 279–294. Kracauer himself revised his original position in "Mädchen in Beruf," *Querschnitt* 12, no. 4 (April 1932): 238–243.

40. Reingard Jäkl, *Vergnügungsgewerbe rund um den Bülowbogen* (Berlin: Bezirksamt Schöneberg, 1979), 40.

41. Hessen, *Prostitution in Deutschland*, 63–64.

42. Monika Shafi analyzes Keun's novel from this perspective of the loss of illusions, which she identifies as a process of finding a female identity. See Monika Shafi, "Aber das ist es ja eben, ich habe ja keine Meinesgleichen," *Colloquia Germanica* 24 (1988): 314–325.

43. Wolfgang Schivelbusch, *Disenchanted Night: The Industrialization of Light in the Nineteenth Century* (Berkeley and Los Angeles: University of California Press, 1988), 60, 64.

44. Walter Benjamin, *Charles Baudelaire: Ein Lyriker im Zeitalter des Hochkapitalismus* (Frankfurt am Main: Suhrkamp, 1974), 48.

45. "Die Frau in der Öffentlichkeit," in *Die praktische Berlinerin*, no. 13 (Berlin: Ullstein, 1925), 1.

46. Andrea Kuner, "Bürgerliches Frauenbild und 'gefallene' Mädchen (1830–1923)," in *Ich bin meine eigene Frauenbewegung: Frauen-Ansichten aus der Geschichte einer Grosstadt*, ed. Petra Zwacka (Berlin: Edition Hentrich, 1991), 165–172.

47. On the varying positions on the question of marriage within the women's movement, see Heide Soltau, *Trennungsspuren* (Frankfurt am Main: Extrabuch, 1984), 148–185.

48. Keun, *Das kunstseidene Mädchen*, 55.

49. Ibid., 92.

50. Ibid., 117.

51. Ibid., 116.

52. Else Kern's *Wie sie dazu kamen* (Munich: Ernst Reinhardt, 1928) and Wilhelm Hammer's *Zehn Lebensläufe Berliner Kontrollmädchen* (Berlin: Seemann, 1930), are but two examples of the large number of volumes of interviews with prostitutes from this period. The contribution of Dr. Anna Pappritz, who was actively engaged in the discussion centering on effectively combating prostitution, sheds light on the development of state and medical supervisory measures as the ultimate goal of such interviews: "And yet ultimately it will have to come down to the fact that doctors are able unencumbered to find ways and means for decreasing the growth of lifestyles that generally lead to women falling victim to vice." Anna Pappritz, "Lebenslaufforschung von Prostituierten," in *Freie Wohlfahrtspflege* 3, no. 118 (Berlin: Franz Dahlem, 1929).

53. Keun, *Das kunstseidene Mädchen*, 55.

54. Ibid., 50.

55. Ibid., 78.

56. See Verena Stefan, *Häutungen* (Munich: Frauenoffensive, 1976), 26.

57. Keun, *Das kunstseidene Mädchen*, 63.

58. Abigail Solomon-Godeau, "The Legs of the Countess," *October* 39 (Winter 1986): 76.

59. Keun, *Das kunstseidene Mädchen*, 99–100.

60. Hans Ostwald, *Sittengeschichte der Inflation* (Berlin: Neufeld und Henius, 1931).

61. For a discussion of the question of women's living situations, see Soltau, *Trennungsspuren*, 108 ff.

62. Keun, *Das kunstseidene Mädchen*, 53.

63. Ibid., 56.

64. Ibid., 132.

65. Christoph Asendorf, *Batterien der Lebenskraft* (Giessen: Anabas, 1984), 98.

66. Walter Benjamin, "Die Wiederkehr des Flaneurs in Berlin," in Franz Hessel, *Ein Flaneur in Berlin* (Berlin: Arsenal, 1990), 279.

67. Alice Rühle-Gerstel, "Zurück zur guten alten Zeit," *Die literarische Welt* 9, no. 4 (27 January 1933): 5–6.

68. In her interpretation of Virginia Woolf's essay "Street Haunting," Rachel Bowlby posits walking on the street as the basic prerequisite for writing: "The move outside involves the removal of individuality for anonymity. . . . A corollary . . . of the move from self to anonymity is the change from 'I' to 'eye.' " In contrast to Keun's protagonist, who, as we have already seen, cannot develop an unmediated perspective on the city, Woolf's female narrative "I" emancipates herself from the role of the female passerby being seen by becoming the flaneuse who sees. In that Doris withdraws from the street into the space of the apartment, she deprives herself of the possibility of finding her own identity. See Bowlby, "Walking Women and Writing: Virginia Woolf as Flaneuse," in *New Feminist Discourses*, ed. Isobel Armstrong (London: Routledge, 1992), 26–47.

69. The space outside the parameters of the city was considered reactionary in leftist discourse. For example, the communist youth in Brecht and Eisler's film *Kuhle Wampe* distances itself from the revisionist older generation in the garden colony. In prefascist discourse, the garden location was a positive counterimage to the uncontrolled wilderness, which was engendered as female in the same way that the chaos of the city was: "In a society that has subjected everything to rationalization, the free wilderness of sexual life, in so far as it serves to rejuvenate the body of the Volk, must give way to a garden plot." Claus Schrempf, *Diktatur der Tatsachen* (Berlin, 1932), cited in Helmut Lethen, *Neue Sachlichkeit* (Stuttgart: Metzler, 1975), 38. Doris's rejection of a free life at the cost of material security and a sense of being home with Karl should also be read within this context.

70. Keun, *Das kunstseidene Mädchen*, 59.

NINE

In the Mirror of Fashion

Sabine Hake

Every season brings in its newest creations some secret flag signals of things to come. Those capable of reading them would know in advance about new art movements as well as about new laws, wars, and revolutions.—Without doubt therein lies the greatest attraction of fashion but also the difficulty of using it productively.
—WALTER BENJAMIN, *DAS PASSAGENWERK*

"A European chronicler in the year 1999 who wanted to describe the time around 1925 would have to begin as follows: 'It was the time of the pageboy, it was the time of the short skirt, of flesh-colored stockings.'"[1] The date chosen by Hans Janowitz is still a few years away, but his predictions have turned out to be quite accurate. Fashion is mentioned in most accounts of Weimar culture, whether as a fixture in its urban settings, a constant reference point in new designs for living, or a compelling allegory of modernity. Many descriptions of the so-called New Woman revolve around fashion, and cultural historians seem to agree that fashion played an important role in defining modern femininity: as a marker of economic status and social ambition, as an expression of female narcissism and beauty, and as the focus of consumerist fantasies and commodified versions of the self. The growing presence of middle-class women in the public sphere and their entry into office- and service-related professions changed traditional gender roles and resulted, among other things, in the demand for less confining modes of dress. With the introduction of *Reformkleidung* (reform clothes) during the prewar years, fashion emerged as the most visible sign of women's newly gained freedom of movement, literally and figuratively. The production of inexpensive *Konfektion* (ready-to-wear clothes) and their attractive display in department stores made fashion available to larger groups in society, thus elevating it to a signifier of the modern and the new. No longer the prerogative of a cultured elite, fashion came to be associated with a variety of causes, from the fight for sexual freedom and women's rights to the conservative campaigns against rampant consumerism and the Americanization of Germany. Especially during the stabilization period from 1924 to 1929, when Weimar democracy thrived on the promises of economic stability and technological progress, women's fashions stood at the center of heated debates that used the changing styles to address problems of modernity and articulate its contradictions in gendered terms. Such overdetermined readings are not unusual. For as an expression of the zeitgeist, fashion, to quote Eduard Fuchs, "is ruled not by anarchy but by strictest regularity. Its subordinate elements are organically linked to the entire culture and follow its laws. Thus it is a very accurate expression, in every single part, of all culture and reflects it in the most faithful way."[2]

Fashion is able to represent other spheres because of its own involvement with representation and difference. Its practices and products create a semiotic field where changes in society can be traced through the close study of surface phenomena and where the culture/nature dichotomy can be overcome through a more fluid definition of social and sexual identities. As such a metadiscursive category, fashion was enlisted by Georg Simmel, Siegfried Kracauer, and Walter Benjamin in their attempts to develop new critical categories from the experience of everyday life. Inspired by their writings, I propose to look more closely at 1920s women's clothing and explore its cultural and critical relevance through the problem of sexual difference and the eroticism of the commodity. The big city provided the stage where the newest trends could be seen, where style became a matter of almost existential significance, and where the cult of youth and androgyny found its most willing followers. Fashion promised sexual liberation, social mobility, and narcissistic gratification outside the confinements of traditional identity politics. However, women's desire for new self-images also subjected them more strongly to mass-produced fantasies that, with their ever-changing forms, reproduced the old distinctions within a different framework, now based on the rhetoric of functionalism. To understand this dynamic on the level of articulation (i.e., as a signifier) and not confuse it with its implied meanings (i.e., its signified), one needs to approach fashion as a phenomenon that reveals as much as it hides—a phenomenon that simultaneously affirms and subverts the order of things. It is with these implications that I want to reconstruct the discursive formation ruled by the term "fashion" during the Weimar years.

Let me begin with an obvious example, the so-called *Bubikopf* (pageboy). Weimar critics argued passionately over its merits and demerits as if the fate of modernity depended on the length of women's hair. Conservatives saw the disappearance of long hair, the crown of true womanhood, as a sign of cultural decline, and held the inevitable masculinization of women responsible for everything from sexual perversions to social tensions. Erich Fromm's famous 1929 survey of attitudes among workers included the question "Do you like short hair in women?" The reactions were for the most part positive: "Yes, short hair is an advance on 'the good old days.'" Only middle-class men, betraying their conservative attitudes, objected categorically: "No, a woman should make herself beautiful with that which nature has given her."[3] Following the example of Victor Margueritte's 1922 *La Garçonne* (The Bachelor Girl), novelists used the Bubikopf to describe emancipated young women whose search for self-fulfillment was exciting but, not infrequently, paid for with personal unhappiness. Some writers enlisted the length of women's hair in political struggles. In Willy Bredel's 1933 proletarian novel, *Der Eigen-*

tumsparagraph (The Property Clause), two young women attend a Nazi rally and one remarks to the other, "We must not stand out. They have already started keeping tabs on us. Your page boy catches the eye."[4] And this is how Martin Kessel's 1927 novella, *Der Spritzenrotor* (The Turbo Rotor), opens:

> Progressive as she is, Frisca Weill, the strict but fragile Frisca, a teacher by profession and single for forty years, had her hair cut in the fashionable pageboy style, despite her stringy hair and gray, stretched skin around the chin. For long hair, she argues, is both a burden and a handicap, is also uneconomical and, already for that reason, pointless.[5]

In addition to its appearance in contemporary novels, the new haircut inspired numerous essays about fashion and modern mass society. Heinrich Mann praised the Bubikopf not only for its practical nature but also for its democratizing effect: "There are things where female worker and society lady think alike,"[6] he said about the new styles. For others the growing fashion consciousness illustrated the trend toward standardization. Vicki Baum used the example of the Bubikopf, and of hundreds of thousands of women rushing to the hairdresser, to reflect on a basic contradiction at the heart of fashion, the contradiction between originality and uniformity: "It is fashionable to be original. Thus all modern women are original. Since all of them are original at the same time, none of them actually is."[7]

The Bubikopf first appeared in the United States during the war years. First adopted by movie stars like Louise Brooks, Colleen Moore, and Anna May Wong, it became the trademark of the emancipated city woman, known as a flapper or jazz baby. Through Coco Chanel and Isadora Duncan, the new style reached Germany in the early 1920s and soon could be spotted on Berlin's main boulevards and in trendy nightclubs and cafés. Bubikopf wearers included prominent women—most of them brunettes—from all areas of cultural life, including the writer Marieluise Fleisser, the artist Hannah Höch, the dancer Valeska Gert, and film stars like Asta Nielsen, Pola Negri, Tilla Durieux, Aud Egede Nissen, and Mia May. In its basic shape, the Bubikopf or *Pagenkopf* refers to a straight cut around the head, with the length level with the tips of the ears and the face framed by even sides and distinctive bangs. Later variations exposed the hairline in the back in a style referred to as shingling, which accented the cut's angular shape, or they imitated men's styles by further trimming the hair and adding a part on the side. Known as the Eton crop, the latter was favored by the sculptress Renée Sintenis and the actresses Elisabeth Bergner and Herta Thiele. With the short hair came small, close-fitting, and brimless felt hats like the ubiquitous cloche, which hid much of the wearer's face and emphasized the head's sculptural features. Soft berets also gained in popularity, especially in sportswear, while embroidered or beaded bandeaux were the adornment of choice for evening wear. In the early 1930s, softer, wavy cuts parted on the side gradually replaced the Bubikopf, and the severe masculine look gave way to distinctly feminine styles.

It is a critical commonplace that periods of great upheaval are often followed by a masculinization of women in dress and manners. The new look, from short hair to silk stockings, celebrated the spirit of the Weimar Republic. To be sure, the straight silhouettes and the simple styles were already popular before the war, namely, as part of reform clothing and its campaign against corsets and other forms of disciplining the female body. And hemlines had already begun to rise during the war years in response to growing female employment and shortages in textile production. However, beginning in the postwar years, fashion was increasingly identified with the desire for new lifestyles and identities. Between 1924, the year of the currency reform, and 1929, the year of the stock market crash, mass consumption changed dramatically, promising not only satisfaction of basic needs but also participation in symbolic acts. The tastes and styles associated with the stabilization period reflect this development, from the emergence of woman as the modern consumer to the exploitation of emancipatory movements in fashion trends. There is no doubt that the new dress styles had much to offer to the young office workers and sales girls who sought freedom in the big cities, the working-class women with the double burden of family and job, and the wealthy socialites eager to take up tennis, boxing, and motor touring. Now terms like "simplicity," "functionality," and "versatility" began to define clothes in use-oriented terms. Physical fitness became the distinguishing mark of the streamlined, machinelike body. Yet the myth of instrumentality and the obsessive pragmatism also betrayed a continuous anxiety over sexual difference that could not be relieved through any promises of liberation, equality, and casual dressing.

In general, women's wear during the Weimar years was characterized by short hemlines that showed off legs in flesh-colored silk stockings and low waistlines that emphasized tubular forms; previously cherished features such as a small waist or large bust were suppressed. With the disappearance of form-conscious shapes came unstructured bodices and brassieres, which made the fit, slender body an even greater necessity. The androgynous look challenged traditional notions of female beauty, but also forced more voluptuous women to flatten out their curves with the help of girdles and corsets. The jumper dress, in its basic shape or in modifications like the tunic, dominated daytime fashions and convinced through clear lines, tubular silhouettes, and soft fabrics. The basic outfit chosen by most office workers consisted of a sporty jumper blouse, often worn with a vest or cardigan, a straight or pleated skirt, and medium-high pumps with straps or ankle boots. New or improved fabrics like jerseys, knits, and, most important, artificial silk—rayon, as it was called after 1926—brought greater comfort and mobility, while modern textile design, in its preference for colorful geometrical prints, added a playful, creative touch.

Evening wear, however, remained glamorous and ultrafeminine, with low-cut gowns, sleek silhouettes, and accessories like ostrich feathers, fox stoles, and artificial flowers. Satins, taffeta, chiffons, and silks highlighted the generous cuts of the gowns and conveyed a sense of luxury that had been exorcised from the functional world of daytime fashion. Joined by famous film stars and the wives of war profiteers, high-society women continued to follow the change of seasons that, in subsequent years, brought Turkish harem pants, Egyptian headgear, Chinese pajamas, and Spanish shawls. The fact that French couturiers at one point tried unsuccessfully to eliminate the short skirt reveals the growing influence of celebrities as unofficial fashion leaders. The vanguard function of this new leisure class can be seen in the growing popularity of casual wear, which, through the understatement in the choice of fabrics and cuts, offered an illusion of democratic culture while preserving its exclusiveness; hence the popularity of cardigans and trousers modeled on distinctly British class sports like tennis and golf.[8]

The relationship between fashion and role-playing came to the fore in the changed attitude toward makeup. Until the war, only prostitutes and demimondaines wore makeup during the day. Respectable middle-class women may have used face powder but typically found rouge and mascara too unnatural, too closely linked to the specter of sexuality. Fromm's survey indicates that the resistance to the New Woman was most pronounced in matters of makeup, with the image of red painted lips uniting different social groups against the threat of a liberated femininity. Younger women nonetheless welcomed the new products introduced by cosmetics firms like Helena Rubinstein and Max Factor. Two basic styles predominated, the sporty, tanned look that limited the use of makeup to foundation and rouge and the pale look for the evening, with plucked and penciled eyebrows, dark eye shadow, bright red lips, and heavy perfumes like Mitsuko and Shalimar.[9] Both aspects of fashion, dress and makeup, treated sexuality as a spectacle and identity as a construction. Yet whereas the one expanded gender definitions to include images of androgyny, the other dramatized older assumptions about female beauty and eroticism through its use of the mask. This division of labor helped to ease anxieties about possible gender transgressions and confirmed the link between woman and culture, while at the same time acknowledging her physicality.

At this point, it might be useful to look at two images that not only depict Weimar fashions but also participate in the construction of fashion as the apotheosis of modern life. My first example is August Sander's famous photograph of a secretary at a radio station. Working on his project "People of the Twentieth Century" throughout the 1920s, Sander portrayed several representatives of the New Woman (fig. 9.1). If it is true that, in the words of Friedrich Theodor Vischer, "the degree of self-mirroring that characterizes the physiognomy [of fashion] is modern, is a fruit of the sharpening in reflexivity"[10] since the Enlightenment, then one should be able to find traces of this process in images specifically designated as modern. And indeed, Sander's radio secretary conveys a strong sense of ironic detachment that manifests itself in her reliance on the attributes of fashion. She acts out the tensions between the search for other images of femininity and woman's inevitable objectification by fashion as a commodity. Removed from her work environment, the woman is photographed against a neutral backdrop. The division

Figure 9.1. August Sander, *Radiosekretärin* (Radio Secretary) (1931). Reprinted courtesy of Schirmer-Mosel Verlag, Munich.

between the bright wall on the left and the dark curtain on the right creates spatial depth and heightens the sense of ambivalence in the woman's self-presentation, from the cigarette in her right hand to her skeptical gaze. Seated on a chair, she turns her upper body and face toward the camera while her crossed upper legs remain on the side. This strained body position bears witness to the compromises between provocation and reserve that inform so many fashion statements. Repeating the chiaroscuro effect of the backdrop, shadows highlight the woman's angular cheeks and jawbone and show off her sharp profile. A small curl softens the severity of the shortly cropped hair. Similar effects—of tension and of compromise—structure the juxtaposition of her fair complexion with the shiny blackness of her hair and dress. The simplicity of the collarless, black satin jumper finds a counterpart in the stylized floral embroidery on the front; the cut of the dress suggests that it ends well above the knee. With her slender frame, flat chest, delicate hands, and chiseled face, the radio secretary personifies the physical ideal of the androgyne.

Otto Dix's 1926 portrait of the writer Sylvia von Harden relies on very similar visual markers of ambivalence, including the same contorted body position, the provocative look toward the onlooker, and the use of a cigarette as a distancing device. The writer is seated on a chair, with a cocktail glass and a monogrammed cigarette case on the marble table in front of her. Under Dix's scrutinizing gaze, von Harden becomes a caricature of the New Woman, complete with monocle and Eton crop. With the reddish backdrop evoking the excesses of the brothel, the short red plaid jumper gives her skin an unnatural color. Her silk stockings form creases around the knees. Von Harden's face, from the parted lips to the dark circles around her eyes, suggests boredom, arrogance, and despair; the elongated fingers make her look sickly. The woman seems tragically caught in her own scenarios of self-presentation. With these implications, Dix's portrait of von Harden resembles his critical portraits of German philistines but also adds a distinct element of misogyny to stage a vengeful drama of modern femininity.

The correspondences between fashion, femininity, and modernity remain a theoretical construct if they are not linked to the dramatic changes in clothing manufacture and consumer culture that made fashion so central to the realignment of cultural practices after World War I. Werner Sombart has used terms like "collectivization of consumption," "uniformization of taste," and "urbanization of demand"[11] to demarcate the field in which fashion began to mediate between the cult of individualism and the inescapable trend toward uniformity and standardization. With a view toward new markets, the fashion industry in the prewar years had begun to differentiate its products, making them both more available and affordable. While the haute couture continued to offer expensive, custom-tailored designs, more and more companies specialized in prêt-à-porter, with their manufacture-based system a good compromise between cost and quality. They introduced industrial methods into the fabrication of the so-called Konfektion sold in large department stores like Wertheim and Tietz. Product differentiation was necessary to attract new customers, especially among members of the lower middle class who often realized their personal and social ambitions through fashion as a substitute.

The intense preoccupation with fashion reflected dramatic changes in consumer behavior. Products were sought out to satisfy narcissistic desires, and the act of shopping was experienced as an intoxicating celebration of the self. Displayed in the temples of consumer culture and scrutinized on the pages of the feuilleton, fashion—here to be understood both as an object and as a quality inherent in the object—epitomized the spectacle of the commodity and its promises of instant gratification and permanent self-transformation. With clothes as the most visible status symbol in the anonymous urban crowd, novelty and originality became more important than usefulness or durability. In the big cities, styles appeared and disappeared with increasing speed, and while the urban middle classes became fully conversant in the idioms of fashion, the old upper classes withdrew from the frantic celebration of the new and sought refuge in quality and tradition. As a mode of distinction that brought everything under its spell, fashion, however, continued to extend its influence into other areas of daily life, from furniture and interior design to table manners, cultural tastes, and political opinions.

The modern metropolis provided a stage for the display of women's fashions. As the center of the fashion industry and the illustrated press, as the city of the emancipated woman and the artistic avant-gardes, Berlin started new trends and was alternately glorified and vilified as an embodiment of the modern. On Kurfürstendamm and Tauentzienstrasse, the latest fashions were exhibited in the windows of department stores and exclusive shops for luxury goods. The spectacle of the commodity attracted the wealthy socialite and the fashion-conscious secretary, the modern *flaneuse* and, in the words of Curt Moreck, the "Tauentziengirl"[12] who strolled on the boulevards to see and be seen, thus making the rituals of fashion an important part of public life in the big city. Through the cinema and the illustrated press, fashion became an inescapable presence in everyday life and constantly redefined everything along its shifting lines of demarcation. Mass publications like the *Berliner Illustrirte Zeitung* showed snapshots of beautiful celebrities at the gala premieres of Berlin's first-run cinemas and at benefits organized by exclusive tennis clubs. *Der Bazar,* the leading fashion journal, reported regularly about international fashion shows and emerging designers. As the most popular women's magazine, *Die Dame* offered practical advice about everything from flirting to driving and printed informative articles about fashion, lifestyles, and the arts; it also advertised the popular Ullstein paper patterns.[13] On and off the screen, film stars like Lya de Putti and Mia May influenced the female audience—from their tastes in men to their choice of cars. "The Berlin woman enjoys elegance and luxury in the flickers—instead of a chinchilla, she buys a movie ticket and studies the gowns of the fashion house of Flatow-Schädler/Mosse in Fritz Lang's *Dr Mabuse, der Spieler*,"[14] noted one journalist derisively.

While high fashion continued to cultivate its international orientation, its significance within Weimar culture cannot be separated from the reemerging nationalisms and the remapping of Europe after World War I.[15] Before the war, the leadership role of Parisian couturiers—and of London clothiers, in the case of men's wear—had been undisputed. Confronted with growing mass markets, the French developed better marketing strategies (e.g., Jean Patou's cosmetics line) and introduced new styles geared toward the independent modern woman (e.g., Coco Chanel's garçonne style). Textile design found inspiration in modern painting and took to heart the call of the avant-garde for a transformation of all aspects of modern life. Such creative efforts found an unlikely ally in the textile industry, which, through the introduction of manufactured fibers like rayon (since 1910) and acetate (since 1924) and the improvement of imitation materials ranging from artificial pearls to fake leather, made many of these ideas available to the average consumer. Last but not least, the 1920s saw the rise of Americanism as the main paradigm of mass culture. American fashions not only redefined the meaning of fashion through their antielitist pretensions, a contradiction essential to its appeal, and their deliberate allusions to the world of work and sports. They also used the new mass media for launching new trends, thereby replacing the old downward model of dissemination (i.e., of fashion trends started by the social elites and then adopted by the masses) with a more complicated system of product tie-ins as well as cross-cultural references.

In trying to balance international perspectives and national developments, the fashion industry in Berlin was especially affected by the shift toward the Right and the rise of anti-Semitism. Concentrated around the Hausvogteiplatz in the city's east, clothing manufacture had thrived in Berlin since the nineteenth century and included everything from exclusive fashion houses to countless specialty shops and sweatshops. Although there were many Jewish firms in Berlin, Hermann Gerson and Nathan Israel being the largest ones, their numbers have been grossly exaggerated by the Nazis in their attempt to "Aryanize" this traditional center of the German fashion industry. The campaigns against foreign influences also extended to stylistic choices. During the war, anti-French feelings had elevated the choice of German designers to a patriotic act. In the years following, French couture was increasingly associated with the kind of aristocratic culture against which the representatives of the Weimar Republic formulated their vision of a democratic mass culture. With the Dawes Plan, American culture emerged as the preferred model because it united the cult of functionalism with the promises of social equality. It streamlined the female body to make it both more sexual and less feminine. And it glorified the commodity as a means to personal fulfillment as well as a compensation for the inevitable failures of such plans. The enthusiastic reception of things American was part of a globalization of mass culture that erased regional differences and celebrated mass-produced goods as the perfect union of social and aesthetic concerns. Not surprisingly, conservative and right-wing critics used fashion to describe the dangers of a homogeneous international culture. Modern styles, in their view, originated in a conspiracy of French couturiers and Jewish *Konfektionäre* against Germany's indigenous traditions. Calling for a return to folk costume, some wanted to reintroduce regional and ethnic elements into a largely metropolitan phenomenon and appealed to women to reject androgyny for the authentic look of motherhood—without much success. The world economic crisis in 1929, not the rise of fascism, prepared the ground for the return to more feminine styles—styles, to be sure, that, after the Nazi takeover of the German fashion industry, distinguished themselves only through their complete lack of originality.

To what degree fashion and, by implication, modern notions of beauty relied on national stereotypes can be seen in Elsa Maria Bud's *Bravo, Musch!* (1931). The novel focuses on the experiences of a young woman, a medical student at the

University of Berlin, who supports herself by working part-time as a fashion model. During a fashion show in the Netherlands, she charms the audience through her naturalness, a key concept in 1920s fashions. The apotheosis of the "liberated lady" brings together all the relevant female and national stereotypes.

> With the many changing images the sympathies of the audience gradually became apparent: One of the guest models, a French girl, has a wildly spirited manner; she bounces around as if on springs, she rushes by, more like a harlequin than a girl, a redhead with a snub nose, very pretty actually. Mabel's boyish swinging around delights several times; then she disappears in the crowd. Antje has the sympathies of the Dutch ladies who even in the new times have not lost their traditional heaviness. Musch is as she always is. Spontaneously, she presents each dress in the style in which it looks the best. She is brash, reserved, is melancholy or sober; at all times there is a dark gleam of desire and excitement in her gray eyes.[16]

As to be expected, the program ends with the crowning of the German girl as the most beautiful model.

It was in the context of white-collar culture that fashion became an entirely new way of looking at the world. In his famous study on *Die Angestellten* (The White-Collar Workers, 1929), Kracauer links this phenomenon to the "moral-pink skin color"[17] that captured their mentality in a physical attribute. The emphasis on a pleasant appearance in the workplace, he notes, made modern fashion and body culture an effective weapon in the streamlining of a workforce that would eventually have to come to terms with its own going out of style. Whereas Kracauer emphasizes the need for distinguishing oneself, if only for purposes of self-promotion, his contemporary Max Rössiger speaks of the employees' strong need for "social mimicry."[18] Adopting middle-class personas, Rössiger argues, the white-collar workers hope to escape both the fate of proletarization and the equalizing forces of mass society. Alice Rühle-Gerstel even uses a fabric to describe the precarious class position of white-collar workers, calling them a "fifty percent silk profession, fifty percent silk like their soul and their mind."[19]

Though motivated by the desire for a precise analysis of class, the identification of white-collar culture with artifice and deception is marred by highly problematic distinctions between surface and essence, falseness and authenticity. What fashion reveals to these critics, and what makes it so attractive to certain segments of Weimar society, is precisely its ability to grant social status through the mere display of its attributes. That this promise can never be fulfilled is almost part of the attraction, for it leaves open other possibilities. Mass culture makes sure that everyone can participate in the illusion of selfhood through consumption, and democracy provides the images that endow the products with meaning. From that perspective, the turn to fashion among white-collar workers must be regarded as a progressive move. It was a decision against the confinements of identity, against the normative effects of physiognomy, and against the ethics of belonging. Fashion to them represented the most effective way of translating social ambitions into aesthetics terms. In their study of masquerading and posturing, Weimar's most perceptive cultural critics would detect the first signs of a homogeneous middle-class society in which differences were reduced to a mere game. But fashion also showed them ways of overcoming the limitations of the cult of identity with its problematic assumptions about body, gender, and the self.

In articles about the corrupting influence of fashion consciousness on white-collar culture, women were regularly mentioned as the main culprits. Just as the diatribes against white-collar workers highlighted their "feminine" characteristics (e.g., the lack of class consciousness, the greater susceptibility to outside influences), negative portrayals of modern women focused on their "masculine" qualities—notwithstanding the fact that both groups were to a large degree identical. Rosa Mayreder rejected such gender essentialism in favor of a sober analysis of the changing social conditions experienced by the New Woman.

> She does not want to wear masculine clothes but clothes appropriate to her lifestyle, her athletic tendencies, and the modern means of transportation. She hardens her body against external forces because she wants to live without male protection. From there develops that naturally slender body . . . [and] clothing [that] automatically adopts the forms found in men's clothing. . . . The woman does not become masculine. She merely becomes an independent being.[20]

Because of its assault on gender as a normative category, fashion allowed its detractors to express anxieties about women's emancipation, their entrance into the workplace, and changes in sexual behavior. In accordance with the widespread notion that female identity resides in the body, the look of 1920s fashions was often used to "explain" the myth of the New Woman, and vice versa—with the effect that both could then be dismissed as passing fancies and products of media hype. Again it was clothing that seemed to bring out the "pathology" of the female body, from the rejection of motherhood to the embrace of homosexuality. Traditionally invoked to celebrate femininity, the artifice of fashion was blamed for severing the bond between woman and nature and turning her body into an instrument of egotistical self-actualization. Hence Moreck's warning: "When the modern woman . . . strives fanatically toward equality with the man and uses the means of fashion to demonstrate her masculinization by suppressing the female and imitating the male secondary sexual characteristics, the sexual instinct is bound to be irritated and enter the dangerous field of perversion."[21]

Even fashion styles inspired by the aesthetics of Taylorization used these formal elements for rehearsing the drama of modern eroticism, without necessarily paying attention to their original function. Whereas unproductivity was the image conveyed by women's fashion at the end of the nineteenth century, the postwar identification of fashion with work, whether real or imaginary, invariably introduced the question of gender transgressions. The dynamic between the eroticizing of the functional and the functionalization of the erotic is nowhere more evident than in the public reactions to the Garçonne style. Characterized by her masculine attire and short haircut, the Garçonne appropriated the look of the other sex and, in so doing, challenged existing notions of sexual difference, often with the explicit goal of scandalizing her surroundings. While the athletic look signified health and leisure, the Garçonne emphasized the performative and aesthetic aspects of sexuality. The flirtation with masculinity involved a playful staging of identities that was predicated on the full achievement of gender equality, and, given the imaginary nature of such assumptions, often highly ironical and self-reflexive in its effect. Public anxieties about a thus liberated female sexuality found a convenient stereotype in the lesbian "butch" and the rituals of a homosexual subculture where, so it seemed, gender was reduced to a choice of costumes. Tailored suits and ties first appeared in Berlin's lesbian subculture and artistic circles before they were popularized by Marlene Dietrich in the 1930s to become part of the myth of Weimar decadence. Renée Sintenis's appearances on Kurfürstendamm, complete with top coat, girlfriend, and fox terrier, played into such perceptions, as did the spectacle of transvestism displayed to a thrill-seeking international audience in famous bars like Berlin's Eldorado. The *Berliner Illustrirte Zeitung* even organized a contest under the title "What in the world do you say about Miss Mia?" and invited readers to contribute funny captions for the image of a young woman with short hair and tailored suit. Submissions included "*Sachlichkeit* (objectivity) transformed into *Sächlichkeit* (neuterness)," "Clothes don't make the man; what counts are the naked facts," and, as a variation on a German folk song, "Say who may the little man be?"[22] These humorous comments on male identity, of course, raise the question of to what degree the perceived masculinization of women also addressed unacknowledged homosexual tendencies in men.

The widespread fascination with the Garçonne, whether as a fashion phenomenon or the embodiment of lesbianism, draws attention to the close relationship between women's fashion and the female body. While late nineteenth-century styles imposed their forms on a passive, malleable body, modern dress required slender bodies that could support soft, unstructured outfits. The modern body gave life to the functional clothes; by the same token, clothes became the means to its self-actualization. As an ideal, *the femme enfant* or, to use the terminology of the times, the *Girl* [*sic*] possessed a slim, almost angular body with narrow hips, small breasts, and long legs. The deemphasizing of all secondary sex characteristics, especially of bust and buttocks, betrays a fixation on youth and a symbolic rejection of the maternal as the most oppressive element in traditional gender roles. Achieving and maintaining this kind of body shape required rigorous dieting, various kinds of massages and medical baths, and, of course, regular exercise; cosmetic surgery was discussed controversially in many literary journals.[23] The popularity of swimming, skiing, tennis, and even boxing further confirms the influence of Anglo-American body consciousness and its equation of beauty with health. While the athletic body of American provenance, complete with blond hair and tanned skin, became the physical ideal of the successful and the ambitious, young city dwellers with no opportunities or no desire for social advancement cultivated the look of the night: dark eyes, pale skin, and almost anorectic bodies. Like the *femme fragile* of the turn of the century, this female stereotype was often associated with sexual excess and drug use. Confirming such associations, the well-known Berlin designer Valentin Manheimer even created a special "cocaine outfit."[24]

A recurring theme in fashion journals, novels, and films was the beauty of women's legs; adjectives commonly used include "long," "muscular," "slender," "strong," and "lean." After years of shame associated with woman's legs, the provocative display of calves and knees caused some concern among contemporaries. In accordance with the rhetoric of functionality, defenders of the short skirt pointed to the gain in mobility. But these benefits, of course, were paid for with a lack of proper protection during the cold months and the unavoidable runs in silk stockings. More than anything, the emphasis on women's legs betrayed a fetishistic interest in the female body that, to invoke Freud's analysis of fetishism, introduced the question of lack. As is well known, fashion always emphasizes particular body parts that are considered sexually attractive. The fashion historian J. C. Flugel has examined these shifts for the time period in question: "The fashions of the last few years have thus been based upon a certain upward displacement of modesty, an accentuation of the body rather than of clothes, an idealization of youth rather than of maturity, and a displacement of erotic value from the trunk to the limbs."[25] Flugel links this idealization of youth, and hence immaturity, to the threat of the emancipated woman or, to phrase it in psychoanalytic terms, the denial of female castration through the fixation on legs, shoes, and stockings.

The power of women's fashion to illuminate Weimar culture as a whole is predicated on the assumption that fashion, in playing with social and sexual identities and in embracing transitoriness and ambivalence, can be read as an allegory of modernity. Simmel was one of the first to look at fashion as a theatricalization of social processes and to describe it as a mediation between the need for imitation, and hence social adaptation, and the need for differentiation, and hence individualism. The main function of fashion, he argues, is to unite and separate, to define one social group and distinguish it from all others. The more societies emphasize difference, the more they rely on such systems of demarcation. Simmel goes on to explain how fashion embraces change through its insistence on novelty; how it turns transitoriness—that is, the eventual disappearance or co-optation of new styles—into an aesthetic principle; and how it comes to symbolize the present, and therefore the modern. If things are perceived as fashionable because of their ephemeral status, then fashion consciousness is always guided by an acute awareness of temporality. The conditions under which Weimar women gained equality and the precarious circumstances under which they enjoyed the benefits of fashion confirm this link between social experiences and aesthetic choices. If the essence of stylization lies in compromise, defined by Simmel as "this delusion of individual poignancy, this generalization beyond the uniqueness of the personality," then 1920s styles thrived because they reinvented the personal as the general. Fashion gave expression to a psychological conflict experienced by many female white-collar workers: to leave behind their class origins and, at the same time, to make up for these transgressions through their uniform appearance. According to Simmel, the vacillation between social obedience and individual differentiation, between domination and submission, made fashion particularly attractive for those without power but with a strong need for asserting their individuality. Women's allegedly greater susceptibility to fashion, as well as their stricter adherence to social norms, is for him directly linked to an experience of ongoing discrimination that makes them more outer-determined and, therefore, more alike. His conclusion that "fashion gives woman a compensation for her lack of position in a class based on a calling or profession" captures accurately the dilemmas faced by women in the Weimar Republic.[26]

Simmel's brilliant analysis of fashion as an integral part of modern culture also sheds light on its discursive functions. For him, urbanism, modernity, and, one might add, femininity are inextricably linked to the emergence of fashion as a new cultural paradigm. Hence his conclusion that it "may almost be considered a sign of the increased power of fashion, that it has overstepped the bounds of its original domain, which comprised only personal externals, and has acquired an increasing influence over taste, over theoretical convictions, and even over the moral foundations of life."[27] Fashion assumes these roles, Simmel concludes his reassessment of modernity in the spirit of fashion, while "the great, permanent, unquestionable convictions are continually losing strength, as a consequence of which the transitory and vacillating elements of life acquire more room for the display of their activity."[28] Unlike the traditional arts, fashion responds almost instantaneously to changes in the public sphere and contributes to the heightened level of sensory stimulation described already in Simmel's groundbreaking essay of 1903, "The Metropolis and Mental Life." In a world where nothing is fixed and everything is always new, fashion dissolves the old distinctions between the sexes and the classes—but only to introduce new ones based on its own definition of boundaries.

In the context of Weimar culture, the function of what Joan Finkelstein has called the "fashioned self"[29] must be described as one of rehearsing and reenacting the changing social and sexual boundaries. As has been suggested by the sociological studies of Fromm and Kracauer, one important aspect of Weimar fashion, apart from the play with gender roles, was its ability to transgress class boundaries. The possibility to improve or maintain one's social status through the means of clothing points to a growing porosity of class-related categories. In the preference for functionalist clothes, these two contradictory positions found equal articulation: the belief that complete identification with the Taylor system, that the conflation of body and machine, would bring greater freedom and mobility; and the suspicion that the aestheticizing of the working body amounted only to a more insidious system of exploitation. While the promise of a new social identity was instantly available in the department stores and on the movie screens, the fleeting nature of fashion implicated the white-collar workers more deeply in the circulation of commodities.

Not surprisingly, the styles of the 1920s frequently reconfigured social and sexual identities. Sexual roles were redefined through social categories, and social conflicts were expressed in sexual terms. For the most part, such processes involved the appropriation of male attire and its representative functions. Yet the erosion of femininity as a norm also opened up the possibility of using typically feminine clothes as a defense against accusations of masculinization or associations with feminism and lesbianism. In both cases, fashion functioned as a mask that, to quote Simmel, "conceals the real features and can furnish this service only by means of a wholly uncompromising separation of the feelings and the externals of life."[30] In this relationship of femininity and masquerade, 1920s fashions emphasized and, at the same time, distracted from the actual accomplishments of female emancipation. Precisely because the short hair and short skirt symbolized the spirit of revolt, they could be used in the new promotional strategies that turned terms like "beauty" and "freedom" into qualities of the commodity. Precisely because the new fashions still defined woman through the body, she could realize her desires under the disguise of traditional images and become aware of the artificiality of gender roles. That is why Weimar fashions always involved the staging of ambivalences. It foregrounded the promises and the betrayals of modernity itself and, through that association, became a powerful tool of self-reflection. Kracauer once defended the need for distraction in modern mass society by claiming that the "emphasis on the external has the advantage of being *sincere*. It is not externality that poses a threat to truth. Truth is threatened only by the naive affirmation of cultural values that have become unreal." As I hope to have shown, his call "for a kind of distraction which exposes disintegration instead of masking it"[31] also applies to fashion.

NOTES

1. Hans Janowitz, *Jazz* (Berlin: Die Schmiede, 1927), 9, 10. All translations are mine unless noted otherwise. For a similar attempt to predict future trends, compare Paul Poiret, "Die Mode in 30 Jahren," *Der Querschnitt* 7 (1927): 30–32.

2. Eduard Fuchs, "Ich bin der Herr dein Gott" (1906), rpt. in *Die Listen der Mode*, ed. Silvia Bovenschen (Frankfurt am Main: Suhrkamp, 1989), 163. On the appeal of fashion, especially in relation to modern eroticism, also see Helen Grund, "Im Klima der Mode," *Der Querschnitt* 5 (1925): 514–515.

3. Erich Fromm, *The Working Class in Weimar Germany: A Psychological and Sociological Study*, trans. Barbara Weinberger, ed. and introd. Wolfgang Bonss (Providence, R.I.: Berg, 1984), 158. Fromm's statistics suggest that positive attitudes toward modern women's fashion were equally strong in left-wing and right-wing political groups. By contrast, the representatives of the middle class showed the greatest degree of opposition and resistance.

4. Willy Bredel, *Maschinenfabrik N & K, Rosenhofstrasse, Der Eigentumsparagraph* (Berlin and Weimar: Aufbau, 1975), 34, 439.

5. Martin Kessel, *Betriebsamkeit: Vier Novellen aus Berlin* (Frankfurt am Main: Iris, 1927), 27.

6. Heinrich Mann, "Der Bubikopf (1928)," in *Essays*, 2 vols. (Berlin: Aufbau, 1956), 2:162. In 1925 and 1926, the *Berliner Illustrirte Zeitung* (*BIZ*) devoted numerous articles and il-

lustrations to the popular new haircut. Examples for 1925 include "Der Bubenkopf," *BIZ* 24 (1925): 742; the cover for *BIZ* 33 (1925), "So was gibt's noch? Die staunenden Bubenköpfe von Heringsdorf"; and the letter of an angry subscriber canceling his subscription because of too many pageboy references in *BIZ* 49 (1925): 1648. Examples for 1926 include "Bubikopf und Ehepsychologie," *BIZ* 2 (1926): 38, and the "Bubikopf" jokes and cartoons in *BIZ* 4 (1926): 102.

7. Vicki Baum, "Leute von heute (1927)," in *Die Dame*, ed. Christian Ferber (Berlin: Ullstein, 1980), 166. On the changing role of the hairdresser, also see Ilia Vilko, "Der moderne Damenfriseur," *Der Querschnitt* 7 (1927): 318.

8. Critical contributions on the new styles appeared even in a special issue of the avant-garde journal *Die Form* 1 (1926); see the individual articles by Marlice Hinz, "Bekleidungskunst," 307–312; Renate Richter-Green, "Probleme der Mode," 414–423, Wilhelm Lotz, "Typus und Individuum in Kleidung und Mode, 428–435. For articles from the early 1930s that reflect the new conservatism, see Beverley Nichols, "Gericht über die heutige Frauenmode," *Der Querschnitt* 14 (1934): 5–8, and Richard Dillenz, "Modische Aphorismen," *Der Querschnitt* 15 (1935): 417–419.

9. On changes in makeup and its influence on gender definitions in early twentieth-century American society, compare Kathy Preiss, "Making Faces: The Cosmetics Industry and the Cultural Construction of Gender, 1890–1930," *Genders* 7 (1990): 143–169. Many of her conclusions apply to the German situation as well.

10. Friedrich Theodor Fischer, "Mode und Zynismus" (1879), rpt. in Bovenschen, *Die Listen der Mode*, 61.

11. Werner Sombart, "Wirtschaft und Mode: Ein Beitrag zur Theorie der modernen Bedarfsgestaltung" (1902), rpt. in Bovenschen, *Die Listen der Mode*, 80–105.

12. Curt Moreck, *Das Weib in der Kunst der neueren Zeit* (Berlin: Askanischer Verlag Carl Albert Kindle, 1925), 384. Compare his description of the New Woman on pp. 394–395.

13. For evidence of the growing links between publishing and modern fashion, see the promotion of *Ullstein-Schnittmuster* in *Die Dame* 9 (1929): 26–27.

14. Quoted by Uwe Westphal, *Berliner Konfektion und Mode, 1836–1939: Die Zerstörung einer Tradition* (Berlin: Edition Hentrich, 1986), 74. Westphal's interesting study documents how the continuous need for social distinctions prompted designers to introduce labels like "Modellgenre," "gehobenes Genre," "besseres Genre," "Mittelgenre," and "Damenkonfektion." On the Berlin fashion industry, also see Cordula Moritz, *Die Kleider der Berlinerin: Mode und Chic an der Spree* (Berlin: Haude & Spener, 1971), 69–76. The working conditions in clothing manufacture, including the resistance to unionization, have been described in Werner Turk's novel *Konfektion* (Berlin: Agis, 1932).

15. On the connections between fashion and modernity in a European context, see Mark Wigley, "White Out: Fashioning the Modern," in *Architecture: In Fashion*, ed. Paulette Singley and Deborah Fausch (Princeton: Princeton Architectural Press, 1994), 148–268.

16. Elsa Maria Bud, *Bravo, Musch!* (Berlin: Die Buchgemeinde, 1931), 247–248. To what degree the model became a figure of literary interest can be seen in Polly Tieck, "Das Berliner Mannequin," *Der Querschnitt* 5 (1925): 985–986.

17. Siegfried Kracauer, *Die Angestellten: Aus dem neuesten Deutschland* (Frankfurt am Main: Suhrkamp, 1974), 25. Compare his amusing piece on suspenders in "Die Hosenträger," in *Schriften*, ed. Inka Mülder-Bach (Frankfurt am Main: Suhrkamp, 1990) 5, 1:385–388.

18. Max Rössiger, *Der Angestellte von 1930* (Berlin: Sieben-Stäbe Verlag, 1930), 70.

19. Alice Rühle-Gerstel, *Das Frauenproblem der Gegenwart: Eine psychologische Bilanz* (Leipzig, 1932), 299. The metaphor of artificial silk can also be found in the title of Irmgard Keun's novel *Das kunstseidene Mädchen* (1931), published in English as *The Artificial Silk Girl*, trans. Basil Creighton (London: Chatto and Windus, 1933).

20. Rosa Mayreder, quoted in Hanna von Vollmer-Heitmann, *Wir sind von Kopf bis Fuss auf Liebe eingestellt: Die zwanziger Jahre* (Hamburg: Ernst Kabel, 1993), 44.

21. Moreck, *Das weibliche Schönheitsideal im Wandel der Zeiten* (Munich: Franz Hanfstaengl, 1925), 282.

22. "Was sagen Sie bloss zu Fräulein Mia?" *BIZ* 51 (1927), 2127–2128. The reference is to "Sag, wer mag das Männlein sein?" from the children's song "Ein Männlein steht im Walde." Young women's androgynous looks inspired a similar contest under the title "Bub oder Mädel?" *BIZ* 21 (1928): 912.

23. For example, see Jean Lasserre, "Das Schönheitsgeschäft," *Der Querschnitt* 12 (1932): 638–643.

24. Mentioned by Westphal, *Berliner Konfektion und Mode*, 79.

25. J. C. Flugel, *The Psychology of Clothes* (New York: International Universities Press, 1971), 162.

26. Georg Simmel, "On Fashion," in *On Individuality and Social Form: Selected Writings*, ed. Donald Levine (Chicago: University of Chicago Press, 1971), 310.

27. Ibid., 303–304.

28. Ibid., 303.

29. Joanne Finkelstein, *The Fashioned Self* (Philadelphia: Temple University Press, 1991), 9. As an example of the renewed interest in fashion from a feminist perspective, see Shari Benstock and Suzanne Ferris, eds., *On Fashion* (New Brunswick: Rutgers University Press, 1994).

30. Simmel, "Fashion," 312.

31. Kracauer, "Cult of Distraction: On Berlin's Picture Palaces" (1926), trans. Thomas Y. Levin, *New German Critique*, no. 40 (Winter 1987): 94, 96.

TEN

Lustmord:
Inside the Windows of the Metropolis

Beth Irwin Lewis

When this essay was conceived in the early 1980s, it could well have been titled "An incredulous view into gendered discourse in art history." As a historian wandering into the fields of art historians, I was stunned by the images of mutilated women's corpses that I kept uncovering and was even more appalled to find that the infrequent treatment of the images in catalogs managed to contain them fully within the formalistic mode of composition and colors. Otto Dix's *Lustmord* watercolor (1922)—a birthday present to his wife—was considered, by one writer, to present a particularly beautiful melding of diagonal forms and liquid reds. Haunted by the ferocity and technical brilliance of the works, I offered an intense graduate seminar at the University of California, Los Angeles, in the winter of 1985, "Violence against Women in 20th-Century German Art," in which we wrestled over the genesis and significance of these mutilated bodies. When I presented the first tentative version of the paper, a distinguished art historian accused me of voicing an interpretation that was dangerously congruent with National Socialist attacks on German avant-garde art and artists. Instead, he argued, these disfigured and dismembered bodies should be read as part of the symbolic vocabulary of political dissent raised by left-wing artists against a corrupt society.

In the decade since that day, the scholarly world, provoked and inspired by feminist critics, has produced a plethora of books and articles that explore the representation of violence in modernist art forms and that take seriously the gendered historical specificity of the human body. We have learned to look at what is represented, instead of only seeking symbolic formulations. From the pioneering work of Carol Duncan, Susan Griffin, and Susan Gubar[1] to the recent ambitious book on *Lustmord* by Maria Tatar,[2] we have come to understand how deeply misogynist violence is embedded within modernist thinking and art forms. This is not the place to attempt a review of the literature, I only want to underline the profound shift that has occurred when Weimar sexual cynicism[3] has become an accepted topic in the intellectual scene.

It is, however, appropriate to celebrate those publications that consider these Lustmord images. Several early studies examined aspects of specific paintings by Grosz, Dix, and Davringhaus.[4] Hanne Bergius has touched on sexual murder within the chaotic dadaist visions of the metropolis.[5] Reinhold Heller has argued that calculated provocation and commercial success were crucial factors in the creation of these images.[6] Kathrin Hoffmann-Curtius has published significant studies that deconstruct Grosz's images to demonstrate the multiple layers of political and gendered meaning contained in the works.[7] Most recently, Maria Tatar has provided us with a complex book on Lustmord that ranges from the sensational serial murderers of Weimar through the art of Dix and Grosz to Döblin's *Berlin, Alexanderplatz,* Fritz Lang's *M,* and Alfred Hitchcock's *Psycho.* Her stated aim is "making the victims visible and understanding the cultural significance of the violated female corpse" in these works of art.

My short essay, reprinted here, shared that fundamental aim of insisting on the female identity—the human integrity—of the violated corpses, rather than accepting their use as empty bodies to be manipulated for extraneous significance. Our studies differ, however, not only in length and breadth but also in approach. Written at a time when many were still skeptical about feminist approaches to history,[8] my essay searched historical sources to explore the multiple social and cultural issues surrounding the "woman question," whereas Tatar draws on recent literary and film theory to find an aesthetic and psychological understanding of the inner motives of the artists and writers. Since my essay was written in an effort to draw attention to these disturbing images, it seems appropriate to present it as it was written with only minor changes, recognizing that others have extended and deepened the discussion in remarkably satisfactory ways.

At the end of June 1917, two months after being discharged from a military asylum, George Grosz, writing to his close friend Otto Schmalhausen, discussed his new large paintings of city scenes. His description of the chaotic street scene intermingled violence and sex with the technology of the modern city. Screams of women giving birth, jangling telephones, knuckle-dusters and Solingen knives resting in the trouser pocket of the pimp, Circe turning men into swine, gramophone music, and murder by strangling in a dusty cellar—all these Grosz called the "emotions of the metropolis," which he executed with a remarkable palette of reds.[9] In this letter, Grosz was probably referring to two of his major paintings of 1917–1918, *Metropolis* and *Dedicated to Oscar Panizza;* however, the theme of the suspicious and bestial world of the streets and of the life inside the windows was not a new one for him. It was the dominant subject in his first published works, both drawings and poetry, in journals and portfolios. In the *Erste George Grosz Mappe* (1917), seven of the nine lithographs were street scenes in which windows in multistory buildings revealed scenes of seduction, assault, and suicide. In the twenty prints of the *Kleine Grosz Mappe* of the same year fourteen showed street scenes, and the long, expressionist title-page poem was a verbal counterpart to the drawings in which the windows of the city displayed drinking, sex, murder, and mayhem.[10]

The windows serve as a catalog of the signs of degeneracy—the stigmata of a pathological age, according to Max Nordau—attributed to the modern metropolis.[11] In his poem Grosz expressed this view of the degeneration within the city characterizing those who inhabit the dingy streets and toppling tenements as

> an always evil people, degenerate,
> meaty-handed, with ball-like feet.

Looking from the outside in, Grosz presented domestic scenes during the First World War in which people commit suicide, fight and murder, or stare in bleak desolation out onto streets where funeral hearses mingle with respectable burghers and degenerate figures.

The first critics who wrote about Grosz concentrated on his brutal vision of the metropolis and his disturbing view inside the windows. Theodor Däubler, in the earliest review of his work in 1916, described Grosz's penchant for portraying the windows of the city with violent scenes within and, in the following year in a major art journal, stated that in Grosz's drawings one did not look, as is usual, *out* of a window but instead looked *into* windows like stacked boxes containing quarrelsome, sentimental, murderous people. Even the deep cellars, Däubler said, contained raging suicides, sadists, drunks, gamblers, and whores.[12]

By 1918, Däubler developed his theme further, seeing Grosz as passionately affirming violent modern urban life, even the bitter life within the tenements of the great city. Grosz's tenements virtually exploded, said Däubler, from the force of the emotions raging within: itching, cringing, rioting, rutting.[13] Each of Däubler's articles was accompanied with drawings and poems by Grosz that confirmed his observations (fig. 10.1).

Within this catalog of passion that Grosz portrayed in word and line and that critics discussed was the Lustmord (sex or sexual murder). In the second part of the title-page poem, published in 1932 under the title "Berlin, 1917," Grosz intimated a scene of sexual violence.

> Gloomily the overcoat flaps at the pimp's bones,
> Back bent, brass knuckles fixed,
> Descending with a sharp Solingen knife
> Deep into tenements
> Into fur shops and silk houses
> Or coal cellars
> Afterwards one sometimes finds a bloody
> Piece of taffeta or a wool stocking
> Or the bill with a handprint.[14]

In his drawings and paintings of sexual murders, Grosz was more explicit. Several of the paintings were published in the early reviews of his work and the descriptions by avant-garde critics are surprisingly matter-of-fact, concentrating on the formal elements of the works. For example, Däubler wrote in 1917, "Grosz also

Figure 10.1. George Grosz (German, 1893–1959), *Menschen in der Strasse* (People in the Street) (1915–16), from the portfolio *Erste George Grosz-Mappe*. Reprinted courtesy of the Los Angeles County Museum of Art, The Robert Gore Rifkind Center for German Expressionist Studies. Museum Number: M.82.288.71e.

painted many a Lustmord. . . . The red of the blood stains and marks intertwines with the arabesques of the imitation Genoese damask carpet."[15]

This acceptance of sexual murder as an expected manifestation of the nasty underworld of the metropolis can be viewed as an extension of the bourgeois preoccupation with the degeneracy and corruption of urban life at the end of the century. Grosz himself clearly viewed the prostitute, both alive and dead, as very much part of bourgeois life. In *World of the Bourgeoisie,* drawn in July 1918,[16] Grosz integrated both respectably conventional prostitutes and those engaged in sadistic practices into a crowded urban scene presided over by a top-hatted aristocrat and a straight-laced burgher seated at a table. In this corrupt metropolis, Grosz included a truncated image of the Lustmord: a bloody knife and a dismembered female torso with lash marks on her buttocks rest on the table of the burgher. Furthermore, the bloody knife connects the torso to the profile of the artist himself.[17]

In this essay, I shall address the question of why Grosz and other avant-garde artists of his generation chose to present images of violated and dismembered women in bleak urban settings. I shall argue that these artists portrayed domestic violence in its extreme form—the Lustmord—because of pervasive social anxieties about the role of women that many of the artists and intellectuals shared with the urban middle classes in this period. These urban anxieties were transposed into the "woman question," which *Brockhaus* defined in 1898 as "the totality of problems and demands that have most recently been called forth by the transformation of society and its ways of life, with respect to the position of the female sex among modern peoples." The driving force that raised these problems and demands was, according to *Brockhaus,* the women's movement that made "the principle of the relation of the sexes one to another" into an issue.[18] A second theme of the essay is that these artists, who constituted the second generation of German expressionists or the generation of 1914,[19] consciously turned to popular urban culture for artistic themes to express their own anxieties.

Scholars have convincingly demonstrated the misogynistic response of artists and writers at the turn of the century to social changes within the industrial world, particularly the increasingly visible women's movement and the unsettling of gender roles within the bourgeoisie. Artists of the 1890s, they argue, objectified their anxiety about women in the images of the seductive femme fatale and the dangerous animalistic woman.[20] The artists who came of age on the eve of the war—the generation of 1914—were affected by a different complex of cultural and social changes. As adolescents, they consumed the violent and pornographic trash literature and itinerant films that had their heyday in Germany in the decade before the First World War. As young men, they became enamored with the misogynistic ideas of the earlier generation of symbolists, shortly before most of them had to confront service in the war, which was, for many, traumatic. Most of these young men were aware of the turn-of-the-century sexology that sought to define normative sexual activity for both male and female. At the same time, troubling social problems associated with the metropolis—such as the rising visibility of prostitution, contraceptive usage, abortion, venereal diseases, sexual promiscuity, and pornography—combined with Darwinian ideas produced a preoccupation on the part of many intellectuals with degeneracy that was linked with woman. A critical factor was the uncertainty and anxiety occasioned by the disruption of bourgeois sexual roles that accompanied these social changes brought about by urban modernization and intensified by the First World War.

Grosz started drawing sex murders in 1912–1913, several years before the war. The earliest examples of the Lustmord theme in his work were presented in a hazy, stylized fashion, clearly inspired by images from popular culture and from his reading of horror novels. Grosz often recounted in later years that he was fascinated as a child by the horror stories shown in primitive peep shows in country fairs. He liked to read newspaper accounts of sensational murders and he devoured trashy pornographic, adventure, and detective novels. A voracious reader of fantastic and demonic writers, he was particularly fond of Gustav Meyrink, Hanns Heinz Ewers, and Edgar Allan Poe; hence, the title of one of his early depictions of a man murdering a woman: *Double Murder in the Rue Morgue*, dedicated to E. A. Poe. In the decades before the war, pulp novels, sold in installments, and cheap pamphlet stories constituted a lucrative trade throughout Germany, so extensive that one scholar has claimed that "the world picture of millions of late 19th-century Germans was formed more by pamphlet stories than anything else."[21] Estimates of annual sales on the eve of the war range from 25 million to 300 million. The most popular colporteur novels combined violence and sex; Victor von Falk's *The Executioner of Berlin*, possibly the best-selling novel in nineteenth-century Germany with over a million copies sold, included graphic descriptions of murders, executions, dismemberments, torture, and kidnapping in its three thousand pages.[22] Beginning in the 1880s, the covers of the pamphlet stories displayed multicolored scenes of sensational, violent acts.[23] Itinerant films, introduced in 1895, did not lag far behind in portraying endless cycles of violence and sadism. The cinemas spread so rapidly that by 1914, millions of lower-class Germans were viewing films each day in over twenty-five hundred cinema houses.[24] Together, the trash novels and the cinema constituted a burgeoning urban culture, providing the working urban classes with escape into the windows of distant exotic worlds or nearby urban underworlds.

Grosz attested to the power of the pamphlet novels and primitive films over his imagination in his autobiographical statements, first published in 1929, where he recounted both titles and plots of the ones he most relished and reproduced an illustration from *Jack the Mysterious Maiden Killer*, a childhood book he still owned.[25] In 1943 he planned to dedicate his autobiography to several men, including the author of his favorite dime novels.[26] Not surprisingly, given Grosz's penchant for expressing the same ideas in written and visual form, a long series of Grosz drawings from 1912 to 1914 have the gruesome and exotic quality of the pulp novels. Scenes of harems, family tragedies, modern Bluebeards, and sailors of death disposing of female victims mixed with the predominant image—that of the

Lustmord. These sex murders took place in prostitutes' rooms, disordered, with indications of alcoholism and debauchery, both believed at that time to be characteristics of urban degeneration. The sense of uncanny agitation in most of these images was emphasized by Grosz's use of fine, spidery lines to envelop the figures.

Although Grosz reveled in these tales, many in the educated middle and upper classes did not. Reacting against the widespread popularity of these cheap, colorful, and trashy manifestations of popular culture, middle-class crusaders by the late 1890s mounted campaigns against the pornographic and violent books and films, which they charged had deleterious effects on young people and the lower classes. Forming a large number of Morality Associations, the purity crusaders agitated in journals, newspapers, and demonstrations in front of various city councils and state legislatures. By 1912, limited forms of censorship were put into place. These crusades were significant for the public debate and attention that they generated over the linked themes of sexuality and violence in popular culture at the time when Grosz and his peers were adolescents. Scholars who have examined these crusades speak of the "unprecedented obsession with and fear of sexuality" at that time.[27]

This obsession with sexuality also emerged in the high culture of the prewar period. The fear of women became visible in misogynist writings by intellectuals and in the preoccupation with sexuality in the medical world throughout Europe. The science of sexology that emerged in the late nineteenth century was both a response to and a manifestation of anxiety about moral and national degeneracy. Sexology was an attempt to define and then regulate sexual pathologies that were perceived to underlie patterns of national degeneration. A basic axiom among sexologists was that sexuality was biologically determined, not socially constructed. The concern was to define respectable bourgeois roles or, conversely, to liberate people from social constraints and enable them to fulfill "normal" biological needs. Whether reformist or conservative, the sexologists agreed that woman is determined by her biology, that her being is overwhelmingly sexual, and that her purpose is reproductive.[28] This concentration on woman's sexual nature and reproductive purpose indicated that underneath the concern for respectable and healthy sexual norms lay considerable anxiety about the threat to the traditional male-dominant role that the "woman question" was posing. That a woman's normal nature was fulfilled by sexual relations and reproduction was a powerful argument for maintaining traditional roles against women's demands for equal rights and independence.[29]

The assumption of the fundamentally sexual nature of woman underlay the misogyny of writers in Germany, Austria, and France who cultivated a reactionary view of women. Drawing on Schopenhauer's pessimistic study *On Women*, which was reissued in 1908 in an edition of fifty thousand,[30] on Nietzsche's brief aphoristic condemnation in *Beyond Good and Evil* of woman as a mindless and soulless being, and on Strindberg's unbounded hatred of and fascination with strong aggressive women, writers and artists compulsively explored the nature of the battle of the sexes. In *Die Frau und die Kunst* (1908), Karl Scheffler, editor of *Kunst und Künstler,* attacked the women's rights movement because it denied the fundamental, eternal, and natural polarity of the sexes. "Seldom," he wrote, "has the ancient trial between man and woman been conducted so noisily and indecently as in our day."[31] Arguing that man's true nature is active, creative, and individualized but that woman's true nature is passive, imitative, undifferentiated, and childlike, Scheffler insisted that man fulfills his nature by creative activity. When woman, however, attempts to become active or creative, she either becomes a poor imitation of man or destroys herself.[32] In his book Scheffler, an influential critic, echoed the ultimate statement of pseudoscientific sexology presented by Otto Weininger in his 1903 book *Sex and Character,* in which he defined woman totally as a sexual being (*Geschlechtswesen*) who has no consciousness, no soul, and no existence beyond her sexuality. As pure sexual being, the female, living only for the phallus, threatens all that is transcendent and godlike in the male. Men, as moral beings, can only be destroyed by the immoral sensual omnipotence of the female.[33] Weininger himself chose suicide after he completed his passionate discourse, but Weininger's woman, possessed by her sexual organs and her omnivorous appetite for the phallus, emerged in startling clarity in the images of the femme fatale.[34] The expressionist receptivity to Weininger's writing was reflected in Herwarth Walden's posthumously published articles in 1910 in the first issues of *Der Sturm.*

Weininger's woman appeared around 1912 in a series of Grosz's drawings of Circe, whose imperious sexuality reduced men to degraded cringing animals. In other drawings, under her direction an ape with knife and ax slaughtered and beheaded a man, handing her the gory head. The images conflate Salome, Judith, Circe, Poe, and cheap novels. Grosz's drawings, expressing the pessimism of high culture, were indebted to the images of urban mass culture. When he came to Berlin in 1912, Grosz was not only reading horror novels, he was enamored—as were most of the young artists—by fashionable writers, all of whom were noted for agonizing over woman's sexuality: "We worshiped Zola, Strindberg, Weininger, Wedekind—naturalistic enlighteners, anarchistic self-tormenters, devotees of death, and erotomaniacs."[35] Filled with the diatribes of Nietzsche and Schopenhauer, Grosz was particularly drawn to "the truly great Huysmans and Strindberg,"[36] whose works he read, admired, and wrote about throughout his life. He remembered seeing a series of Strindberg plays in Berlin at this time. His letters, poetry, and drawings were awash with his own fascination, influenced by his reading, with sex and death. In a letter to his friend Otto Schmalhausen in 1916, he used language from Weininger to analyze Otto's problems.[37] Däubler, describing the denizens of Grosz's street scenes in 1917, referred to "a criminal, in Weininger's sense." Yet Grosz also shared Weininger's awe before the eternal reproductive power of women. Writing about a childhood experience—whether actual or fantasy—of peering through a window and finding within a woman undressing, Grosz, transfixed by the fleshy vision, concluded, "It was as if someone I don't know had shown me a symbol, something eternal—for as long as we exist, there will be the symbol of nudity: woman as the everlasting source and continuation of our species."[38] Enthralled by the power of sex, fearful of women embodying that power, Grosz and his generation of artists, like Bohemians before them, glorified and vilified the prostitute. He read Flaubert and de Maupassant and reveled in the prostitutes of Berlin, for, as he said, "The Friedrichstadt was alive with whores."[39]

Grosz's observation coincided with contemporary controversies over the conspicuous growth and visibility of prostitution in German cities in the decades before the First World War. As a result of social and economic changes produced by rapid industrialization, prostitutes not only increased in numbers but also spread out of the old police-regulated bordellos into the streets of the industrial cities in Germany. In 1897, Berlin police regulated 3,000 registered prostitutes, but estimated there were another 40,000 to 50,000 unregistered prostitutes in the city. By 1900, estimates for prostitutes in Germany varied between 100,000 and 200,000; by 1914, they had reached 330,000.[40] In addition to prostitutes becoming more visible and, therefore, more threatening to middle-class morals, a whole lower-class entertainment industry grew up around prostitution in the cities: cafés, cabarets, beer halls, and music halls. With the prostitutes also came venereal diseases that reached epidemic proportions in the early years of the century; according to one source, VD was second only to tuberculosis in the number of cases treated in hospitals.[41] Women, as prostitutes, were perceived as carriers of sickness and death. The connection between sex and death was concrete and physical. Prostitutes, usually as victims, were also involved in the rising crime statistics. The number of sexual crimes and homicides increased: in Prussia in 1900, 191 women were killed; that number rose to 365 in 1914. While the raw numbers seem low to our violence-saturated minds, they caused alarm in the prewar period, particularly the female homicides, because the newspapers tended to run lurid stories on murdered women, heightening the perception of women as victims of the industrial city. Women who were single, living and working independently in Berlin and other cities, were more likely to be murder victims than women who remained in traditional roles in rural areas.[42] Women, therefore, became visible symbols for fears about the degeneration and corruption produced by industrial city life. Morality Associations, in addition to crusading against pornographic books and films, were actively trying in the years before the war to cleanse the city streets of the social disorder represented by the prostitutes.[43]

Another form of degeneration—again connected with women—that raised national anxieties at this time was the declining birthrate and rise of abortions in Germany. Both of these phenomena were occurring in other European countries, but the proportions of each in Germany were sufficient to alarm authorities who began to talk about a "birth strike." The downward trend of the birthrate, begun in the 1870s, became most visible after the turn of the century, and declined precipitously during and after the First World War. In 1914, there were 27 births per thousand persons; in 1922, 11.5 per thousand.[44] Particularly worrisome was the declining birthrate among the lower middle and lower classes. Motivation for the re-

fusal to bear children appears to have gone, in many cases, beyond fear of pregnancy to a rejection of male sexual demands.[45] Despite increased prosecution of
women, abortions increased from an estimated one hundred thousand in 1912 to
one million in 1931. In 1914, half of all German women were estimated to have
had at least one abortion. By 1930, that estimate became two abortions per
woman and abortions exceeded live births.[46] Already by 1914, fears raised by ille-
gal abortions and by the specter of a birth strike brought debates in the Prussian
parliament and the Reichstag. Newspaper articles not only blamed socialism and
feminism for this decline of births, but charged the birth strike with undermining
the health and strength of the nation.[47]

Anxiety over all these forms of urban degeneration, from venereal disease,
pornography, and crime to abortions and the falling birthrate, reached levels of
active agitation and publicity in the decade before the war. Observers believed
that sexuality and confused sexual roles lay at the basis of the degeneration. As
early as 1888 in his exhaustive catalog of contemporary sexual pathologies,
Richard Krafft-Ebing had posited that advanced urban cultures generated degenerate sexuality that would undermine the nation unless controlled.[48] The locus of
this degenerate sexuality was generally seen to be the modern metropolis that accelerated vice and perversions. For many, a fundamental factor in urban degeneracy was the women's movement with its heatedly debated effort to overturn traditional sexual roles. It was in the cities—Hamburg, Berlin—that women were
organizing and clamoring for rights that had hitherto been the prerogative of
men. Both the liberal and the socialist women's movements, begun in midcentury,
came actively to the political scene in the 1880s. Their period of most vocal and
radical agitation lasted until women were granted the right of assembly in 1908.
This coincided, as outlined above, with the period of the most intense agitation
and discussion on questions of prostitution, pornography, and sexuality. Karl
Kraus, an acerbic observer of his time, complained in a lead article in *Die Fackel* in
1912, "My head is whirring from the women's movement, the women's exhibition,
and such things at home and at work. Everywhere people are jewing [*jüdeln*]
about problems, sexual problems."[49] After 1908 women's organizations increased
substantially in number and size, although some historians argue that they became
less militant. After supporting the war effort, in part, by entering the workforce in
large numbers, women were granted the vote in the November Revolution of
1918.[50] Among the women's continuing demands were the rights to education, to
enter the professions, and to gain civil and marital equality.

Most of the avant-garde artists and writers in Germany were not receptive to
these demands that would bring women into equality within bourgeois society.
There was sympathy among some—for example, *Die Brücke* or the circle around
Otto Gross—for freeing women from the moral strictures of bourgeois marriage,
but this was based on a view of woman as essentially a sexual being who should be
free to become totally sexual—and freely available to men. Women, in this view,
should not aspire to education or careers because that might inhibit their sexual-

ity.[51] Grosz expressed a Nietzschean rejection of intelligent women in a 1918 letter, even as he was later in his autobiography to exalt their reproductive force and sexuality.

> Between us: I shit on profundity in women, generally they combine it with a hateful predominance of masculine characteristics, angularity, and skinny thighs; I agree with Kerr (the critic): "I alone have intelligence."[52]

All of his drawings, letters, and poems in the years before and during the war indicate that Grosz not only was unsympathetic to the women's movement but that even while he was fascinated by woman, he saw her as a creature of the city who demonstrated various degrees of sexually degenerate behavior. This became focused during the war for Grosz, and many other young artists, into the harshly punitive image of the Lustmord.

An acquaintance in the circle of friends around Grosz in Berlin suggested an explanation for this violent turn against woman. Magnus Hirschfeld, a radical sexologist who founded the Institute for Sexual Science in Berlin in 1919 and who strongly supported the women's movement, claimed in the twenties that the war constituted a major turning point in moral history, marked by the emergence of women in considerable numbers in the workforce and by the dissolution of the old bourgeois moral standards.[53] Women were mobilized during the war to take positions of all kinds left by men called to the front. They entered into the heaviest forms of construction work and outnumbered men by 75 percent in light industry. The proportion of women in industrial jobs rose from 22 percent in 1913 to 35 percent in 1918. Not only did women leave domestic work to invade the industrial sector, they were increasingly employed in visible official positions such as mail carriers, postal clerks, and railroad guards.[54]

Although women became a decisive economic factor in the war machine, male resistance to women stepping into male jobs began almost immediately. Magda Trott, writing in 1915, described organized action in offices by men against the new "intruders."[55] Meta Kraus-Fessel, a colleague of Hirschfeld's, agreed with him about the great changes wrought by the war in women's economic and social position, but she also pointed out that men were threatened by the possibility of women achieving equality with them and made considerable efforts during and after the war to curtail those gains.[56] Hirschfeld himself cited frequent instances of brutal and violent acts by returning soldiers against wives who were suspected of exhibiting too much freedom. He accused newspapers of deliberately fostering suspicion and violence on the part of the veterans against women. He also, however, charged women—as did other writers, including Freud—with widespread sexual aggressiveness that elicited the violent male response.[57]

Popular medical books about sex-starved women appeared at the time with titles like *The Rape of Men by Women* by Hans Menzel or *The Sexual Unfaithfulness of Woman*.[58] The latter was written by a much-published physician, E. Heinrich Kisch, in 1917. Within a year, it had gone through three editions and had been enlarged from 208 pages into two volumes, *The Adulteress* and *The Mercenary Woman* (Weib). These titles and the violent acts against women suggest the heightened anxiety about sexuality that the war engendered. As early as September 1914 at a meeting of the medical Society for Sexual Science, a speaker discussed the problem of antisocial perversity being released by the war, especially the danger of sexual inversion or crossing of sexual lines as women wanted to become soldiers and men refused to bear weapons. The implication of the talk was clear: that the war was a proving ground for masculinity and that failure to meet that test could create disturbances in sexuality and sexual roles.[59] The disruption of traditional patterns on the home front, the threat that women posed to male jobs, and the sexual anxiety produced by the war experience appeared early in the war in the work of artists.

During the war years, Kokoschka, Kirchner, Klinger, and Barlach—all artists who had already achieved recognition—created graphic cycles and paintings on the theme of the artist's violent struggle against a woman who would stifle his creativity. Kirchner painted his *Self-Portrait as a Soldier* in 1915 after a brief period of artillery service. In it he expressed his neurotic anxiety about the destruction of his creative ability—through his fear of war, but also through his fear of woman. The castration imagery of the bloody stump and the female nude behind him connect the fear of loss of artistic potency with contact with woman. This fear seemed to have been precipitated for Kirchner, and for other older artists, by the war. In 1905 and 1918, he executed two graphic cycles in which man and woman encounter each other. In the first woodcut cycle, the meeting is untroubled, though rather odd. The same meeting portrayed after his military service in the 1918 cycle is tense and fraught with hostility. In the whole second cycle, Kirchner made it very clear that the "wide and dreadful" battle could only be resolved through the woman's submission to the artist's need for creative dominance.[60] Shortly before the second cycle, Kirchner created a series of explicit lithographs of perverse forms of sexuality—a visualization of Krafft-Ebing's catalog of sexual perversions.[61] In the middle of the war, an older artist, Max Klinger, shifted from allegorical portrayals of women to an eerie series of images in a graphic cycle depicting the demonic power of woman and the necessity of violently subduing that power.[62] Klinger, whose work was closely based on his reading of Schopenhauer, seemed haunted by both phallic and castration images.

While the older artists seemed to link their attack on woman to fears of loss of their already established artistic power, the younger generation moved to an artistic assault on woman that is stylistically much more nasty and vicious. Grosz served for six months in the military before being discharged as unfit for service in May 1916. Until he was recalled to service in January 1917, he experienced a period of intense dread of being called up again that resulted in the poetry and drawings discussed at the beginning of this essay. Three images drawn by Grosz at this time demonstrate the basic iconography of the Lustmord that emerged in his work and the work of other artists: the degenerate man wielding fist or knife and the sexually aggressive female. The hostile relationship between them is epitomized in *Married Life* (Ecce Homo, pl. 63), where the symbolic battle of the sexes of the late nineteenth century has turned into an ugly fistfight in a barren boxlike tenement room with windows looking out onto the factories of the industrial city. Grosz leaves no doubt in this scene that the man will brutalize the woman.[63] In a 1916 self-portrait drawing,[64] Grosz portrayed himself as the artist dandy or voyeur of the violent relationship that takes place in the modern metropolis. Significantly, Grosz here linked himself not only with the bloody body of a woman but also with the stereotype of the urban criminal degenerate, defined by Cesare Lombroso and recalling his own poetic assertion that cities are inhabited by "böse Menschen, entartete." In a drawing done in 1915, Grosz's identification with the degenerate criminal was more explicit (fig. 10.2). The brutal figure, barely recognizable as a human, standing over a bloody distorted woman's body, carries the slender reed cane, Grosz's trademark that he adopted from reading Barbey d'Aurévilly.[65]

Grosz's second brief tour of duty was spent in a hospital and a mental asylum, from which he sent vivid descriptions of his nightmarish experiences, his overwhelming sense of death, his longing to escape to exotic lands, all conveyed with a heavy dose of sex and obscenity. Writing to Schmalhausen from the sanitarium in April 1917, he exclaimed,

> Where have the nights gone, Pierrot? . . . Where are the women? The adventurers??—And my friends hacked up, scattered, duped, bewitched into battle-gray comrades of slaughter!! . . . Oh finale of the inferno, of vile murdering here and murdering there—end of the witches' sabbath, of the most gruesome castration, of slaughter, cadaver upon cadaver, already green rotting corpses glow among the rank and file!—If only it would end soon!![66]

He was released from the asylum when Magnus Hirschfeld testified that he was not fit to serve.[67] Back in Berlin, he produced two of his strongest and best-known drawings: *Sex Murder in Ackerstrasse* (fig. 10.3) and *After It Was Over, They Played Cards* (fig. 10.4). The fanciful quality of Grosz's prewar sex murders gave way here to hard, crisp depictions of matter-of-fact brutality. "Jack, the Killer"—another title for the first drawing that recalls Grosz's favorite book, *Jack the Mysterious Maiden Killer*—is washing his hands after his bloody assault on the woman whose head is nowhere to be seen. This room displays all the symbols of a petit bourgeois existence in the metropolis. Located in a working-class district of Berlin that can be glimpsed through the window, it is identified by the reference in the title to Akerstrasse, a tough street in Wedding.[68] In the second drawing, the criminal degeneracy of the murderers is displayed by their casual card play after dismembering, with ax and razor, the female body in the box. Grosz carefully delineated the basement tenement room in which live these Lomborosian figures or urban apaches, one of whom displays his wealth with his cigar and watch chain. Another *Sex Murderer* from 1916 depicted an aggressive, degenerate man, knife in hand, trousers open, standing in a barren room between a bed with two muti-

Figure 10.2. George Grosz, untitled ink drawing (1915). Reprinted courtesy of George Grosz Estate, Princeton, New Jersey.

lated women's bodies and a table topped with liquor bottle and glass.[69] All of these works were rooted in the themes of the prewar pulp novels or newspaper accounts of murders, but the stylistic shift to brutal clarity must be related to Grosz's own experience of the insanity of the war and grotesque encounters with men in the hospitals.

muse behind them

32

Figure 10.3. George Grosz (German, 1893–1959), *Lustmord in der Ackerstrasse* (Sex Murder in Ackerstrasse) (1916–17), from the book *Ecce Homo*. Reprinted courtesy of the Los Angeles County Museum of Art, The Robert Gore Rifkind Center for German Expressionist Studies, purchased with funds provided by Anna Bing Arnold, Museum Associates Purchase Fund and Deaccession Funds. Museum Number: 83.1.73.32.

Figure 10.4. George Grosz (German, 1893–1959), *Apachen* (After It Was Over, They Played Cards) (1916–17), from the book *Ecce Homo*. Reprinted courtesy of the Los Angeles County Museum of Art, The Robert Gore Rifkind Center for German Expressionist Studies, purchased with funds provided by Anna Bing Arnold, Museum Acquisition Fund and Deaccession Funds. Museum Number: 83.1.73.58.

By 1918, Grosz moved from drawings and watercolors of Lustmords in shabby rooms to oil paintings of assaulted women in the streets of the metropolis. Titled variously *The Little Woman Killer,* or *John the Woman Killer* (fig. 10.5), these paintings present desperate males—"böse Menschen, entartete, grosshändig"—who have just slaughtered a woman. The degenerate character of the men is firmly established in all of these drawings and paintings not only by the vicious act but also by the stigmata of urban degeneration that had been defined by criminologists and anthropologists in the nineteenth century: sloping forehead, large nose, jutting jaw, small eyes, dark visages. In one image, there is the strong suggestion that the murderer is a Jew, a factor that further emphasizes the urban locus of the degenerate act.[70] Wielding knives, teeth clenched, the men grimly pursue their victim or leave the mutilated and bloody body in the street. Fully clothed in all of these murder scenes, they are dwarfed by the sexually powerful woman whose hacked-off head and arms serve to emphasize her potent and threatening sexuality by focusing attention on her breasts and torso.[71] Ravished and decapitated, the corpse remains palpably and bloomingly sexual. In all of these works Grosz used cubistic

Figure 10.5. George Grosz, *John der Frauenmörder* (John the Woman Killer) (1918). Reproduced courtesy of Hamburger Kunsthalle. © Elke Walford (photographer).

displacement and windows that are simultaneously mirrors to create an interpenetration of interior and exterior space in the urban world in which these crimes take place.[72] A similar interweaving of perspectives and complicated exterior and interior urban spaces marks *Metropolis* (1916),[73] an oil painting in which a living prostitute on the street and an identical headless body sprawled on a bed form the center of sinister, lascivious, and innocent lust from male flaneurs.

Images of despoiled women and degraded men were not confined to the works of Grosz at this time. In 1918 Max Reinhardt, for whom Grosz was later to design sets, was able to mount the first public production in Berlin of Frank Wedekind's *Pandora's Box,* in which Lulu, the precocious, flamboyantly sexual femme fatale, became the victim of Jack the Ripper. In the last years of the war, another friend of

Figure 10.6. Heinrich Maria Davringhausen, *Der Lustmörder* (The Sex Murderer) (1917). Reproduced courtesy of Bayerische Staatsgemäldesammlungen, Munich.

Grosz's, Heinrich Maria Davringhausen, painted a series of oils in which he picked up the theme of the sex murderer whose actions take place in commonplace rooms within the city. In *The Sex Murderer* of 1917 (fig. 10.6), an Olympia-like woman, modeled on Manet's portrayal of aggressive sexuality, shares the canvas space with a huge window overlooking a cityscape crowded with high apartment buildings. The relaxed domestic scene with a cat on the end of the bed is disturbed by one other figure in the room: a man under the bed, looking at a pistol on the bedside table.[74] This oil was displayed at the Goltz Gallery in Munich in 1919, where two of Grosz's "Woman Killer" paintings were exhibited the following spring.

Another artist infamous for his appalling depictions of ravaged women was Otto Dix, a friend of Grosz from their Dresden days who was as laconic a writer as Grosz was effusive. Dix spent the whole war at the front, where he had firsthand experience of conditions in the trenches and behind the lines. Examining those conditions throughout the war, Hirschfeld insisted that the war produced five years of "unchained atavistic impulses" and, at the same time, a repression of normal sexuality.[75] Months spent in the trenches, he wrote, produced pathological and perverse forms of sex. Military brothels behind the front lines resulted in the brutalization of sex.[76] In his *War* portfolio (1924), Dix both portrayed soldiers raping nuns and depicted whores, obscenely bloated from their lucrative trade, dwarfing soldiers who have returned from the front. Strongly influenced by his reading of Nietzsche, Dix wrote brief aphorisms in his war diaries in which he suggested an integral relationship between war and sexuality: "Money, religion, and women have been the impetus for war, but not the *fundamental cause*—that is an *eternal law.*" And again: "Actually, in the final analysis *all* war is waged over and for the vulva."[77]

On his return to civilian life, Dix continued to explore the Nietzschean cycle of life and decay, of sexuality and death.[78] From 1920 to 1922, this took the form of a series of grotesque sex murders. In 1920, he produced *Altar for Gentlemen,* an oil painting on a wood panel of an extravagantly bosomed woman and a student walking past a city residence with large shuttered windows. This innocuous work, however, masked Dix's vision of the disparity between external appearances in postwar Dresden and the inner reality of the metropolis. The shutters open up to show scenes of a brothel, in which the central window becomes an adoration of two prostitutes by wealthy customers (fig. 10.7). The right shutter of this altar is dominated by a disproportionately large prostitute, stabbed, with her throat cut, and draped off a bed—in what we could call Dix's favorite Lustmord pose. To emphasize the sexuality and death found within the respectable facades of the city, Dix also unveiled the smartly dressed, voluptuous young woman to reveal an ancient hag with enlarged genitals whose clothes contained patented false breasts, buttocks, and thighs. The fraternity student's head opened to a steamy racist brain filled with right-wing anti-Semitic slogans.

Dix's penetration behind surfaces and windows applied to himself and his own world. In two self-portraits, Dix presented himself, standing in his own Biedermeier room, dismembering a woman with vicious glee. Dix created the image, which he titled *Sex Murderer, Self-Portrait,* both as an oil painting and as an etching that was included in a major graphic cycle (fig. 10.8). Fully clothed like a cosmopolitan dandy, Dix wildly waves a bloody knife and a detached leg; pieces of a gigantic woman litter the room; her decapitated head is still screaming; blood gushes from the limbs and from his mouth. Dix dissected her with a surgical precision that allowed for a jarring anatomically correct rendition of the genitals and reproductive system that is particularly clear in the etching. He then placed his own bloody handprints all over the pieces of the figure in the oil painting, as if to paw brutally over the body. Dix executed both of these works in 1920, when he was back in Dresden as a student at the Art Academy. A fellow student years later recalled going to Dix's room—the scene of these murders—and watching Dix show off this self-portrait by standing behind the oil and moving the arm with the bloody knife.[79] Another friend recalled Dix telling him that if he had not been able to create these artistic sex murders, he could well have committed actual murder.[80] Whether either of these reminiscences was accurate, Dix definitely chose to culti-

Figure 10.7. Otto Dix, *Altar für Kavaliere* (Altar for Gentlemen) (1920). Copyright © 1996 Artists Rights Society (ARS), New York/VG Bild-Kunst, Bonn.

vate the myth of being a wild man capable of mayhem and murder.[81] In 1921, he portrayed another fantasy vision of himself surrounded by prostitutes, including one marked by the sores of venereal disease. Directly in front of his face, he placed a female corpse, raped, bleeding, and disemboweled. He balanced this with a castrated penis on the other side of the watercolor.

The following year, Dix created five more versions of raped and violated fe-

Figure 10.8. Otto Dix, *Der Lustmörder* (Sex Murderer, Self-Portrait) (1922). Copyright ©
Artists Rights Society (ARS), New York/VG Bild-Kunst, Bonn.

male corpses sprawled in urban interiors. He gave a watercolor of a woman with
her throat slit, sprawled off a pillow on the floor, titled *Scene II (Murder)*, to his wife
on her birthday.[82] Several other watercolors include a man in the scene, one of
which presents his attack and rape of a woman and another his departure from
the murdered woman. He included a gruesome disemboweling and slashing of a
woman in a cycle of graphic works called *Death and Resurrection*. Copulating dogs in
the foreground of this etching underlined the sexual nature of the murder and the

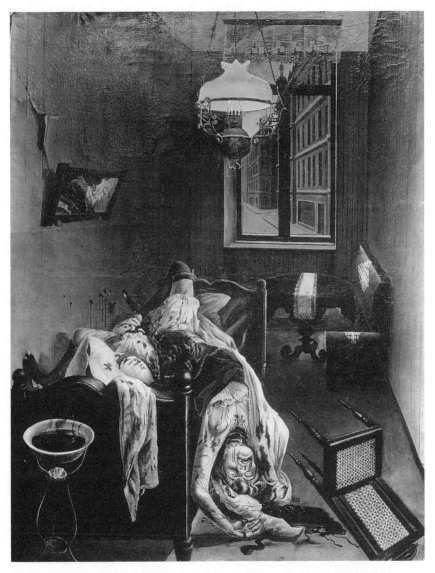

Figure 10.9. Otto Dix, *Lustmord* (Sex-Murder) (1922). Copyright © 1996 Artists Rights Society (ARS), New York/VG Bild-Kunst, Bonn.

bestiality of sexual intercourse. Another even more shocking oil painting depicted a meticulously detailed corpse whose throat and torso have been slit splattering blood across the bed and the floor on one side of the neat bourgeois room (fig. 10.9). She is draped half off a bed, again in Dix's student room in Dresden. In this room, Dix painted with fastidious care his lamp, an overturned cane chair, elaborately embroidered table covers, filmy curtains, a blood-filled washbasin, and a mirror placed strategically to reflect the mutilated body. Outside the large window that dominates the back wall is a view of orderly middle-class apartment buildings.

Dix's fascination with death and dismemberment led him to study corpses in morgues and police photographs of horrendously mutilated corpses. The iconographic source of at least two of Dix's ravaged women was in police photographs of viciously mutilated bodies at the scene of crimes, which were published by Erich Wulffen in his 1910 book, *The Sexual Criminal*.[83] Dix was reported to have owned and carefully studied this book shortly before he did the *Lustmord* oil of 1920.[84] Paul Westheim, writing in *Das Kunstblatt* in 1924, recognized that Dix's sex murders were virtually illustrations to Wulffen's text.[85] In the late twenties, Wulffen published a study in which he argued that both art and crime were human responses to the explosive drive of sexuality; therefore, he explained, criminal sexual acts were a natural and consistent theme in the history of art. His book was illustrated by visual images of Lustmord executed by contemporary German and French artists, including two of these by Dix and others by Willi Geiger, Alfred Kubin, Walter Trier, Max Beckmann, Frans Masereel, Käthe Kollwitz, and Ernst Stern.[86]

Dix's Lustmord images all date from the immediate postwar inflationary period, a period perceived at the time, even in government reports, as one marked by a wild disintegration of morals.[87] Commentators blamed this moral chaos on the war and the inflation, but particularly on the New Woman, who was loath to give up her work and return to her family role. Hans Ostwald, who published *Sittengeschichte der Inflation* (Moral History of Inflation) cited the women's rights movement as a significant factor in the "hellish carnival" of those days.[88] The eroticism of women in the inflationary years formed a leitmotiv in his book. He devoted a chapter to the social problems resulting from women leaving the home to seek work, though he ended with the certainty that good German women would return to home and hearth. Ostwald was not alone. A chorus of voices held the New Woman responsible for the breakup of the family, the epidemic of venereal diseases, illegitimate children, abortions, dancing, and cultural decadence.[89] Men blamed women for taking their jobs, even though the demobilization laws required women to give up their jobs to returning veterans. With demobilization, wrote one observer, "a horrible war broke out between male and female over bread and work."[90]

The war may have been over bread and work, but the antagonism had its roots in sexual anxieties. Carried out in visual images, the violent and sadistic attack went beyond Dix and Grosz. In 1920, Georg Scholz, who returned to Karlsruhe from three years at the front, created images of rape and torture, including a sexually perverse crucifixion of a woman that was reminiscent of Felicien Rops.[91] In 1921, Gert Wolheim, who also had three years of frontline duty, created a dreadful collage of a servant girl who was tortured to death with rakes and pitchforks.

Figure 10.10. Rudolf Schlichter, *Lustmord* (Sex Murder) (1924). Private Collection.

The collage combined the newspaper report of her death with a drawn image.[92]
After two years at the front, Erich Wegner enrolled at the Kunstgewerbeschule in
Hannover where he produced a long series of crude sex murders and dismemberments in attic rooms.[93] Also in Hannover, Kurt Schwitters placed a model of an
"abominably mutilated corpse of an unfortunate young girl, painted tomato-red,"

into the Sex Crime Cavern in his Cathedral of Erotic Misfortune.[94] In his drawings and watercolors, Rudolf Schlichter plunged deep into the world of overt sexual perversity popularly associated with postwar Berlin. One of Grosz's closest friends, Schlichter shared Grosz's love of carnival peep shows, trivial literature, and adventure stories. Schlichter, whom Grosz satirized sharply as a foot fetishist, portrayed in his work the underground world of the twenties in Berlin. Like Dix, Schlichter was deeply influenced by Nietzsche's Dionysian negation of traditional values, but Schlichter combined his study of Nietzsche with his fascination over the exotic crimes and massacres of trash novels and films. Sexual murders, suicides, hanging women, murders in public and private proliferated in Schlichter's drawings. The images that emerged from his compulsive fantasies in the early 1920s are, however, almost like calm reports of urban atrocities, visions of lonely women murdered in the great empty rooms and back streets of the modern Babylon of the great metropolis.[95] (See fig. 10.10.)

I have tried to suggest the range and intensity of violent images created by this group of avant-garde artists against woman in the modern industrialized world of the German metropolis during and after the Great War. I have also argued that these images can only make sense if they are viewed in the context of the pervasive cultural and social struggle over sexual roles that took place in German urban industrial society in the first decades of the century. In each of these images, there is an overpowering fascination with sexuality combined with an obsessive dread of woman. In the midst of the profound unsettling of boundaries between the sexes that the war accelerated, these artists' apprehension and anxiety produced vicious images that grew out of complex emotional and social responses to women's changing role. The sentence of death against woman pronounced in these images was a reactionary response that had its roots deep in contemporary cultural and social misogyny. The presence of these Lustmord images in the art of the avantgarde at this time is a sharp reminder that artistic images cannot be understood outside of their social and cultural context. Within that context, these particular images force us to go beyond the celebration of the artist as a perceptive interpreter of the period to recognize the extent to which artists were marked by contemporary fears and anxiety.

NOTES

I have received constructive criticism from presentations of various versions of this essay at Stanford University, UCLA, Pomona College, State University of New York at Stony Brook, Harvard University, and the Universities of Iowa, Wisconsin, and New Hampshire. I also presented closely related papers on dadaist misogyny at the meetings of the Midwest Modern Language Association (1987) and the German Studies Association (1988). I thank Richard Figge for polishing my German translations and Peter Paret, Arnold Lewis, Susan Figge, Joan Weinstein, and Sanda Agalidi for their uncomfortable but sustaining criticism. Peter and Lilian Grosz provided gracious and open access to the George Grosz Archive in their home. I am grateful to the Robert Gore Rifkind Center for German Expressionist Studies, Los Angeles County Museum of Art, in whose extensive library and print collection I was able to complete the research for this essay.

1. Carol Duncan, "Virility and Domination in Early Twentieth-Century Vanguard Painting," *Art Forum* 12, no. 4 (December 1973), 30–39; Susan Griffin, *Pornography and Silence: Culture's Revenge Against Nature* (New York: Harper & Row, 1981); Susan Gubar, "Representing Pornography: Feminism, Criticism, and Depictions of Female Violation," *Critical Inquiry* 13 (Summer 1987), 712–741.

2. Maria Tatar, *Lustmord: Sexual Murder in Weimar Germany* (Princeton: Princeton University Press, 1995).

3. See especially Peter Sloterdijk, *Critique of Cynical Reason*, trans. Michael Eldred (Minneapolis: University of Minnesota Press, 1987), 250–266, 499–520; and Stephen Brockmann, "Weimar Sexual Cynicism," in *Dancing on the Volcano: Essays on the Culture of the Weimar Republic*, ed. Thomas W. Kniesche and Stephen Brockmann (Columbia, S.C.: Camden House, 1994), 165–180. Klaus Theweleit provides overwhelming evidence of sexual cynicism in Weimar in *Männerphantasien* (Frankfurt: Roter Stern, 1977), translated by Stephen Conway as *Male Fantasies* (Minneapolis: University of Minnesota Press, 1985).

4. Heinrich Theissing, "George Grosz, die Morde und das Grotesque," *Festschrift für Eduard Trier*, ed. Justus Mueller-Hofstede and Werner Spies (Berlin: Gebrüder Mann Verlag, 1981), 269–284; Eva Karcher, *Eros und Tod im Werk von Otto Dix: Studien zur Geschichte des Körpers in den zwanziger Jahren* (Münster: LIT Verlag, 1984), and *Otto Dix* (Cologne: Benedikt Taschen, 1992); Wolf-Dieter Dube, " 'Der Lustmörder' von Heinrich Maria Davringhausen," *Pantheon* (April–June 1973):181–185.

5. "Painter & Paster: 'Propagandada' George Grosz," *Das Lachen Dadas: Die Berliner Dadisten und ihre Aktionen*, Werkbund Archiv, Bd 19 (Giessen: Anabas Verlag, 1989), 166–176; "Berlin als Hure Babylon," in *Die Metropole: Industriekultur in Berlin im 20. Jahrhundert*, ed. Jochen Boberg, Tilman Fichter, and Eckhart Gillen (Munich: C. H. Beck, 1986), 102–119; "Berlin: A City Drawn," in *German Realist Drawings of the 1920s*, ed. Peter Nisbet (Cambridge, Mass.: Harvard University Art Museums, Busch-Reisinger Museum, 1986), 15–30.

6. Otto Dix, "Sex Murder (Lustmord)" 1922, catalog entry, in Heller, *Art in Germany 1909–1936: From Expressionism to Resistance* (Munich: Prestel Verlag and Milwaukee Art Museum, 1990), 171–172.

7. " 'Wenn Blicke töten könnten' oder Der Künstler als Lustmörder," in *Blick-Wechsel: Konstruktionen von Männlichkeit und Weiblichkeit in Kunst und Kunstgeschichte*, ed. Ines Lindner et al. (Berlin: Dietrich Reimer Verlag, 1989), 369–393; *George Grosz: 'John, der Frauenmörder'* (Hamburg: Hamburger Kunsthalle, 1993). See also her "Erotik im Blick des George Grosz," in *George Grosz: Berlin/New York*, ed. Peter-Klaus Schuster (Berlin: Nationalgalerie and Ars Nicolai, 1995), 182–191.

8. This was presented as a paper for an interdisciplinary conference, "Culture and Metropolis: Production and Reception of Culture and the Arts in Berlin, 1900 to the Present," organized by Charles W. Haxthausen, Heidrun Suhr, and Gerhard Weiss at the University of Minnesota in October 1987 in celebration of the 750th anniversary of the city of Berlin. It was subsequently published in *Berlin: Culture and Metropolis*, ed. Charles Haxthausen and Heidrun Suhr (Minneapolis: University of Minnesota Press, 1990), 111–140.

9. George Grosz, *Briefe 1913–1959*, ed. Herbert Knust (Reinbek bei Hamburg: Rowohlt Verlag, 1979), 53–54.

10. *Erste George Grosz Mappe* (Berlin: Verlag Neue Jugend, 1917), published in the spring. *Kleine Grosz Mappe* (Berlin-Halensee: Malik Verlag, 1917), published in the fall.

11. Max Nordau, *Degeneration*, introd. George L. Mosse (New York: Howard Fertig, 1968; 1st English ed., 1895). For the development of the concept of degeneration, see J. Edward Chamberlain and Sander Gilman, eds., *Degeneration: The Dark Side of Progress* (New York: Columbia University Press, 1985); and Robert A. Nye, ed., *Crime, Madness and Politics in Modern France: The Medical Concept of National Decline* (Princeton: Princeton University Press, 1984).

12. Theodor Däubler, "Georg [*sic*] Grosz," *Die Weissen Blätter* 3 (October–December 1916), 167–170; and "George Grosz," *Das Kunstblatt* 1 (March 1917), 80–82.

13. Theodor Däubler, "George Grosz," *1918: Neue Blätter für Kunst und Dichtung* 1 (November 1918), 153–154.

14. Grosz, *Gedichte und Gesänge, 1916–17* (Litomysl: Josef Portman Verlag, 1932).

15. Däubler, *Das Kunstblatt*. See also "George Grosz im Spiegel der Kritik," *Der Ararat* 1 (July 1920), 84–86; "George Grosz," *Der Ararat*, Erstes Sonderheft (Munich, 1920); Alfred Salmony, "George Grosz," *Das Kunstblatt* 4 (April 1920), 97–104.

16. Published in Grosz, *Ecce Homo* (Berlin: Malik Verlag, 1923), pl. 18.

17. Grosz recorded in his accounting ledger that Goltz had sold 34 copies of the lithographic version by the end of February 1922.

18. Cited in Ute Frevert, *Women in German History: From Bourgeois Emancipation to Sexual Liberation*, trans. Stuart McKinnon-Evans (Oxford: Berg, 1988), introduction. See also the series of books edited by Gustav Dahms under the general title, *Der Existenzkampf der Frau im modernen Leben: Seine Ziele und Aussichten* (Berlin: Verlag Richard Taendler, 1895–1896); and Grete Meisel-Hess, *The Sexual Crisis: A Critique of Our Sex Life*, trans. Eden and Cedar Paul (New York: Eugenics Publishing Co., 1933, 4th ed.; 1917, 1st English ed.), 14–15.

19. Robert Wohl, "The Generation of 1914 and Modernism," in *Modernism: Challenges and Perspectives*, ed. Monique Chefdor et al. (Urbana: University of Illinois Press, 1986), 66–78.

20. See, for example, Reinhold Heller, *The Earthly Chimera and the Femme Fatale* (Chicago: University of Chicago Press and David and Alfred Smart Gallery, 1981); Bram Dijkstra, *Idols of Perversity: Fantasies of Feminine Evil in Fin-de-Siècle Culture* (New York: Oxford University Press, 1986); Elaine Showalter, *Sexual Anarchy: Gender and Culture at the Fin de Siècle* (New York: Penguin Books, 1990).

21. Ronald A. Fullerton, "Toward a Commercial Popular Culture in Germany: The Development of Pamphlet Fiction, 1871–1914," *Journal of Social History* 12 (Summer 1979): 489–511.

22. Rudolf Schenda, *Volk ohne Buch: Studien zur Sozialgeschichte der populären Lesestoffe, 1770–1910* (Munich: Vittorio Klostermann Verlag, 1977), 310–314; Ronald A. Fullerton, "Creating a Mass Book Market in Germany: The Story of the 'Colporteur Novel,' 1870–1890," *Journal of Social History* 10 (March 1977):271.

23. Fullerton, "Toward a Commercial Popular Culture," 496.

24. Gary D. Stark, "Cinema, Society, and the State: Policing the Film Industry in Imperial Germany," in *Essays on Culture and Society in Modern Germany*, ed. Stark and Bede Karl Lackner (College Station: Texas A&M University Press, 1982), 122–127.

25. Grosz, "Jugenderinnerungen," *Das Kunstblatt* 13 (June 1929), 172–174; and *Ein kleines Ja und ein grosses Nein: Sein Leben von ihm selbst erzählt* (Hamburg: Rowohlt Verlag, 1955), 21–26. The German title was *Jack der geheimnisvolle Mädchenmörder* (Berlin, 1899). For an analysis of

the Ripper murders in London in 1888 and the construction of the Jack the Ripper myth, see Judith R. Walkowitz, "Jack the Ripper and the Myth of Male Violence," *Feminist Studies* 8 (Fall 1982):542–574.

26. In his typed notes, he listed several names, including James Fenimore Cooper and Adolph von Menzel in one list and then: "UND Arvid von Falk, Verfasser des Romans: Der Räuberhauptmann Zimmermann, der Schrecken der Tyrannen, der Beschützer der Armen, oder Hass und LIEBE oder Zwei Frauen unter einem Dache." Archives of the History of Art, the Getty Center for the History of Art and the Humanities, Los Angeles, Calif., #850703.

27. Gary D. Stark, "Pornography, Society, and the Law in Imperial Germany," *Central European History* 14 (September 1981):203. See also R. J. V. Lenman, "Art, Society, and the Law in Wilhelmine Germany: The Lex Heinze," *Oxford German Studies* (1973):86–113; and Fullerton, "Toward a Commercial Popular Culture," 500–503.

28. The literature on this subject is extensive. See Sander L. Gilman, *Difference and Pathology: Stereotypes of Sexuality, Race, and Madness* (Ithaca: Cornell University Press, 1985); George L. Mosse, *Nationalism and Sexuality: Respectability and Abnormal Sexuality in Modern Europe* (New York: Howard Fertig, 1985); Jeffrey Weeks, *Sex, Politics and Society: The Regulation of Sexuality since 1800* (London and New York: Longman, 1981).

29. For a strong statement of this argument about sexology, see Sheila Jeffreys, *The Spinster and Her Enemies: Feminism and Sexuality 1880–1930* (London: Pandora, 1985).

30. Cited in Eduard Fuchs and Alfred Kind, *Die Weiberherrschaft in der Geschichte der Menschheit*, vol. 3 (Munich: Albert Langen, 1914), supplement to chap. 1.

31. Karl Scheffler, *Die Frau und die Kunst* (Berlin: Verlag Julius Bard, 1908), 5.

32. Ibid., chaps. 2–3. For an analysis of Schleffer's views, see Silvia Bovenschen, *Die imaginierte Weiblichkeit* (Frankfurt am Main: Suhrkamp Verlag, 1979), 24–43.

33. Otto Weininger, *Sex and Character* (London: William Heinemann, 1906; orig. published Vienna, 1903; reprinted New York: AMS, 1975), chap. 12.

34. See Nadine Sine, "Cases of Mistaken Identity: Salome and Judith at the Turn of the Century," *German Studies Review* 10 (February 1988): 9–29; Patrick Bade, *Femme Fatale* (New York: Mayflower Books, 1979); *Gerd Stein, ed., Femme Fatale-Vamp-Blaustrumpf* (Frankfurt am Main: Fischer Verlag, 1984); Virginia M. Allen, *The Femme Fatale: Erotic Icon* (Troy, N.Y.: Whitston, 1983).

35. Grosz, *Ein kleines Ja*, 98.

36. Grosz, *Briefe*, 352.

37. Ibid., 37.

38. Grosz, *Ein kleines Ja*, 35.

39. Ibid., 91.

40. Richard J. Evans, "Prostitution, State and Society in Imperial Germany," *Past and Present* 70 (1976):106–109; Lenman, "Art, Society, and the Law," 89.

41. Lenman, "Art, Society, and the Law," 89.

42. Randolph E. Bergstrom and Eric A. Johnson, "The Female Victim: Homicide and Women in Imperial Germany," in *German Women in the Nineteenth Century*, ed. John C. Fout (New York: Holmes & Meier, 1984), 346–357.

43. See Evans, "Prostitution, State and Society," 120–129.

44. Hans Ostwald, *Sittengeschichte der Inflation: Ein Kulturdokument aus den Jahres des Marktsturzes* (Berlin: Neufeld & Henius Verlag, 1931), 159.

45. Anneliese Bergmann, "Frauen, Männer, Sexualität und Geburtenkontrolle: Die Gebärstreikdebatte der SPD im Jahre 1913," in *Frauen suchen ihre Geschichte: Historische Studien zum 19. und 20. Jahrhundert*, ed. Karin Hausen (Munich: C. H. Beck, 1983), 81–92.

46. Ibid., 86, and Atina Grossmann, "Abortion and Economic Crisis: The 1931 Campaign against Paragraph 218," in *When Biology Became Destiny: Women in Weimar and Nazi Germany*, ed., Renate Bridenthal, Atina Grossmann, and Marion Kaplan, (New York: Monthly Review Press, 1984), 80–81. Grossmann discusses the unreliability of all of these estimated figures.

47. Bergmann, "Frauen, Männer, Sexualität und Geburtenkontrolle," 92–103.

48. Sander Gilman, "Sexology, Psychoanalysis, and Degeneration: From a Theory of Race to a Race to Theory," in Chamberlin and Gilman, *Degeneration*, 77–79.

49. Karl Kraus, "Glossen," *Die Fackel* (31 March 1912), 1.

50. See Richard J. Evans, *The Feminist Movement in Germany 1894–1933* (Beverly Hills, Calif.: Sage, 1976); and Barbara Greven-Aschoff, *Die bürgerliche Frauenbewegung in Deutschland 1894–1933* (Göttingen: Vandenhoeck & Ruprecht, 1981). For a bibliography of the German women's movement, see Fout, *German Women*, 385–394.

51. For analyses of expressionist critics and writers, see Marion Adams, "Der Expressionismus und die Krise der deutschen Frauenbewegung," in *Expressionismus und Kulturkrise*, ed. Bernd Hüppauf (Heidelberg: Carl Winter Universitätsverlag, 1983), 105–130; and Barbara D. Wright, " 'New Man,' Eternal Woman: Expressionist Responses to German Feminism," *German Quarterly* 60 (Fall 1987):582–599.

52. Grosz, *Briefe*, 58. See M. Kay Flavell, "Über alles die Liebe: Food, Sex, and Money in the Work of George Grosz," *Journal of European Studies* 13 (1983):279.

53. Magnus Hirschfeld, *The Sexual History of the World War* (New York: Panurge Press, 1943; German ed., 1930), introduction; *Sittengeschichte der Nachkriegszeit* (Leipzig and Vienna: Verlag für Sexualwissenschaft Schneider, 1931), 1: chap. 1.

54. Ursula von Gersdorff, *Frauen im Kriegsdienst 1914–1945*, vol. 11 of *Beiträge zur Militär- und Kriegsgeschichte*, ed. Militärgeschichtliches Forschungsamt (Stuttgart: Deutsche Verlags-Anstalt, 1969), 20–27, 218–219; "Frauendienst," in *Ein Krieg wird ausgestellt* (Frankfurt am Main: Historische Museen, 1976), 144–154; Frevert, *Women in German History*, 156–159; Renate Bridenthal and Claudia Koonz, "Beyond *Kinder, Küche, Kirche*: Weimar Women in Politics and Work," in Bridenthal, Grossmann, and Kaplan, *When Biology Became Destiny*, 48–49.

55. Magda Trott, "Frauenarbeit, ein Ersatz für Männerarbeit?" *Die Frau* 3 (1915), reprinted in *Women, the Family, and Freedom: The Debate in Documents*, ed. Susan Groag Bell and Karen M. Offen (Stanford: Stanford University Press, 1983), 2:277–279.

56. Meta Kraus-Fessel, "Frauenarbeit und Frauenemanzipation in der Nachkriegszeit," in Hirschfeld, *Sittengeschichte*, chap. 6.

57. Hirschfeld, *Sexual History*, chaps. 2, 11.

58. E. Heinrich Kisch, *Die sexuelle Untreue der Frau: Eine soziale-medizinische Studie* (Bonn: A. Marcus & E. Weber, 1917). His earlier book, *Das Geschlechtsleben des Weibes in physiologischer und hygienischer Beziehung* (Berlin, 1904), was translated by M. Eden Paul in 1910 and went through six English editions by 1931.

59. E. Burchard, "Sexuelle Fragen zur Kriegszeit," *Zeitschrift für Sexualwissenschaft* 1 (January 1915):373–380.

60. *Zwei Menschen* or *Mann und Weib*, 1905; *Petrarca, Triumpf der Liebe*, 1918. See Günther Gercken, *Ernst Ludwig Kirchner: Holzschnittzyklen* (Stuttgart: Beiser Verlag, 1980).

61. Annemarie Dube and Wolf-Dieter Dube, *E. L. Kirchner: Das graphische Werk* (Munich: Prestel Verlag, 1980), nos. L 266–274. Titles included, among others, *Der Sadist, Der Masochist, Der Busenfreier, Der Fussfreier.*

62. *Zetl, Opus XIV,* 1915. See Alexander Dückers, *Max Klinger* (Berlin: Rembrandt Verlag, 1976), chap. 7.

63. For a remarkable playing out of this image of violence against a woman, see the multiple variations on Grosz's drawing created by Concetto Pozzati, *Dal Suicido di Grosz* (Bologna: Galleria de' Foscherari, 1972).

64. *Autoportrait,* 1916, reproduced in *George Grosz: Dessins et aquarelles* (Paris: Galerie Claude Bernard, 1966).

65. Grosz, *Ein kleines Ja,* 84.

66. Grosz, *Briefe,* 49–50. Ellipses in the original text were characteristic of Grosz's letter-writing style.

67. Lothar Fischer, *George Grosz* (Reinbek: Rowohlt, 1976), 42.

68. According to notes in his accounting ledger, Grosz sent one proof and fifty lithographs of this drawing to Hans Goltz in December 1920. All were sold by the end of February 1922.

69. Reproduced in the catalog *Ohne Hemmung: Gesicht und Kehrseite der Jahre 1914–24 schonungslos enthüllt von George Grosz* (Berlin: Galerie Meta Nierendorf, 1963).

70. On attempts to identify Jack the Ripper as a Jew, see Walkowitz, "Jack the Ripper," 555–556.

71. For interpretations of dismemberment of female bodies in art, see Renate Berger, "Pars pro toto: Zum Verhältnis von künstlerischer Freiheit und sexueller Integrität," in *Der Garten der Lüste: Zur Deutung des Erotischen und Sexuellen bei Künstlern und ihren Interpreten* (Cologne: DuMont Buchverlag, 1985), 150–199; and Gubar, "Representing Pornography."

72. Grosz recounted a curious footnote about these paintings in a letter he wrote to Marc Sandler on 6 June 1952. Sandler had evidently sent a photograph of one of the paintings to Grosz, who urged him to buy it. He then wrote that the last time he saw the work, it was hanging in the bedroom of the Hannover art dealer Herbert von Garvens. The room, decorated in black, featured one of the "kleinen Frauenmörder," several Ensors, and cactus plants. Garvens threw a costume ball in Grosz's honor, which Grosz described as "eine höchst unheimliche Affäre: es war, als ob ich von lauter kleinen oder grösseren Frauenmördern umgeben wäre." Garvens, he reported, was rumored to have been mixed up in the case of the mass murderer Haarmann (*Briefe,* 457). Grosz himself did not shrink from playing the role of "Frauenmörder" in a scene that he documented with the well-known photograph of Eva, whom he married in 1920, posing provocatively before a mirror while he crept up with a knife clenched in his hand (photograph in the George Grosz Archive, Akademie der Künste, Berlin).

73. Museum of Modern Art, New York.

74. Dube, " 'Der Lustmörder.' " See also *Heinrich Maria Davringhausen: 'Der General,' Aspekte eines Bildes* (Bonn: Rheinland Verlag, 1975), 22–28.

75. Hirschfeld, *Sexual History,* 21; see also chaps. 17–18.

76. Ibid., chaps. 8–9.

77. Dix, "Kriegstagebuch," quoted from Otto Conzelmann, *Der andere Dix: Sein Bild vom Menschen und vom Krieg* (Stuttgart: Klett-Cotta, 1983), 133.

78. For a thorough analysis of this theme, see Eva Karcher's *Eros und Tod im Werk von Otto Dix* and *Otto Dix* and her essays in exhibition catalogs on Dix at the Rupertinium Salzburg (1984) and the Villa Stuck, Munich (1985).

79. Lothar Fischer, *Otto Dix: Ein Malerleben in Deutschland* (Berlin: Nicolaische Verlagsbuchhandlung, 1981), 23.

80. Diether Schmidt, *Otto Dix im Selbstbildnis* (Berlin: Henschelverlag, 1978),58.

81. Heller, *Art in Germany*, 171–172.

82. Dix inscribed this 1922 watercolor "Mutzli zum Geburtstag." Mutzli was Martha Koch, the daughter of a well-to-do family and wife of Dr. Hans Koch, a surgeon and a patron of Dix's work. In 1922 when these works were created, Martha had left her husband to live with Dix whom she married in 1923. Their marriage lasted until their deaths.

83. Erich Wulffen, *Der Sexualverbrecher: Ein Handbuch für Juristen, Verwaltungsbeamte und Ärzte mit zahlreichen kriminalistischen Originalaufnahmen* (Berlin: Dr. P. Langenscheidt, 1910), 459, 476.

84. Fischer, *Otto Dix*, 81–82. Fischer also states that there was a copy of Hirschfeld's book on sexual criminals (possibly *Geschlecht und Verbrechen* published in 1932) in Dix's library in Hemmenhof.

85. Paul Westheim, "Dix," *Das Kunstblatt* 10 (1926), 144.

86. Wulffen, *Sexualspiegel von Kunst und Verbrechen* (Dresden: Paul Aretz, [1928?]). The Dix works were the oil painting of 1922 and the self-portrait oil of 1920.

87. Atina Grossmann, "The New Woman and the Rationalization of Sexuality in Weimar Germany," in *Power of Desire: The Politics of Sexuality*, ed. Ann Snitow, Christine Stansell, and Sharon Thompson (New York: Monthly Review Press, 1983), 156.

88. Ostwald, *Sittengeschichte der Inflation*, 7.

89. Grossmann, "The New Woman," 156–157; Bridenthal, Grossmann, and Kaplan, *When Biology Became Destiny*, 1–14. See also Hirschfeld, *Sittengeschichte*, chaps. 1 and 8.

90. Matilde Wurm, quoted in Claudia Koonz, *Mothers in the Fatherland: Women, the Family, and Nazi Politics* (New York: St. Martin's Press, 1987), 26.

91. *Georg Scholz: Das druckgrafische Werk* (Karlsruhe: Künstlerhaus-Galerie, 1982). I am indebted to Vernon Lidtke for bringing these works to my attention.

92. *Eine Dienstmagd zu Tode gemartert*, 1921; reproduced in *Am Anfang: Das junge Rheinland: Zur Kunst-und Zeitgeschichte einer Region, 1918–1945*, ed. Ulrich Krempel (Düsseldorf: Städtische Kunsthalle, 1985), 210.

93. *Erich Wegner: Bilder, Aquarelle und Zeichnungen der XXer Jahre* (Munich: Michael Hasenclever, 1987).

94. John Elderfield, *Kurt Schwitters* (London: Thames & Hudson, 1985), 161.

95. *Rudolf Schlichter 1890–1955* (Berlin: Fröhlich & Kaufmann and Staatliche Kunsthalle, 1984).

CONTRIBUTORS

Lynne Frame is a doctoral candidate in the German Department at the University of California, Berkeley. Her dissertation on women in Weimar popular and scientific discourses brings together her literary interests with her background in human biology.

Anke Gleber is Assistant Professor of German at Princeton University. She has published on Nazi cinema, G. W. Pabst, film theory, and travel literature of the Weimar Republic. She is currently working on a study of filmic perception and flanerie entitled *Flanerie: The Art of Taking a Walk*.

Sabine Hake is Associate Professor of German at the University of Pittsburgh. She has published extensively in the area of German film and is the author of *Passions and Deceptions: The Early Films of Ernst Lubitsch* (1992) and *The Cinema's Third Machine: Writings on Film in Germany 1907–1933* (1993).

Beth Irwin Lewis is an adjunct professor of art history and research associate at the College of Wooster. She is currently writing, with Joan Weinstein, a social history of modern German art. Her publications include *George Grosz: Art and Politics in the Weimar Republic* ([1971] 1991), *Grosz/Heartfield: The Artist as Social Critic* (1980), and *Persuasive Images: Posters of Art and Revolution from the Archives of the Hoover Institution* (with Paul Paret, 1992). Her essay in this collection is part of an extended study of misogynist attitudes and images among German artists in the early decades of this century.

Janet Lungstrum is Assistant Professor of German Studies and Comparative Literature at the University of Colorado at Boulder. She is the coeditor of *Agonistics: Arenas of Creative Contest* (forthcoming), and has published articles on Nietzsche and modernist theories of creativity in Kafka, Proust, Musil, Sartre, and Rilke, as well as on Kleist and Wittgenstein. She has articles forthcoming on Weimar German film, and she is writing a book on urban visual culture of the Weimar Republic. She is a member of the executive committee of the Kafka Society of America.

Annelie Lütgens is Assistant Curator at the Kunstmuseum Wolfsburg. Her primary scholarly interest is to record the significance of women in the visual arts from Angelika Kauffmann to Hannah Höch. She is the author of a study on Jeanne Mammen, *"Nur ein paar Augen sein": Jeanne Mammen-Eine Künstlerin in ihrer Zeit* (1991).

Maria Makela teaches art history at the Maryland Institute, College of Art. She is the author of *The Munich Secession: Art and Artists in Turn-of-the-Century Munich* (1993), and has published widely on German art of the Empire and the Republic. She has co-curated a retrospective exhibition of the work of Hannah Höch for the Walker Art Center in Minneapolis and is also at work on a book on Lovis Corinth and politics.

Nancy Nenno is Visiting Assistant Professor of German at Wellesley College. She was a recipient of a Fulbright grant to Berlin for the academic year 1993–1994. Her dissertation, "Masquerade: Woman Nature Modernity," investigates the trope of masquerade in Weimar Germany, focusing particularly on the female performance of identity.

Patrice Petro is Associate Professor of English and Comparative Literature at the University of Wisconsin, Milwaukee. She is the author of *Joyless Streets: Women and Melodramatic Representation in Weimar Germany* (1989) and editor of *Fugitive Images: From Photograph to Video* (1995).

Katharina von Ankum has taught at the Claremont Colleges and at Cornell University. She is currently at work on a book-length study on gender and modernist utopias. Her articles on Weimar popular culture have appeared in the *German Quarterly*, the *Women in German Yearbook*, and *Colloquia Germanica*. Aside from the Weimar Republic, her research focuses on the reevaluation of GDR literature and on issues of memory in a united Germany. She is the author of *Die Rezeption von Christa Wolf in Ost und West* (1992) and the recipient of a Charles Phelps Taft postdoctoral fellowship.

INDEX

Designer: U.C. Press Staff
Compositor: Impressions Book and Journal Services, Inc.
Text: 10/12 Baskerville
Display: Baskerville
Printer & Binder: Edwards Bros.